MARK SALZMAN

True Notebooks

Mark Salzman is the author of *Iron & Silk*, an account of his two years in China; *Lost in Place*, a memoir; and the novels *The Laughing Sutra*, *The Soloist*, and *Lying Awake*. He lives in Los Angeles with his wife, the filmmaker Jessica Yu, and their daughter, Ava.

True Notebooks

True Notebooks

A WRITER'S YEAR AT
JUVENILE HALL

MARK SALZMAN

VINTAGE BOOKS

A DIVISION OF RANDOM HOUSE, INC. | NEW YORK

FIRST VINTAGE BOOKS EDITION, SEPTEMBER 2004

. . . we would assume that what it was we meant

would have been listed in some book set down
beyond the sky's far reaches, if at all
there was a purpose here. But now I think
the purpose lives in us and that we fall

into an error if we do not keep
our own true notebook of the way we came,
how the sleet stung, or how a wandering bird
cried at the window . . .

—LOREN EISELEY

Contents

True Notebooks

1 / Somebody

Mr. Jenkins unlocked the bolt and pushed the steel-frame door to K/L unit open with his shoulder.

"Look who's back. Nice trip?"

"Very nice." I had just returned from my sister's wedding in Connecticut. "Did we lose anybody while I was gone?"

"Paulino's in the Box, but he'll be back."

"Hey Mark! Whassup?"

Three of the boys in my juvenile hall writing class were already in the library, their folders and notepads spread out on the table. Toa, a seventeen-year-old Samoan with a linebacker's build, stepped forward and gave me a hug. "So you bring us any maple syrup, or what?" he asked.

"Maple syrup?"

"I know 'bout that 'cause a watchin' *Mr. Rogers* when I was a kid."

Raashad's eyes opened wide. "You seen that show too?"

"Every kid seen that show, fool. Nothin' else to do in the mornin' 'cept break toys an' shit."

"Yeah, I was always like, where *that* neighborhood at? Nobody got drunk or beat his ass or nothin'."

"Yeah," Toa said, "but check it out: that show be *fake*. Know how I figured it out? People always be walkin' in and outta his door and he never locked it. He'd'a had all his shit jacked if it was real."

"Yeah! Homies be like, *'It's a beautiful day in the neighborhood*—now gimme that train set, fool.'"

"So how was your sister's wedding?" Antonio asked me as I handed out pencils.

"Beautiful. Perfect weather, too."

"Any fights break out?" Toa asked.

"At the wedding?"

"Nah, at the reception."

"No, no fights. Where are the rest of the guys?"

"The chapel. They got some kinda meditation retreat over there this morning. Could you gimme another pencil, Mark? This one don't got no eraser."

Toa frowned. "'Cause you bit it off, fool. I just seen you."

"I didn't bite nothin' off. It was already gone, I was just chewin' on the metal part."

"I went to that meditation thing once," Antonio said. "I went 'cause I heard the instructor was this hot female, but then I got there and it was some bald guy in a robe playin' a harmonica. Fuck that."

Raashad checked the eraser on his new pencil, then said, "Yeah, you suppos'ta close your eyes an' picture yourself goin' down some stairs into your workshop in the cellar where you got all yo' tools."

"Your tools?"

"Yeah, 'tools for life.'" Raashad rolled his eyes. "You suppos'ta choose what tools you need and put 'em on your belt, like you some kinda superhero. First of all, I say to myself: What nigga you know got a workshop? What nigga you know got a cellar? Right off I knew this shit ain't for me."

We joked around for a while, talked about a former class

member who had just been sentenced to fifty years to life, then the boys settled down to write. After forty minutes, when they had all written something, I asked who would like to read aloud first.

"Let Carter start," Antonio said. Although I addressed them by their first names, the boys followed the example of the staff and referred to each other by last name only. "Carter got some good news last week."

Raashad nodded, propped his notepad on one knee, and read:

> At about 2:33 a.m. the night staff came to my door and unlocked it. The sound of the key turning woke me up immediately, that sound always wakes me up alarmingly. The staff said, "Hey Carter, get up." I said, "Man what the hell." He said telephone. The first thing I thought was it was the police telling me someone in my family was dead. As I'm walking to the phone my heart was beating extremely hard like if you could see it beating through my shirt. When I picked up the phone I was relaxed by the sweet soothing sound of my companion and fiance Amika telling me she just gave birth to a little girl. The feeling inside me was indescribable. It was amazing, she said she weighed in at 8 lbs 4 oz. I felt so happy my body felt so numb. I was astounded by the information I had just received. I feel so great. Ever since that day I've been happy and just waiting to see her. I heard her giggle on the phone the feeling was great. I can't wait until the day when I can hold my daughter.

"Congratulations," I said.

He half smiled. "I'm pretty excited about it. I just pray to God I win my case so I can get out soon."

Toa volunteered to read next, promising to take everyone's

mind away from prison and back to the freedom of "the outs."

> *My family weddings are cool and all but my family can't get along. During the wedding it's cool and all but the party that's after it ain't nothin' nice. It's like warfare. As soon as they down a few cases everybody all of a sudden feels like Superman. For example my cuzzin's wedding was beautiful, everything's going smooth, even the party until my brothers showed up. Apparently my brother had shot one of the groom's cuzzins and he was paralyzed. And the best man was that fool's older brother. They weren't trippin' but my brother was. He banked the best man up on the dance floor in front of everybody. People was already drunk and shit so they start jumpin' in wanting to scrap too. My stupid ass cuzzin threw a chair in the crowd and it hit this old man. Everybody stopped right then and there because the old man was the priest. The priest's son started trippin' so we fucked that punk up in the parking lot. That's why I kinda hate family weddings.*

As promised, the essay took Raashad's and Antonio's minds off their surroundings. They compared stories of family gatherings that had turned into brawls until we had only five minutes left for class, then Antonio read last.

> *I am lying in my room incarcerated at Central Juvenile Hall looking at the white painted walls in my room, and how my door is shut with a steel bolt lock to show that I am locked up. It's weird but this room relates to my life I once lived outside, over the walls laced with barbed wire. I was locked in a world where nothing would come in and nothing would go out. I was trapped in my gang life, that's all I knew and all I wanted to know. I chose to stay in my room*

and not let anybody control me. I had too much pride to open my door and let somebody in. I neglected the people who really cared about me, my family and my loved ones. Sure, at the time it was all fun, but was the consequences really worth it? To me, no, but I was the steel bolt that kept myself from realizing that the world is a lot bigger than a room (my gang). There are a lot more things out there than your homies and homegirls. Don't get me wrong, I got love for them, but how are you going to be with people that are holding you back from blossoming and showing your full potential? I now realize how precious life really is. It's too bad that I am probably never going to be able to show the world what I have to offer. As I sit in my room thinking what would have happened if I would have opened my door and not just stayed in my room.

"This is why we get into so many fights around here," Raashad said. "You don't wanna be thinkin' shit like that, it's too depressing, so you start somethin' with your roommate, and before you know it you both be poundin' on each other till you fall asleep. It's a distraction."

Mr. Jenkins tapped on the glass, letting us know it was time for the boys to return to the dayroom for lunch. Meanwhile, the inmates who had attended the meditation retreat were just returning. They shuffled across the yard single file with their hands clasped behind their backs and most of their heads bowed forward. When everyone had come inside and the door to the unit was closed, one of the boys crossed the dayroom to say hello to me.

"How you doin', Mark? We missed you."

"I missed you, too, Santiago. It's good to be back."

"Sorry about not comin' to class today. I wanted to try meditation, see if it could make me relax."

"How was it?"

"It kinda sucked. The instructor was a guy."

"But you look happy," I said.

"I am happy! Something good happened to me today, Mark." Santiago grew serious for a moment. "I been feelin' really stressed 'cause I started trial last Friday. This morning the chaplain saw me and he asked me what was wrong. I said, 'I feel like a piece of shit stuck under somebody's shoe.' I told him how I had to hear the prosecutor say all this bad stuff about me in front of everybody. It was the worst day of my life. My whole family was there. I felt like I let everybody down. So the chaplain looks at me an' he puts his hand on my shoulder like this, an' he says, 'Diaz, you gotta remember something: *You are somebody*. Don't ever forget that.' So I thought about it, and I realized—damn, he's right! Nobody could take that away from me. I *am* somebody! I—"

"Diaz, get your ass over here so we can eat."

Santiago glared at the messenger and gave him the finger. The messenger pointed at Santiago and yanked his hand back and forth to simulate masturbation. The two boys exchanged threatening looks until honor had been restored, then Santiago turned his attention back to me.

"What were we . . . ?"

"The chaplain," I said.

"Oh yeah! I *am* somebody," he said once more, grinning this time. "Somebody awful!"

2 / Just Say No

When I can't make up my mind about something, I start a notebook. I use it to think aloud; I fill it with questions, arguments, and reassuring clichés. My notebook from August 1997 read:

REASONS NOT TO VISIT
DUANE'S WRITING CLASS AT JUVENILE HALL

—students all gangbangers; feel unqualified to evaluate
  poems about AK-47s
—still angry about getting mugged in 1978
—still angry about having my apartment robbed in
  1986
—still angry about my wife's car being stolen in 1992
—wish we could tilt L.A. County and shake it until
  everybody with a shaved head and tattoos falls into
  the ocean
—feel uncomfortable around teenagers

On the next page, I wrote:

REASONS TO VISIT DUANE'S CLASS
AT JUVENILE HALL

—have never seen the inside of a jail
—pretended to be enthusiastic when Duane
 mentioned it

The trouble started after I mentioned to Duane Noriyuki, a friend and writer for the *Los Angeles Times*, that I was having problems with my novel about a cloistered nun. "What kind of problems?" he asked. I didn't want to reveal the full extent of it: the plot had collapsed, the main characters seemed lifeless, the dialogue rang false, I had lost sight of the theme, and the setting felt wrong—so I limited myself to telling him about Carlos. Carlos was a minor character in the story, a juvenile delinquent with a terminal illness. Although I had given Carlos tattoos and a bald head, he failed to impress my editor. She thought he needed a personality. And "please please please," she urged in one of her notes, "give him a different name."

Los Angeles is the youth gang capital of the world, so I figured Duane must have had to write about them at some point. I asked if he could recommend any good books about juvenile delinquents that I could use for research. He thought about it, then answered, "Not really."

I figured that was the end of that, but then he said, "But I volunteer down at juvenile hall twice a week. I teach a writing class there. If you'd like to come down and visit sometime, the guys could tell you more than any book."

I didn't respond immediately; I wanted him to think I was giving it serious thought. Then I asked, "Are you *sure* you can't recommend any books?"

MORE REASONS NOT TO VISIT DUANE'S CLASS

—Jack Henry Abbott/Norman Mailer debacle. Who cares if thugs write well? They're still thugs.
—Crime victims don't get free writing classes, why should the criminals?
—I gave free readings for the L.A. Library and Planned Parenthood this year, I did my bit.

And then there was my deep-seated prejudice against writing classes. I taught creative writing once; at the end of that semester I vowed never to put the words "creative writing" and "class" together in the same sentence again. During our first meeting, a female student read aloud a nonfiction piece about the day her mother discovered her father had been having an affair. As she came to the part of the story where her mother, driven hysterical with anger, scratched her father's face and drew blood, the memory was so painful that she burst into tears and barely made it to the end. When she finished, an uncomfortable silence hung over the room. I was the teacher; it was my job to think of something to say that acknowledged her grief but kept the focus on writing. Should I compliment the way she made the scene more immediate by putting it in the present tense? Should I praise her use of dialogue without tags, i.e., how she always managed to keep the two voices distinct through style and context?

> *"I have no idea what you're—"*
> *"Liar!"*
> *"You're not letting me—"*
> *"Bastard!"*

Before I could decide what to say, a shrill male voice rose out of the silence:

"Your *mother* scratched your father's *face* just because he was having an *affair*?"

The man who was to make the next three months a living hell for me—a middle-aged adult education student who wrote stories about middle-aged adult education students living in Japan who discover love with underage, gender-unspecified Asians with skin like bean curd milk and hands like lotus buds—rolled his eyes and hissed, "She sounds like a real *bitch* to me."

The class was supposed to run from 6 p.m. to 10 p.m., but I concluded that meeting at seven-thirty, went out to the parking lot, and hyperventilated in my car.

Most of the students were taking the class because they needed a minimum number of English credits to graduate. They turned in handwritten assignments on paper torn out from spiral notebooks; they came in late and wandered out of class early; they wrote about dogs that could water-ski, memorable hangovers, and the true meaning of love:

> *I'm there for you*
> *And your there for me*
> *Our beatiful baby*
> *Makes three.*

The student who wrote the poem about her *beatiful* baby was a senior, one semester away from her goal of becoming a public school teacher. I asked if, in her next draft, she could perhaps tell us more about her baby. Describe the baby, tell us how the baby is beautiful, make us see the baby—avoid generalizations, be specific. She shrugged and said, "I don't have a baby."

REASONS NOT TO VISIT ANY WRITING CLASS

—exposure to student writing
—exposure to students

There was one more reason I did not want to visit Duane's class, but it was too depressing to face, even in the privacy of my notebook. What if Duane's students asked if I believed writing was worth the effort? If they were as cunning as their reputations suggested, they might sense how lost I felt as a writer and realize that I had nothing to offer them. Then, I imagined, they would beat me up.

My notebook for that season ends with a solution:

—Remove juvenile delinquent character from novel.

3 / Gentlemen

Sometimes I heed the advice I give myself in my notebooks, sometimes I don't. The ratio works out to about 50 percent—the kind of result one gets flipping a coin. This is one reason I suspect that free will is an illusion, but it is an illusion I can't seem to live without. So I keep filling notebooks.

Central Juvenile Hall was easy to find. I exited the freeway in East L.A., drove toward County Hospital, and then followed the razor wire. I pulled up to a flimsy-looking guardhouse at the entrance, where a sign announced that identification was required to pass but no guard was anywhere to be seen. I drove through and parked in the lot next to a sedan with tinted windows and a bumper sticker that read *My Kid Beat Up Your Honor Roll Student.*

As I waited for Duane to meet me at the entrance, a police cruiser pulled up beside me and stopped in front of a pair of eighteen-foot-high metal doors set into a concrete wall. A bored-looking teenager was sitting in the backseat with his hands cuffed behind him. A red light on top of the doors flashed and an alarm went off, then the metal panels screeched open like a giant mouth. The cruiser passed inside and the doors slid shut.

Duane showed up on time and crossed the parking lot with a knapsack slung over his shoulder. As we shook hands the alarm went off over the metal doors again. The concrete monster opened its mouth and spat the police cruiser out. The boy was gone; he, I presumed, needed to be digested for a while before being shit into the adult prison system or puked back out onto the streets.

"Some place, huh?" Duane asked.

He led me to an aluminum-sided trailer where someone gave him a key in exchange for his driver's license. We used that key to pass through a battered metal door into an alley. "This is just a temporary entrance," Duane explained. "The regular entrance was damaged in the earthquake, but it hasn't been repaired yet." The earthquake he was referring to had occurred more than three years earlier.

We followed the alley between a smog-blackened wall and an abandoned building. I peeked inside one of the broken windows and saw iron bed frames lying helter-skelter, covered along with everything else in a thick layer of dust. The alley ended at the entrance to a weedy yard, several acres in size, bordered by a series of concrete bunkers. Detention facilities are not meant to be cheery places, but this looked like something out of a Dickens novel. My impression was confirmed not long after that visit, when a Los Angeles County grand jury—called upon to investigate the medical, mental health, and educational programs and the living conditions in the county's juvenile detention facilities—concluded that Central "can best be described as falling apart."

The place felt deserted, but I noticed a shadowy movement all around us. I tracked one of these shadows and saw that it was a feral cat. These miserable-looking animals seemed to be everywhere, slinking around with their tails lowered and their half-chewed ears tilted back.

We passed by a guard station in the center of the yard, where a spectacularly obese man snored. His chin rested on his chest, and the front of his T-shirt was moist with drool. As we passed by him, Duane explained that each building represented a separate "unit," allowing the facility to keep minors of different ages, genders, and criminal sophistication isolated from each other. He taught his writing class in a unit reserved for HROs, or high-risk offenders—they were, as one law enforcement official put it, "the cream of the crud." Most of the HROs at Central were charged with murder, rape, or armed robbery, and were declared unfit to be tried as juveniles, meaning that their cases had been shifted to adult court. No Youth Authority camps or guaranteed release at age twenty-five for members of this group; if convicted, they received adult-length sentences and went straight to prison.

I could make out human figures standing in the windows of some of the cells. The glass was tinted so I couldn't see any faces, only the outlines of heads and torsos. I heard thumping noises and realized the inmates were pounding on the windows to get our attention.

When we reached the farthest building, Duane led me into a dark stairway. I felt slightly claustrophobic when he locked the steel door behind us. At the top of the stairs, he fumbled in the darkness with yet another lock, then used his hip to shove open the final door leading to the unit.

After our dramatic journey across the yard and through the steel doors, my first view of the inside of juvenile hall proved anticlimactic. There were no bars anywhere, and the two dozen or so inmates sat in molded plastic chairs watching television. They wore identical orange uniforms, and were almost all either Latino or black. A few of them turned their heads to look at us, but most seemed engrossed in the movie, a crime drama. They sat quietly, in neat rows with their arms folded across their laps. A guard wearing combat fatigues, a black T-shirt, and paramilitary boots stood nearby to keep watch over them, while two other guards chatted in a control room separated from the prisoners by thick glass windows. None of the staff carried weapons, which surprised me, given the large number of inmates and the fact that most of them were accused of violent crimes.

Duane approached the guard dressed in fatigues, who was white, and introduced me as a visiting author come to speak to the writing class. The guard made no sign of having heard. He kept his eyes on the inmates and did not acknowledge us with even a nod. When enough time had passed that the message was unambiguous—our presence was not appreciated— he barked out a command to the inmates: "Writing class. Get your things and take it down to the kitchen, *gentlemen*."

Four young men stood up, clasped their hands behind their backs, and shuffled out of the room. They kept their eyes lowered and their faces blank. When they returned, they carried brown accordion-style folders with them. Duane and I followed them to a windowless room with a sink and some shelves in it. As soon as the door to the kitchen closed behind us and the guard was out of sight, the inmates' zombielike expressions relaxed. They talked quietly as they pulled up chairs and opened their folders, like students settling into any classroom, but I felt like a ghost—even though there were six of us in a room the size of a large closet, they managed to seem completely unaware of my presence. This was done so skillfully, however, that I didn't feel unwelcome so much as invisible.

I also felt nervous. Duane had mentioned that all of the members of his class had been charged with murder, and while they were all under eighteen years of age, they were physically mature—all but one of them stood taller than me. I remembered hearing somewhere that violent criminals (or was it dogs?) don't like it if you look them in the eye, they take it as a challenge. I didn't want to challenge anyone, so I struggled to keep my gaze from meeting any of theirs. But where to look? It was like trying to find a neutral spot to look while standing in a crowded elevator. Eventually my eyes settled on the inmates' hands.

Two of the young men were Latino, one black, and the fourth white. The white guy scared me the most. A tall, broad-shouldered skinhead with tattoos on his arms and hands, I imagined he was seething with hatred for his darker-skinned classmates and would start a brawl at any moment.

Duane opened his knapsack and handed out yellow legal pads and pencils (inmates aren't allowed to keep pencils in their cells, Duane had told me, because they can be used as weapons), then introduced me. "This is Mark. He's a friend of mine, and a professional writer. The book he's working on now has a character in it from juvenile hall, but he's having trouble making the character seem real. I thought maybe you guys could help him out." The movie showing in the adjacent dayroom seemed to be reaching its climax. The sounds of gunfire and explosions bounced around the concrete walls and smeared into an irritating roar. Duane's students seemed oblivious to it.

"Since we only have an hour," Duane suggested, "why don't we start with some reading. I'd like for Mark to see the kind of work you're doing."

The young men opened their folders and pulled out examples of their writing, but then everything in the room seemed to stop. It was like seeing a group of people in bathing suits run up to a swimming pool on a hot day, then halt right at the edge and look everywhere but at the water; no one wanted to be the first to jump in. I thought Duane would call on someone, but he showed no sign of being in a hurry. He sat quietly and let them sort it out on their own. Eventually one of the Latino inmates shifted in his chair and asked, "So who's gonna start?"

"Go ahead, Barreda."

"Yeah, kick it."

"Aw, come on, somebody else go for a change."

"Naw, you go, homeboy."

He clicked his tongue and frowned. "OK, then, I will." He held one of his essays out in front of him, then turned toward Duane. "The ending's weak."

Duane brushed his hair behind one of his ears thoughtfully but did not say anything. The boy sighed, straightened up in his chair, and held the sheet higher in front of him. "My name's Ruben Barreda," he said, then he cleared his throat. He leaned back in the chair, tossed his left ankle over his right knee, and propped the essay on his thigh.

With my gaze lowered prudently, I could not help noticing that the squirming and throat-clearing were mere diversionary tactics. The real battle was taking place in Ruben's hands: they trembled so badly from stage fright he could barely hold on to the page. When he began reading, his voice sounded the way his hands looked. But he forced himself through it nevertheless.

CLOUDS

Clouds, this is just a word. Where did this word come from? Who was the one to say that those white shapes that float in the blue skies are clouds? I never put serious thought into this subject, maybe because it was irrelevant to the life I lived. I never took the time to look up at a cloud and just stare at it. I was too busy with my everyday routine. The things I looked forward to were tagging on the walls, kicking back with the homies. I was so focused on these insignificant things that I didn't take time to look around at the beauty the environment had to offer. I didn't appreciate anything. Hey, if I didn't care about myself or others, how could I have possibly cared for a cloud?

As I think of these things, I realize how much I've changed. I look out this window, which is covered with gang engravings, and I see a nice puffy white cloud just slowly floating by, and I think to myself, "Where will this cloud go? Where does it come from? Why is it that it floats so perfectly like a boat on the water, yet there is nothing to support or hold up this cloud? Whose will or power lets this cloud continue to cross this beautiful blue sky?"

I will never know where this cloud is headed. Does it have a particular destination to reach? I wonder if someone I know will set eyes on this exact same cloud. It's not like I can ask anyone, "You didn't happen to see a puffy, white cloud floating in the air around 5:00 did you?" They might say yes, but I know deep inside it wasn't the same one. There's just too many beautiful clouds out in the sky to be able to pinpoint the one I'm talking about.

Like a boy stares into a pet shop for his new puppy, I stare out my window and from a distance I see a few clouds beginning to emerge. I stop and look at the engravings on the window which keep me from clearly seeing the process of nature unfold: Flaco, King Kobras R13V, Sotel, Smiley Highland Park, Big Top Locos. All these gangs are carved into this window. I stop and think back. A year ago, I wouldn't have seen beyond the graffiti, and putting "Malo Avenues" would have been my first reaction. I put some thought into how I would have reacted, and I realize that for the five years of being a gang member I have missed out on so much. I didn't appreciate the beauty life and nature gives us on a daily basis. My gang had me so hypnotized *that if I had tried to look out into the sky, my eyes wouldn't have seen past the gang writing that scars the window.*

As I think about this it fills me with disappointment because I know some of my peers will enter this room that I now sit in. They will look out this window and be so focused on the gang engravings that they will never be able to see the beauty of a cloud. At least I have come to a point where I can really look and stare at a cloud with gratitude and not be distracted by stupidity or nonsense.

4 / Trip to the Museum

Ruben's essay took me by surprise; I was still reeling from it when Duane and I left the building that night. As we made our way across the yard, he pointed out a woman with close-cropped white hair and wire-rimmed glasses standing nearby, talking to a group of Catholic volunteers.

"That's Sister Janet," Duane said. "She's the person who convinced me to start the class. Anything you want to know about this place, she's the person to talk to."

As soon as the nun saw us, she bade the volunteers good night and walked over. "You must be Mark," she said. "We're delighted you could visit."

Sister Janet Harris was nearly seventy years old but looked two or three decades younger. She had a lovely smile and a pleasing voice—I wanted to like her right away—but the fact that she was a nun and that she worked in a prison made me wary. I couldn't help thinking of the film *Dead Man Walking*, which I disliked in spite of not having seen it.

Even after Susan Sarandon won an Academy Award for her portrayal of Sister Helen Prejean, the real-life nun who ministers to condemned inmates, I avoided seeing the movie. I had a problem with the basic premise: a nun, after dedicating her life to helping the needy, prays for guidance and ends up helping Sean Penn. Or rather, the character Sean Penn plays in the film—an unsavory, cold-blooded killer. This was the neediest person she could find? I rented *Unforgiven* instead.

Now there's a movie! Like *Dead Man Walking*, it portrays the moral ambiguity of vengeance. By the film's end, however, when Clint Eastwood gets drunk and hunts down the sadists who lynched Morgan Freeman, we know we're all rooting for him. If a nun had walked on-screen and talked Clint out of it, citing the judgment-impairing effects of alcohol and the need for due process, audiences would have rioted.

"What was your impression of the class?" Sister Janet asked, eyeing me steadily.

I told her it wasn't like any writing class I had ever attended. I actually enjoyed it.

She seemed pleased but her gaze held firm, reminding me of a phrase Chinese martial artists use to describe the ideal kind of strength: an iron bar wrapped in velvet.

"And what did you think of their writing?"

I tried not to gush. These were delinquents, I reminded myself. Was their writing technically sophisticated? No, and from a quick glance at their handwritten work, I guessed that none of them had ever won a spelling bee. On the other hand, were they writing coherently? Yes. Were they writing about things that meant a great deal to them? Yes. Did they write about those things in a way that would draw a reader in? Yes. Did their writing show that they were actually *thinking*? Yes. And nobody called anybody's mother a bitch! I went ahead and gushed; I told Sister Janet that if my college students had made this kind of effort, I might still be teaching.

"Did you tell the boys that?" Sister Janet asked.

"I did."

Her reserve gave way. "You can't imagine how much a compliment means in a place like this! You may have changed one of those boys' lives tonight."

As the three of us made our way toward the parking lot, Sister Janet explained that she'd been Catholic chaplain at the hall for years, but the increasingly punitive trend in the juvenile justice system made her feel that ministry was not enough; she stepped away from her role as spiritual adviser in order to dedicate herself full-time to advocacy work and coordinating volunteer activities. The activity closest to her heart, she told me, was a writing program that she and author Karen Hunt had created only a year ago. It was still a fledgling project—when Duane started his class the program doubled in size—but Sister Janet assured me that one day, every unit in the hall would have a writing class in it.

"The goal of Inside Out Writers is to give these young people a chance to express themselves, and feel that someone is listening. Karen and Duane don't tell their students what to write, or tell them that gangs and crime and drugs are wrong. They *listen*. They encourage their students to think for themselves, and then to write those thoughts down. You've seen the results. Would you ever have imagined that kids in a place like this could write like that?"

When we reached our cars, Sister Janet removed the ID badge from her front pocket and dropped it into her purse. "If something's meant to happen, it will. It has to be your decision, not something you felt pushed into."

"What decision?" I asked.

"But I will say that even if you decided you could come only once or twice a month—whatever your schedule would allow—we could work around that. Don't feel any pressure."

Duane laughed.

· · ·

In the days that followed my visit to the writing class, I tried
not to feel any pressure. I even started a new notebook:

REASONS NOT TO GET INVOLVED

—What if a kid with no father gets too attached to me?
  What if he gets released and shows up at my house
  asking for help staying off drugs or out of the gang?
—The cliché problem: white guy with everything going
  for him telling dark-skinned kids in prison that art
  matters.
—The futility problem: art doesn't matter enough.

ON THE OTHER HAND

—Knowing it's futile means I can't fail.
—White volunteer teacher better than no volunteer
  teacher.
—If one of those kids ever gets released, he's not going
  to want to move to Glendale.

I debated like this for a week, filling my notebook and losing sleep but coming no closer to a decision. In the end, my
wife—who does not understand the concept of indecision—
settled the matter for me. After I'd told her about the opportunity, had listed the pros and cons and described my conflicted
emotions, she said, "You don't get out of the house enough."

"You'll be fine," Sister Janet insisted as we passed the guard
station, where the large man was snoring again. "All you have

to do is be genuine with them, be yourself, and the rest will follow."

I noticed that each time Sister Janet spoke, she stopped walking, as if to give full attention to the topic at hand. I, more accustomed to continuous motion and shallow conversation, couldn't get my feet to follow her example. As she talked, I stepped in place.

"These children are in crisis," she continued. "Most of them never had a chance, never got the guidance and attention they needed from adults. Is it any surprise they join gangs? The gang makes them feel part of something, it provides structure, and it gives them opportunities to prove themselves. How can we compete with the gangs if we can't offer them something better?

"Look at this place—it's awful! It's falling apart, it's depressing, it's unsafe. What message does that send to these kids? That they are garbage, that's what. It tells them that society simply wants to dispose of them. It's obscene, it's unconscionable that we aren't willing to do better than this! We have given up hope on rehabilitation. That says more about us than it does about these children." She shuddered with anger, then her expression softened and she touched my shoulder. "That's why what Karen, and Duane, *and now you* are doing is so important. You are making a difference."

If it had been at all unclear before, I now understood why Duane described Sister Janet as the most persuasive person he'd ever met. I expressed my concern that while I had not met Karen yet, I knew for sure that I was no Duane Noriyuki. He got those boys to behave like honors students, yet seemed to accomplish this telepathically. During the hour I spent in his class, he couldn't have spoken more than two dozen words, but he managed to convey enthusiasm, compassion, and authority all at once. Sitting next to him that night, I felt like a rodeo clown sitting next to Black Elk, the Sioux mystic.

Sister Janet took a step forward, then stopped again. "Duane has a special gift, it's true, but you'll find your own way. It all boils down to one thing, really: the kids want to feel that they matter to someone. They want to please adults, they want to fit in, they want to model themselves after someone they respect. It's just that most of them have been brainwashed into thinking they aren't capable of it."

Before we could resume our progress toward the unit where I would be teaching, Sister Janet looked over my shoulder and waved to someone coming toward us from the other side of the yard. He appeared to be trying to avoid us by walking through the grass rather than on the path.

"There's a member of the staff. I'll introduce you." She called out to him, "Good morning, Mr. Stone."

The man, who wore a black cap and a policeman's mustache, returned the greeting but did not change course. "Morning, Sister."

"Don't be shy, come join us for a second. There's someone I'd like you to meet."

He adjusted the bill of his cap, grimaced, then walked over.

"Mr. Stone, this is Mark Salzman. He's a very well-known writer. One of his books won a Pulitzer Prize."

"Actually," I said, feeling both flattered and embarrassed, "it was just nominated for one. A lot of books get nominated."

"Well, it should have won," Sister Janet continued without missing a beat. "He's going to start a writing class in K/L unit."

"Ah," Mr. Stone said, looking me over. "A famous writer, huh? Would I have heard of any of your books?"

I named the titles. He smiled—a bit too broadly—and shook his head. "Sorry, never heard of those. You ever work in a place like this before?"

"No."

"Well, let me give you a bit of advice. Don't ever forget

where you are, or who you're dealing with. It's no college campus."

"It certainly isn't," Sister Janet agreed. "And that's what Mark is here to do—to make it more like one."

Mr. Stone folded his arms across his chest and nodded. "It's nice that you people come here to help out. We appreciate our volunteers. But in my opinion, there's a tendency to see what you want to see, to see what makes you feel good. You see the kids at their best, and then think that's the reality."

Although he was looking at me as he spoke, I sensed that his comments were meant for Sister Janet.

He went on: "These kids can seem like the nicest people you'd ever want to meet, oh yes. And when you hear their sad stories, you feel sorry for them, you really do. But Ted Bundy seemed nice, too. My cousin worked at the prison where they held him. Saw him every day. Said you couldn't meet a nicer guy." He tipped the bill of his cap. "Nice to see you, Bob. Have a great morning, Sister."

After he'd left us, Sister Janet peered at me over the rim of her glasses. "Bob indeed! Now you see what I have to deal with every day. Don't expect a warm welcome from the staff. Some of them are caring, but unfortunately, you have a lot of people working in law enforcement who are in the wrong profession."

She closed her eyes. "It's crucial for them to believe, you see, that the kids are not salvageable—they're all just little Ted Bundys. If the kids are monsters, then it's appropriate to dehumanize them, you see how it works? On the other hand, if you or I suggest that the kids are still developing, and could actually benefit from counseling and education, we spoil the whole picture. We're seen as a threat."

Then she grinned at me. "Little did you realize what you were walking into! But don't worry, all of this will become irrelevant as soon as you sit down with the boys. All that matters is what happens between you and them."

When we reached the entrance to K/L unit, which was just downstairs from where Duane taught, Sister Janet had to try several keys before finding the one that worked. It seemed to take forever. Then we passed into a dayroom that looked exactly like the one upstairs, although this one was empty. There were no boys watching television, no boys anywhere in sight. We walked across the linoleum floor, still wet from having just been mopped, to the control room where three staff members—two of them black, one Latino—were mock-arguing over a plate of nachos.

"I'm telling you, you don't want to put that hot sauce on here."

"I like hot sauce."

"Not this shit, you won't. Renteria's mother brought it, it's from a part of Mexico they don't even show on the map."

"I had some of it, it ain't so bad."

"Yeah? When did you have it?"

"Just now, when you were out front."

"Oh man—that's what I was trying to tell you! You don't notice it when you put it in your mouth. It's at the other end where it kicks in."

None of them paid attention to Sister Janet or me standing in the doorway a few feet away. The bantering went on until Sister Janet cleared her throat.

"Could you give us just a moment of your time?" she asked, using a tone of voice familiar to anyone who has been addressed by an angry schoolteacher. "I know you're all very busy."

The three men fell silent but would not look at us. I wanted to run away.

She fixed her gaze on the man sitting at a desk in the middle of the room, leaning back in his chair with his hands clasped behind his head. He was black, tall, and looked around fifty years old. He had a former athlete's build: broad shoulders, powerful chest and arms, long legs, slightly thickening waistline. His body language conveyed ease and authority, while his face registered annoyance.

"Mr. Sills, this is Mark Salzman. He's a very distinguished writer. He's the one who's going to be working with the boys here in K/L. We're very lucky to have him."

Mr. Sills unclasped his hands, leaned forward in his chair, rested his forearms on the desk, and turned to look at me.

"How ya doin'," he asked without smiling. He looked tough, definitely not someone to be messed with. And I had an awful feeling that, intentionally or not, I had just messed with his morning.

"Fine, thanks," I chirped.

"What can we do for you?"

I froze. I had no idea what he could do for me; I felt so unwelcome there I couldn't even remember why I'd come.

Sister Janet frowned. "I brought a list yesterday with the names of three boys on it, and a letter asking you to have them out of their rooms for us by ten o'clock. I gave it to the person on duty last night and he promised he would give it to you. Did he?"

Mr. Sills shook his head. "Haven't heard or seen anything about it."

Sister Janet removed something from her shoulder bag. "I'm not surprised. I brought a copy of the list, just in case." She handed it to him.

He laid it on the desk in front of him, took his time smoothing it flat with one of his giant hands, then looked it over. "Let's see what we got here. Jackson . . . OK. Wu . . . OK . . ." When he got to the third name, he started chuckling. He glanced up at the Latino guard, who looked like he could bench-press four hundred pounds and wore his LAPD cap with the bill pulled down low over his eyes. "You're going to love this," Mr. Sills said. "They want Javier."

"Javier? For a writing class? Whoa, that's an interesting concept."

"It's your call, Granillo. You want to let him out?"

Mr. Granillo looked at Sister Janet. "You might want to re-consider, ma'am. His behavior has been disruptive lately." His use of formal language contrasted with his tone of voice, which sounded as if he were trying to explain something to a child.

"He won't be disruptive today," Sister Janet said.

Mr. Granillo shared a glance with Mr. Sills, then shrugged. "OK by me, then."

Mr. Sills handed the sheet back to Sister Janet. "Where do you want them?"

"Somewhere quiet where they won't be disturbed by the radio or the television. How about the kitchen? That's where the writing class meets upstairs."

Mr. Sills shook his head slowly. "I don't care what they do upstairs. In my unit, I want 'em where I can see 'em. We'll put your class in the library, that'll be quiet enough."

When none of the men stirred from their chairs, Sister Janet asked, "And you'll do that for us now?"

After an interminable pause, Mr. Sills said, "You go on ahead into the library. We'll get 'em to you."

I wished I could make myself disappear.

Sister Janet led me out of their office to a small room lined with bookshelves. Several windows faced the control room, allowing the staff to keep an eye on things without having to leave their posts. I scanned the bookshelves and saw that about half of them were filled with evangelical tracts, the other half with horror/thriller novels. I slumped into a chair, exhausted from the tension of meeting the staff. And I hadn't even met the criminals yet.

Closing the door behind her, Sister Janet directed my attention to the far corner of the yard, where a group of boys in orange outfits were being marched toward a row of elaborately modified low-rider cars.

"That's what passes for educational programming around here," she said. "Ex-gangsters come in and show off their cars and their girlfriends. Just what these kids need."

I was too upset to pay attention. I took out my pencils and legal pads and stared at the clock on the wall: 10:03.

"When the boys get here," she said, "I'll introduce you and explain what our program is about. But then I think I should go. It's your class, and I don't want you to feel that I'm hovering. I'll come back for you in an hour." She smiled. "I bet you won't want to leave by then."

At that moment, I was fantasizing going back into the staff room with a stone-cold expression on my face, and when the staff challenged me, I would—well—frighten them somehow. The fantasy became vague at that point.

Sister Janet interrupted the daydream by telling me something about the three boys she had picked for the class. "Jimmy Wu was born in Taiwan. He was excited to hear that you speak Chinese. He's a sensitive boy, and very smart—he was an A student before he started getting in trouble—but I'm worried that he's getting depressed. Kevin Jackson is shy, it takes a while to get to know him, but he's one of the nicest boys you'll ever meet. You'll like him right away. And Francisco Javier . . ." She glanced toward the staff room and frowned. "He's somebody with a lot of anger and confusion bottled up inside, but he wants to change his life. The problem is, he's not getting enough support. If no one takes him seriously, then of course he's not going to make much progress. I think this class is going to mean a lot to him."

Through the windows I saw the boys enter the dayroom from corridors on either side, presumably where their cells were. Like the boys in Duane's class, they shuffled slowly, with their eyes lowered and their hands clasped behind their backs. Mr. Sills rose from his chair in the staff room and followed them toward the library. He looked even bigger standing up than I'd expected. He walked in a sort of lope, then shoved the library door open with a callused palm. The boys walked under his arm to get inside, then sat down. Mr. Sills stared at our little Rainbow Coalition for a while, then let the door swing shut and returned to his desk. It was hot and stuffy in the library, and awfully quiet.

Sister Janet stood up and introduced me to the boys, describing me as a very famous writer who nearly won the Pulitzer Prize. The boys kept very still. She explained that the Inside Out writing program was designed to give young people like themselves a chance to discover their own voices, to be heard, and to develop the skills of communication they would need to rebuild their lives. The boys nodded.

"Mark decided to start a class here in K/L after visiting the writing class upstairs. He was *very* impressed by their writing."

Francisco Javier raised his hand. Both of his arms, his neck, and even the back of his shaved head were covered with tattoos.

"Yes, Francisco?"

"That's cool and all, but Sister, they got Barreda and Rocha in that class. Those guys really know how to write. I don't know about Wu and Jackson, but my writing sucks."

"Francisco, I have a feeling your writing is a lot better than you think it is. This isn't a competition—it's about writing honestly. Writing from the heart. Can you do that?"

He nodded, then raised his hand again.

"Yes, Francisco?"

"Can we write whatever we want?"

"Why don't you ask Mark? He's your teacher."

Having been given permission to address me directly, Francisco now looked me straight in the eyes. He had an intense gaze, made all the more hypnotic by his eyebrows, which met in the middle to form an unbroken line. "Can we write whatever we want?" he asked.

"Anything except the details of your case," I said, remembering that Duane had suggested this as a prudent guideline.

" 'Cause it could be used against us," Francisco offered, his gaze beginning to unsettle me.

"Right. The idea here is to write about things that really interest you, that reflect who you really are, or who you would like to be. If you have trouble coming up with topics, of course I'd be happy to help you."

"What about cusswords?" Francisco asked.

"If you need to use them, then use them."

With the boys safely delivered to me and the issue of cusswords settled, Sister Janet wished us a productive morning and left to make visits to the other units. When she had gone, the room got quiet again. Unlike in Duane's class, where a routine had already been established, I could feel the boys wondering what I was going to do next. I thought they might appreciate it if I told them a little about myself, so I gave them some background information and told a few stories about my youthful attempts to become a kung fu master. The boys listened politely and smiled at the appropriate times, but my hope that they would feel comfortable around me immediately proved unrealistic. When I asked them to tell me something about themselves, they shrugged and fidgeted in their chairs, but no one volunteered to go first.

Sensing that Francisco was the most outgoing of the three—and noting that he had been fidgeting the most—I asked him to start. He cleared his throat and said, "Ever since I got locked up this time, I'm startin' to change."

He looked at me as if waiting for me to praise him. When I only nodded, he turned to Jimmy Wu and said, "Well? What about you, fool? Don't make me do all the talking."

Jimmy shrugged. His short black hair was spiked up with gel, giving him a prickly appearance. "We all say we're gonna change. But what good does it do? Who cares if we change now? Nobody, that's who. We might as well be the best fuckups we can be; at least then nobody jacks our shit."

I asked what "jacking somebody's shit" meant.

"It means when fools who think they're on top steal your personals and threaten you if you try to get it back. It's a way of disrespecting you."

"Personals?"

"The stuff you're allowed to have in here. You know, shoes, comb, soap, eyeglasses."

Now Francisco laughed; his changed-man persona from a moment ago seemed to have vanished. "If somebody jacks your shit, man, you gotta deal with it right then. You gotta let everybody know: *Don't fuck with me!* Otherwise you'll get punked every day."

Through all of this, Kevin Jackson had kept his eyes on the table and said nothing. He had a disarmingly sweet face. "How about you, Kevin? What can you tell me that would give me some sense of who you are?"

He paused for a long time, smoothing out the creases in his orange uniform with his palms, then said, "I don't know who I am. Somebody lost, I guess."

Something caught Francisco's attention through the window facing the yard. "Hey—homeboy's back!" He pointed to a boy limping toward our unit with a guard right behind him.

"That's Esquivel. I thought that fool got sent to county?"

"Naw, just to the Box."

As the prisoner came closer, we saw that he had a black eye. Francisco doubled over laughing at the sight of it. "Check it out! Homie's all fucked up! He got his ass kicked! Ha!"

"It happened in school."

Francisco waved this suggestion off. "Naw, it was in court, in the holding tank. Some fool threw up a sign, and homie had to do something."

"That's crazy, man. He's too small to do any damage, look at him."

"Yeah, but he's *loco*, he don't know that." Francisco leaned over and started pounding his fist on the glass until the boy outside looked in our direction. Francisco started blinking hard with one of his eyes, and the boy grinned sheepishly.

Sister Janet had been gone less than five minutes and already the class had drifted out of my control. Imagining how humiliating it would be if Mr. Sills and his posse—who I was sure had sized me up as a flake—had to rescue me, I asked Francisco to sit down and explain to me what the Box was.

"The Box? Oh, uh—I mean 'sir'—it's like . . . if you fuck up on the outs, you come here. When you fuck up in here, you go to the Box."

Jimmy Wu went into more detail for me. "The real name for it is SHU—special handling unit. Basically it's solitary confinement, with a video camera watching you 24/7. You're not even supposed to do push-ups in there. Sometimes, like Javier said, it's used for punishment. But it's also for other things."

"Like what?"

"When guys like us lose our cases, they consider us a suicide risk. Because our sentences are so long. So they take us straight from the courthouse to the Box, where we can't hang ourselves or whatever. It's also for people who would get hurt if they were stuck in with the rest of us."

"Snitches," Francisco hissed. "And homos."

"No," Jimmy corrected, "they put the homos in the sex offenders' unit. With the rapists."

"Oh yeah."

When the room fell silent again, I took the opportunity to suggest we try some writing. "How about if we go for thirty minutes? And don't worry about spelling, grammar, neatness, or any of that. Just write what's on your mind."

The boys picked up their pencils.

"For real—any subject?" Jimmy looked skeptical.

"Think of all the times you've had to write on subjects that were chosen for you," I said. "Well, this is your chance to make up for it."

Francisco, his pencil already moving, said under his breath, "We can even use cusswords, homes. I'm gonna get a fuckin' A in this class."

How slowly can thirty minutes pass? I learned the answer that morning as I found myself with nothing to do except watch three teenage inmates struggle to write. I spent part of the time watching each of them out of the corner of my eye. Jimmy sat up straight as he wrote, while Francisco and Kevin hunched over their notepads with their forearms on the table and their faces only inches away from the page. These two clutched their pencils tightly, and when they made mistakes, they erased with a vengeance. After only ten minutes, Francisco slapped his pencil down, sighed loudly, and announced, "Done. Now what do I do?"

"Would you like to write something else? There's still plenty of time."

"Naw, my brain is tired. Could I go get a drink of water?"

"Sure."

He clasped his hands behind his back and crossed the

dayroom. He walked right past the water fountain and wandered over to the staff room instead. To my surprise, he began chatting with the guards. I saw him pointing toward me, and in a moment they were all laughing.

When Francisco returned to the library, he sat down and began drumming the table with his pencil. I didn't want to shush him, but I didn't want him to disturb Kevin and Jimmy either, who were still concentrating on their writing. I got Francisco's attention and pointed to his paper, then to myself, then gestured as if asking for permission.

"You wanna read it?" he asked loudly.

"If it's all right with you," I whispered.

"Sure, go ahead," he said, still making no attempt to lower his voice.

He slid it to me, put his fists one on top of the other on the table, and rested his chin there. The first thing I noticed was that in spite of the clumsy way he held the pencil, he had the most elaborate handwriting I had ever seen. Each letter was meticulously formed, with curlicues and embellishments and variations in the thickness of each stroke. He had written me a letter:

> *Dear Sir:*
>
> *I am writing this few lines to let you know that I apreciat you coming here. You will help us open ourselves and express our feelings on paper. I never thought I had that talent until now and I believe you will help me develope it. I just want to say thank you sir.*
>
> *Sincerly,*
> *Francisco Javier*

When I looked up at him, he shrugged. I took his pencil and wrote below his message:

Dear Francisco:

Thank you very much. I appreciate that you took the chance to give this class a try. I look forward to reading whatever you write. Since we have ten minutes left, would you do me a favor? Describe yourself in one paragraph. Who are you, besides someone who is locked up?

Sincerely,

Mark Salzman

He read my note, gave me the thumbs-up sign, and hunched over the page again.

At the thirty-minute mark, Jimmy and Kevin put down their pencils. "Gimme one more minute," Francisco said, writing furiously. We waited for him, and when he finished he threw himself back in his chair, shook his hand out, and blew on it. "Damn!" he said, wincing. "That shit hurts! It's hard to be a writer."

I noticed that Kevin was looking over my shoulder and nodding. He said to me, "I think the staff wants you."

I turned around and looked toward the staff room. Mr. Sills pointed at the clock on the wall, then opened his hand and spread his fingers out wide. Five minutes.

I felt that now was time for the last hurdle. Would I be able to convince them to read aloud to each other, the way they did in Duane's class? I expected plenty of resistance, so I had come prepared with a speech about the importance of communication, sharing ideas, getting feedback, and so on. I took a breath and asked,

"OK, we have just enough time to read aloud. Would anyone be willing to go first?"

"Read aloud?" Francisco complained. "You didn't say nothin' about readin' aloud before."

"Well," I began, "there are all sorts of reasons that—"

"I mean, it don't matter to me," Francisco interrupted, "but I'll go first if you want." He picked up his sheet of paper, leaned back in his chair, and frowned. "OK. Here we go. It's just something short, no big thing. I had to write it fast, so—"

"Just read it," Jimmy said.

"I'll read it when I'm ready, don't push me. OK. I call it 'Stress,' 'cause, well, that's what it's about."

He fidgeted some more in his chair, then began to read.

You know something, the thing I hate most about my life is when I stress. There's times when I feel like I'm gonna explode! Like when a .45 caliber bullet at high speed hits a tomato and doesn't leave anything but li'l pieces. That's the way I feel, like if I'm gonna end up in li'l pieces. Yeah, I'm not going to deny it, I have shed many tears in my room here, room 17, and I don't think there is anything wrong when a guy cries. There's been times when I had this li'l voice in my mind saying to me, "Kill yourself!" There's been an occasion where I tried to commit suicide. I tried to cut my veins but thanks to God it was nothing major. I was letting all my problems get to my head. One of my major problems is my case. If a person tells you that you are facing two "life without possibility of parole" term sentences back to back, what are you suppose to think, huh? I use to stress a lot on my case. Sometimes I wouldn't even come out my room. I would stay layin' on my bed, lookin' out my window, thinking why did this have to happen to me, with tears dripping down my face. I would close my eyes and in my mind I would tell God what would be the purpose for me still living, to just let me die. It would really hurt me. I never thought I was going to suffer like this.

I will always remember when my parents would tell me that my homeboys were just sinking me deeper and deeper

*into the hole. And that when something bad happened to
me, we would see just who would be there for me. I should
of listened to them. Ever since I got busted, I have never
received a letter or personals from my homeboys. My parents are the ones that have always been there for me. And I
thank God for letting me have them till this day. I guess I
just had to learn the hard way, huh?*

Francisco laid the sheet of paper down on the table and
fixed his gaze on me. "Is that what you meant?" he asked.

"That's exactly what I meant. Nice job, Francisco."

He looked suspicious. "I know there's gotta be plenty of
mistakes in there."

"Don't worry about mistakes. The most important thing is
being willing to write honestly. To write something genuine
and important. Well, you've done that."

Francisco looked like the Scarecrow in *The Wizard of Oz*
just after the Wizard has given him a diploma. He sat up
proudly, gave a polite little cough, then said, "So who's next?
Don't make me carry the whole fuckin' show."

"I'll read," Jimmy said. "It's about a place in my imagination. My daydreams used to be of beautiful places, or places I
remembered from the outs, but now I keep seeing this other
place and I can't get it out of my head."

*I stand alone and look out at the ocean. Feeling the wind
against my face and hearing the water lap against the
sand, I can't hear or feel anything else. I look around and
see that no one is around. I start to shiver and I feel
my arms covered in goose bumps. As I stand there, I wonder how I became who I am and why I feel nothing but
coldness and loneliness. Where had I gone wrong? Why
am I standing here alone? Why is no one standing here
with me?*

Before any of us could make any comment, Mr. Sills knocked on the window and pointed in the direction of the hallway. The boys stood up immediately.

"Hold on a second," I said to them. "Let me ask if we can stay just five more minutes so Kevin can read."

"Maybe better not," Kevin said. "I can read next time."

Mr. Sills already had the door opened.

"Are you sure?"

Kevin clasped his hands behind his back. "You comin' back?"

"I'll be here Wednesday night. We'll meet twice a week from now on."

"Sounds good," Kevin said. "I'll read then."

The boys filed out silently, then disappeared down the corridor. They had left their essays, along with the pencils and notepads, on the table. I gathered everything and stepped into the dayroom. Mr. Granillo had already opened the main door to the unit for me and was holding it.

"Thank you," I said. "It went really well."

"Have a nice day, sir," he said, looking over my shoulder.

I stepped out into the blinding sunlight, heard the door close behind me, then saw Sister Janet standing nearby in the shade of a tree.

"How did it go?" she asked.

"It ended too soon."

"I told you! Did all three boys write?"

"Yes, but Kevin didn't get to read. We had to end class just before it was his turn. I feel badly about it."

"Don't worry, the boys are used to having to wait for things. He'll get his chance. How about the other two? How was their writing?"

I showed her the two essays. As she read them, she shook her head as if in disbelief. "Can you imagine being seventeen years old and feeling this lonely and confused? Most of them are severely depressed, to the point of considering suicide, but no doctor sees them and they get no counseling at all. What Jimmy writes here about standing alone is absolutely true. These children have been abandoned. Someday, perhaps you'll go to court to watch one of their trials. Then you'll really see what I'm talking about."

She led me out to the key trailer, where I exchanged my visitor's badge for the driver's license I'd surrendered earlier. When we parted at the metal detector she said, "I can't tell you how much even this one visit meant to those boys. Even if you can't do this regularly, the boys won't forget you, I can promise you that. Today will be one of the few good memories they'll have of this place."

I said goodbye, got into my car, and sank into the front seat. I couldn't remember the last time I had felt so exhausted. Still regretting that Kevin had not been able to read his essay, I took it out of my bag and read it in the car.

I remember the time when my third-grade teacher, Mrs. Blue, took me to the museum. I know it might not seem like much to write about, but at that point in my life I needed someone there for me. At the time I was a broken-spirited nine-year-old in desperate need of a shoulder to cry on. The reason I was so down in spirits was because my parents had just been killed in a head-on collision three short weeks before.

After their demise I had a hard time coping with life. I didn't want to eat, go out and play, or participate in any other daily activities except grieving. I had a hard time adjusting back to my regular lifestyle, but after our trip to the museum things just started to seem brighter.

I recall the things we did that day like it just happened earlier today. It was a sunny Saturday afternoon when she arrived at my doorstep. She came in and talked with my grandma for a while. I assume they were talking about the day we had ahead of us. After their brief conference we were on our way. We went to the Museum of Science and Industry in South Central. We saw everything there was to see in the museum: the dinosaur bones, the earthquake room and much more. After we finished our exploration of the museum we went into some gift shops nearby. I played with a few of the things they had but was only interested in one object: a "Slinky." Mrs. Blue saw how fascinated I was by it and purchased it for me. She gave me a hug and told me it was the least she could do. After that we walked around the store and looked at all the other weird trinkets that astounded us. She bought us some freeze-dried ice cream for the first time and we both enjoyed it. After experiencing freeze-dried ice cream, we went across the street to a low-budget hamburger stand for dinner. We sat and talked about the things we saw and did at the museum and about a few other things. Once we finished our food, we got back into her car and I was on my way home from a fun-filled day. My house wasn't that far, so it didn't take us long to get to my house. Before I knew it we were at my front door. She gave me a hug and waited to make sure I made it in safely. Then she left.

Once in the house I went to my room, laid on my bed, and thought about my day until I drifted to sleep. And that concluded my day at the museum. I know it wasn't a spectacular day, but I cherish that day because that was the only person that took time out of their life to help me make it through the death of my parents.

5 / Collision

I met Duane at the key trailer the following Wednesday. After we crossed the yard together, he disappeared up the stairway leading to M/N unit. I knocked on the door to K/L and waited. A female guard answered, opening the door wide enough for us to speak through but not wide enough for me to enter.

"Can I help you?"

"I'm the writing class teacher."

"Writing class? That's upstairs, I believe."

"We started one here. Just last Saturday."

She looked skeptical, but opened the door the rest of the way. This time inmates filled the dayroom, sitting in small groups with an adult at the head of each group. Most of the adults were Latino, and all of them were holding Bibles.

"Have I come at a bad time?" I asked the guard.

"No, it's always busy on Wednesdays. This is religious volunteer night."

She led me to the staff room, where I introduced myself to Mr. Warren—a thin, nervous-seeming black man with a goatee—and explained why I had come. Instead of giving me the silent treatment like Mr. Sills, he talked to me as if I were five years old.

"It's very nice that you've started a little writing class here, sir, but we've got a problem."

"What's that?"

"As you can see, Wednesday nights here are a mess. You've got a lot of movement, a lot of bodies, a lot of contact, but only three of us on the staff. It's hard to keep track of who's doing what, and who's sitting with who. This is not good." He shook his head for emphasis. "Way too much movement."

Hoping to sound deferential, I said, "I don't mean to cause any problems. I'd like for the class to meet twice a week, and was told that Saturday mornings and Wednesday nights were the best time slots. Is there another that would work better for you?"

Mr. Warren kept his eyes on the dayroom. "That's very generous of you, sir, we thank you, but I'm afraid those are the only times volunteer activities are allowed."

I asked myself: What would Duane do? In the mental image I conjured up, he just stood there and didn't say anything. I tried it, and to my surprise, it worked.

"We can't be everywhere at once," Mr. Warren eventually said, speaking more naturally. "I don't know who it is who sets these things up. There's way too much movement in here."

"Who you got in that class?" the third member of the staff asked me. He had a body the shape—and nearly the girth—of the Liberty Bell. He wore a baseball cap with the bill turned backwards, which somehow seemed less threatening than the bill-pulled-way-down-in-front style that the Saturday crew favored.

"Kevin Jackson, Jimmy Wu, and Francisco Javier."

The large man chuckled. "You got Javier to *write*? In a *class*? That I'd like to see."

"He writes pretty well," I said. "All three of them do."

"Yeah? Where'd you guys meet on Saturday?"

"In the library." Checking quickly, I saw that the library was empty, but before I could suggest using it, Mr. Warren shook his head with such vigor that his chin nearly touched each shoulder. "Oh no! I'm not putting a bunch of HROs in there on Wednesday night. I can't see over all these people's heads. No way."

The large man chuckled again. "I can see the library from where I'm at. I'll keep an eye on 'em if you want."

Mr. Warren didn't respond at first, then he rolled his eyes and raised his palms in surrender. "Fine. More chaos. Why not?" Then he threw a towel over his head and stared off into space.

The helpful staff member, whose name was Mr. Jenkins, told me to go on ahead into the library. "I'll get the kids for you. If they start acting silly, you let me know." I thanked him but he waved it off. "Ain't no thing."

A few minutes later Francisco, Jimmy, and Kevin made their way through the crowded dayroom, looking surprised to be released from their rooms. As soon as they made it into the library and closed the door behind them they began talking about a fellow inmate who had just lost his case.

"Guilty, homes. They found him guilty on all five counts."

"But he's not in the Box. Jenkins just told me so."

"That's 'cause he was on the county hit list. They took him straight there, he's gone."

"Damn, he must be trippin' right now. He got forty-eight years to life."

Jimmy glowered at the table. "Everybody knows he wasn't the shooter. They even said so during his trial."

"It don't matter, homes. He was there, that's all they care about."

I thought if I waited patiently, the boys would eventually

stop talking and let me begin the class. But I was wrong; soon they were arguing about lunch servings.

"Jackson, how come you didn't hook me up with an extra sandwich at lunch?"

"There wasn't any extras."

"Bullshit, I saw you give two to Marshall, what's up with that?"

"That wasn't for him, that was for Rodriguez. He's locked down."

"Yeah, but—"

"Good to see you all again," I interrupted. "Shall we do some work?"

"Oh—sorry. Yeah, let's do some work." Francisco sounded contrite, but he was still looking at Kevin. "You gotta hook me up better, homes. Those fuckin' sandwiches, there ain't nothing in 'em but air, I gotta have at least two. Diaz never eats his, man, just let me have that one."

"Why should you get two?" Jimmy asked, his voice edgy. "We all have to eat the same nasty-ass food. You're no hungrier than the rest of us."

While they argued, I passed out notepads and pencils and returned their essays from our first session. I also gave each of them a folder, which I told them they could keep. That held their attention long enough for me to say, "OK, last time we had to stop before Kevin had a chance to read his essay, so I'd like to start with that. Kevin?"

Kevin looked down at his essay and began drumming the table with his pencil. "Could I read it some other time?" he asked.

"No way," Francisco said. "We read ours, homes, now you gotta read yours."

"The atmosphere's not right tonight," Kevin said.

"What's not right about it?"

"Too much chattage."

I asked what "chattage" meant.

"Jackson does that all the time," Jimmy explained. "He makes up words out of his head. At lunchtime, he says it's time for eatage. When we get head call, it's time for pissage. Lights-out, and it's time for sleepage."

"That's right," Francisco said, pointing at Kevin's essay, "and now it's time for readage. The teacher said so, man, don't piss him off."

Kevin sighed, picked up his essay, and leaned back in his chair. My stomach tightened; I wondered if it was such a good idea after all to push him to read, given the content of his essay. He read it straight through, however, without apparent difficulty. When it was over, he slid the paper into his new folder and started drumming again with his pencil.

"Damn," Francisco said, looking subdued. "Sorry to hear that."

Kevin shrugged. "Can't do nothin' about it now."

Francisco perked up right away. "Yeah, that's what I say. No use cryin' about what happened in the past. Wanna know somethin' fucked up? Sometimes I don't even mind bein' in jail, I can forget I'm here. But when I think about life on the outs, all that shit from the past—that's when it hurts. It's like a knife goin' right into my heart and then gettin' twisted around, like Chucky goin' crazy on me or somethin'."

"Who's Chucky?" Kevin asked.

"The evil doll, fool. That kills people."

"So what are we writing about it for, then?" Jimmy asked through clenched teeth. "We dredge up all this painful shit, and it only makes it worse. What good is it?"

I admitted to the boys that I didn't know for sure that writing about painful experiences was a good idea. "All I can say," I told them, "is that from an awful time in his life, Kevin cherishes the memory of his teacher helping him out. By cherishing it, he keeps the teacher's gift to him alive, and by writing it down, he passes the gift along to us. It makes me feel good to hear it."

Francisco brightened. "That's real! Hold on, I gotta think about that for a while." He picked up his pencil and tore a fresh sheet of paper out of his notepad. For a moment I thought he was going to start writing without my having to ask, but then he slumped back in his chair. "Damn, I wish they'd let us have conjugal visits in here."

Kevin and Jimmy groaned, which egged Francisco on. "It don't make no sense, homes! They try us as adults, right? They give us adult sentences and send us to adult prison. So how come we can't have conjugal visits? I'm tired a makin' Fifi. I want Gina."

I asked what "making Fifi" meant, but Francisco—for once—demurred. Kevin pretended to be very interested in something outside the window. Shaking his head in disgust, Jimmy volunteered to explain it for me. "Fifi is an artificial vagina," he said in a matter-of-fact tone. "You make it using a county towel and county soap."

"No fuckin' privacy," Francisco complained. "The staff even watches you when you take a shit! There's no doors on the stalls! You can't make faces, you know what I'm sayin'? You know how, like, when you're takin' a shit, it feels good to make faces? You can't do that in here. You gotta sit like this—" He demonstrated by staring straight ahead, expressionless, but holding his breath and pushing until his face turned purple. Kevin and Jimmy laughed so hard I worried that the staff would end our class early.

"Hell," Francisco muttered after he'd let himself breathe again, "you gotta put on this stone-cold mask even then. That's what this place is all about. Puttin' on masks."

"That might be a good topic to write about," I suggested.

"Nobody wants to read about takin' a shit," Francisco argued.

"No, I mean having to put on a mask all the time. What does it feel like? How does it affect you? Does it make you feel as if you lose track of who you really are?"

The boys appeared to be considering this when the door to the library opened and the woman who had let me into the building stuck her head in.

"Any nurse regulars?"

"Naw."

"No."

The female guard leaned against the doorframe and crossed her arms over her chest. "So what kind of writing are you guys doing?"

"We're takin' the negative and turnin' it into somethin' positive," Francisco answered. He held up his essay for her to see, as if to prove that he wasn't lying.

"That's good," she said. "Writing's important."

"That's just what we were talkin' about," Francisco said, erasing the gang moniker he had doodled at the bottom of the page.

"Sometimes you can't think of anything positive," Jimmy said, his eyes fixed on the table. "All you can think about is the negative, because that's all there is in your life. What're you supposed to write about then?"

The guard looked over her shoulder and waved toward the staff room, indicating that there were no "nurse regulars" in the library. Then she said to Jimmy, "You write about the negative, then. If you can write about it, you get it out in the open. It eases the pressure."

"It doesn't change the reality, though. You're still stuck in your fucked-up life. Nothing changes."

"I disagree," she said, pushing off the doorframe. "You *make* the reality. That's my opinion."

When she'd left, Francisco asked me if I knew what a nurse regular was. I said I didn't have any idea.

"Every night a nurse comes in with psych meds. The guys who want 'em line up over there." He pointed to a line of boys standing with their backs to the far wall. One at a time, they went into the staff room and came out a few seconds later.

"What kind of psych meds?" I asked.

"I don't know, but they're strong as fuck. It comes in a little paper cup. You take 'em and you be like—" Francisco's face went slack, his tongue lolled out of his mouth, and he started drooling. "I'd never take that shit. It turns you into a fuckin' zombie."

"If I was stressed enough, I would," Jimmy said. He stuffed his essay into his folder and looked out the window at the yard. "I mean, what good does it do us to hope for *anything*? It doesn't matter what we do anymore. Nobody cares about a bunch of criminals. When I was on the outs, I never thought once about people in jail, so why should I expect anybody to think about me?"

"Don't say that kinda shit, Wu," Francisco said, hunching over his notepad and writing as he spoke. "You gotta have hope, otherwise you go all crazy and shit. Fuck it, I'ma write something *good* tonight."

"How can you do that?" Jimmy asked.

" 'Cause there's shit-all else to do, that's how."

"No—I mean how can you write and talk at the same time?"

Francisco snorted. " 'Cause I gotta fucking split personality, which is what I'm tryin'a write about, so shut up already and write, otherwise Mark ain't gonna come here no more 'cause all we do is fuck around."

Kevin smiled. "Not enough writeage."

"Yeah. So write another one of them depressing stories, Wu. Fat-ass Jenkins said he was gonna make sure we all wrote something tonight, or he wouldn't let us come outta our rooms next week."

The boys settled down and wrote for twenty minutes, but the noise from the dayroom was a distraction. They kept looking up from their work to see what was going on out there, and to mouth silent questions to cell mates and friends. When it looked like they had all finished, I asked who would like to read aloud first.

Once again, no one volunteered. "Do I always got to be the one who goes first?" Francisco complained. Before anyone could respond, he said, "Fuck it, I'll read. I call this 'Collision,' 'cause it's, uh . . . well, 'cause it's . . . fuck it, if I tell you what it's about, then what's the point a readin' it? I'ma just read it."

The angel is coming at full speed in one direction, while the devil comes in the other. The devil with his pitchfork, running at full speed, aiming to hit the angel in the chest, all of a sudden stops with the force of the angel's power. The devil tells the angel that he is going to kill him and that he is going to go to hell, but the angel responds, "I am with God, and the only place where I'm going is to His paradise." The devil then strikes him, sending him to eternal fire. The angel on his knees, weak, all of a sudden gets his energy back and strikes the devil with his wings and sends him to heaven. There they are, throwing blows, wrestling, doing what they can to win.

All of a sudden they're running full speed towards each other when they collide and become one. That one is me.

"That's real," Jimmy said. "Everybody in here wakes up in this place hoping that at last, the bad part of him is gone and everything's gonna turn around. But something always happens. Somebody says something, or looks at you a certain way, or you remember that you've ruined your life, and the bad part all comes back. You're back where you started."

Kevin raised his arms over his head to stretch, then yawned, his face settling into a weary smile. "It's a collision all right, but it's like watchin' a car crash on video where the replay button is stuck. They keep crashin' over and over, but the people in the cars never get it right."

"Yeah! Sometimes I wish I could put my whole life on pause, homes. Just make everything stop for a while so I can figure shit out."

"Not me," Jimmy said. "I want mine on fast-forward. I just want to get to the end. Fuck it."

"What did you write about tonight?" I asked Jimmy.

He looked at the piece of paper in front of him, considered it for a moment, then crushed it into a ball. "I'll try to write something on Saturday. I can't think straight tonight."

I told him not to worry, that he didn't have to write something every session. I said that writing was hard to do and that all of us have days when we feel stuck.

"So that leaves Jackson at the end again," Francisco said. "Hit us with it."

Kevin stretched again, then slid his essay from the table onto his lap.

"Don't got a title for it," he said. "I just thought of it while we were talking before."

Late at night when the reality of being locked up starts to set in, I begin to wonder why was I ever created if I'm gonna spend the rest of my life in prison? The feeling of meaninglessness starts to set deep within my soul as each day goes by. . . .

I know that if I do get the blessing of receiving my freedom back, I will try to do something that will help me to feel like I have a meaning on this earth, but I only have one problem with that, I don't know what I want to be. I don't feel that I'm very good at anything and that just adds to my stress. Sometimes I almost believe myself when I say that I'm a good-for-nothing piece of shit.

"But your life ain't meaningless," Francisco objected. "The Bible says so."

"Yeah, I know. But so far I just can't see it."

"God loves you, homes, you just gotta love him back and then he'll tell you what to do with your life."

Jimmy's eyes narrowed. "My brother loves God and look at all the good it's done him. He got a disease that'll kill him before he's twenty years old."

Francisco threw up his hands. "All I'm sayin' is, Jackson's life ain't meaningless, OK?" He looked at me. "Help me out here, you're the teacher! Tell Jackson his life ain't meaningless."

"If I did that, he would know that I was saying it just to be nice. He has to work it out for himself, which he's already doing. My job is to encourage him to keep working."

Francisco's brow scrunched up for a moment, then relaxed. "That's right," he affirmed, putting his name on the folder I'd given him. "Whatever you just said, that's what I fuckin' meant."

6 / Here I Am

By ten o'clock that Saturday morning the temperature had reached ninety degrees. The sunlight reflecting off the concrete buildings blinded me; as I approached K/L unit, I couldn't see anything through the windows. I leaned in close, shading my eyes with my hands, with my nose pressing against the glass. When my eyes adjusted to the darkness, I saw the inmates sitting with their backs to the walls, legs splayed out in front of them. They were stripped to their underpants and socks. I felt embarrassed at having invaded their privacy and backed away from the entrance. I sat down on the steps, thinking the staff would wait until the boys were dressed to let me in, but a few seconds later the door opened. I kept my eyes glued to the floor because it seemed unfair that I was clothed and the boys were practically naked. I went straight to the control room, where Mr. Sills sat at his desk, feet propped on a file cabinet, talking on the phone. I waved at him and got the usual response, a disinterested nod.

Mr. Granillo, meanwhile, stalked the dayroom like a football coach at halftime. "You think this is *tough*?" he thundered, glowering at the boys from under the bill of his cap. "You think we're *hard* on you? You wanna *complain* to somebody? Well, lemme tell you something. You got a wake-up call coming, gentlemen. And when it comes, you are gonna wish—you are gonna *cry*—for the days when you were here."

He stalked some more, then jabbed the air with a meaty finger. "When you get to the pen, everything's gonna change. You're gonna be boys surrounded by men. Hard men, who'd just as soon shank you as say hello. If you wanna survive, you're gonna have to grow up fast, and you're gonna have to toughen up! You may curse me now, but the day will come when you'll thank me. *The day will come.*"

The boys were drenched in sweat. Mr. Granillo picked up a clipboard and walked over to the staff room. "They're ready, Sills."

Mr. Sills nodded, told the person on the phone that he had business to attend to, then stood up. As he passed by me I saw that the top of my head barely reached his shoulder.

He paced the room slowly, looking at each one of the boys but without saying anything. When he'd come full circle, he paused at the head of the room and was silent for nearly a minute. At last he nodded and said, "OK."

"Take it down," Granillo ordered. The boys jumped up and filed silently down the corridors to their rooms. During all of this, none of the boys had made a sound. When the last of the boys had disappeared, Mr. Sills approached me. "You go on into the library. My kids need to get cleaned up."

The unit's ventilation system did not reach the library. When I opened the door to step inside, the heat sent me reeling. Sunlight poured in through the windows, turning the small room into an oven. I propped both doors open, hoping the air-conditioning from the dayroom would circulate through.

Francisco was the first to join me. "Hey Mark," he said, greeting me with a big smile. "How you doin'?" He looked flushed, and his face and neck glistened with sweat.

"Fine. How about you?"

"Good! My arms and legs are sore as shit, but that's OK, it means I'm gettin' stronger. Granillo had us outside for exercise. He's a sick motherfucker."

Kevin joined us, looking as pumped up as Francisco. I asked what kind of exercises they had done. "Aw, you know—push-ups and sit-ups and running laps and shit. You could barely move when it's done. But it feels good, you know? Better than sittin' in your room all day."

"Does everyone *have* to do the exercises?" I asked. "What happens if somebody doesn't want to do them?"

They looked at each other and shrugged. "If you don't exercise, you don't get to go outside. Man, when you're locked up, you'll do anything to get outside."

"Plus, we gotta get in shape. We got some competition with the other units coming up."

"Yeah, a couple times a year there's contests. We got football, baseball, track, tug-of-war. It's about the only fun you can have in here, so we get into it."

Francisco nodded. "There's a big-ass trophy for the unit that wins. Sills wants that trophy, man! No joke."

"Mr. Sills seems like a no-nonsense guy," I said, curious to know what the boys thought of the staff. I assumed they resented all of the guards, especially the strict ones.

Kevin smiled. "You don't want to get him pissed off, put it that way. But if you're straight with him, he'll be straight with you."

"He's awright," Francisco agreed. "Not like some of the punk-ass staff around here. Dumb motherfuckers, they—"

Francisco halted in mid-sentence. Jimmy Wu entered the

library, followed by another Asian boy who stood with his hands clasped behind his back.

"This is Chumnikai," Jimmy said. "He wants to know if he can be in the class." Jimmy sat down, but the new boy remained standing, as if he were in the army and needed permission.

I asked for his first name.

"Patrick, sir."

"Welcome to the class, Patrick. Have a seat." He was short, had an overbite, and his ears stuck out like acoustical panels. I explained the class to him, how it worked, and promised to bring him a folder if he decided to stick with it. When I asked if he had any questions, he shook his head.

Francisco leaned over the table and glared at the newcomer. "You gotta be serious about this," he said. "This ain't just for hanging out, it's for writing. And you gotta write from the heart. Got it?"

Patrick nodded.

I opened up my bag and took out the boys' essays from the previous sessions. During the week I had typed copies of all of them, explaining that I felt it was helpful to see one's own work in print, the way a reader would see it. Francisco read over his essays, slapped the table with his open palm, and said, "Damn! I had no idea how talented I was!"

When the others laughed, he held one of the pages out in front of him like a cop showing his badge. "Check it out if you don't believe me! There's the title up there: *COLLISION*. In big fuckin' letters! And all the little fuckin' letters underneath tellin' the story, just like in a book. Damn, I'ma send this home."

Delighted with the results of this experiment, I handed out notepads and pencils, and without my having to say anything further, all four boys lowered their heads as if to work.

Then the room started to shake. Somebody was playing rap music on an enormous boom box out in the dayroom, and the bass notes were making everything in the library that wasn't bolted down rattle. The boys jerked to attention, like soldiers hearing a bugle calling for a charge, and sprang into motion: they tapped their feet, they made percussion sounds with their mouths, they rocked in their chairs, they sang along with the lyrics, and more or less did everything a seated person can do except write.

When I got up and closed the doors to the library, the boys looked glum. "You don't have to do that—we can listen and write at the same time! It helps us think."

"It's hot in here, sir."

"Yeah, don't close the door!"

"Let's just try writing without the background music," I said. "You can listen to it after class."

The boys grumbled, but I felt I should stick by the decision so as not to seem wishy-washy. Within minutes the room turned into a sauna, and the boys started fanning themselves with their notepads instead of writing in them. The smell of sweat and disinfectant became overpowering; when one of the boys farted, I broke down.

"Kevin, you may open the doors."

Francisco wiped his brow with his sleeve. "You think this is bad, try spending all day and night in a ten-by-twelve cell. It smells so bad you gotta breathe through your mouth."

Jimmy agreed. "Yeah! Like on a night when your roommate begs to be let out to go to the bathroom, but the staff are too fucking lazy to walk down the hall. So he has to throw a towel in the corner of the room and piss into that. Try breathing then."

"I get the picture. What are you going to write about today, Francisco?"

"I'ma write one a them message-in-a-bottle things. You

know? Like how dudes be stranded on an island and put their last words on paper, and hope some fool finds it?"

"Good idea. How about you, Kevin?"

Kevin shook his head. "I'm stuck."

I asked if he had any other strong memories, like the trip to the museum, that he would like to write down. He smiled but kept shaking his head.

"I don't have a whole lot of memories. Most of my past is like a fog."

"Maybe you could write about that."

"How you supposed to write about nothin'?"

"By describing what it feels like to want to remember things, but to have them seem out of reach."

He kept still for a moment, then shrugged. "I'll give it a try."

I saw that Jimmy was focused on whatever he was writing, so I didn't disturb him. The new boy looked stumped.

"I can't think of anything, sir."

I suggested several topics, but none of them seemed to interest him. Desperate for ideas, I looked out the window and saw a jet leaving a vapor trail across the sky. I wrote the word "distance" on the top of Patrick's notepad and told him to write anything that the word brought to mind.

He nodded, then hunched over the notepad so that no one could read over his shoulder as he wrote.

The boys struggled to concentrate in the heat. After half an hour I could tell they had all had enough, so I asked if anyone would like to start reading. Before Francisco could volunteer, Jimmy pointed out the window. "Check out the front door. We got a visitor."

Sister Janet was using her key to let herself into the unit. As soon as she got inside she froze, squinted toward where the music was coming from, and asked me, "Has this been going on the whole time you've been trying to write?"

"Yeah," Francisco said, "and it's been *really hard* to concentrate." Francisco, I realized, was somebody who knew how to stir up trouble.

Sister Janet's expression hardened. She told us she would be right back and marched toward the staff room.

"Uh-oh!" Francisco said, wringing his hands with glee.

We couldn't hear anything over the music, but could see Sister Janet pointing toward us, then at the boom box on in the hallway, then at Mr. Sills and Mr. Granillo. Their faces remained impassive, but even from across the dayroom I could see their jaw muscles twitching.

The boom box went silent.

Sister Janet returned to the library. "I want to apologize to each of you," she said. "I should have been here earlier to make sure you were being given the help you need. I won't let it happen again."

"Aw, it ain't your fault, Sister," Francisco said. "We coulda asked 'em to turn it down, but we didn't. You know us—we like that music."

"That's not the point, Francisco. It's a matter of adults having respect for what you're trying to do, and supporting it. But that's for me to worry about, not you. Were you able to write today?"

"Yeah, I did! Wanna hear me read?"

"I'd love to."

"OK," Francisco said, taking charge. "But Chumnikai's gotta read first. He's the new guy, he's gotta show he's serious."

Patrick seemed resigned to being told what to do, at least at the beginning. "The assignment was to write something on the word 'distance,'" he said, his voice barely audible.

"Could you speak a little louder?" Sister Janet asked. "When you get to be my age, you don't hear as well as you'd like to."

"I wrote about somebody distant," he said, not much louder than before.

There is a distance between a person and me. He and I are very very close, yet so far away. Far away not like in miles or inches, but something else. He's been there since I was brought to this world and lived with me for a long time. But he is like a stranger to me. He is there to help me, but he does not help me. He is there to take me places to have fun, but he is busy watching TV. He's been there all my life, but it seems like he's not there at all. I'm happy when he visits me here, but he hardly talks and leaves early. So what! I love him! We may not talk to each other much and see each other for a little while, but he traveled far away from his work to see me, and after, he goes back to his work. Even though we are distant, I still love him. I love my dad!

Patrick slid his paper toward me, then appeared to be bracing himself to be teased.

"This was your first day in class?" Sister Janet asked him.

"Yeah."

"And already you were able to write something so beautiful?"

Patrick kept still.

Sister Janet let the room stay quiet for a few moments before asking, "Have you ever told him how you feel? That you love him, but wish you could be closer?"

Patrick shook his head.

"Why not?"

"It's hard to say that kind of stuff."

"Yes, it is." She pointed to the sheet of paper in front of him. "What about sending him this essay? Do you think you could do that?"

Patrick thought about it, then nodded. "Maybe."

"If you did that, I promise you he would cherish it."

"Yeah. I'll think about it."

"Let me know if you need an envelope or a stamp."

"Thanks."

Now Sister Janet turned to face the original three in my group. "Well," she said, smiling, "I'm curious to know what you've been up to. Mark tells me you've done remarkable work. There are a lot of people out there ready to say that nothing good can come out of this place. You're going to prove them wrong, I'm convinced of it."

"They don't know anything about us!" Francisco protested. "All they know is what the newspapers say. They don't know the whole story."

"Then it's up to you to tell them, isn't it? Are you prepared to make that effort?"

Francisco's eyes blazed. "I wanna do somethin' with my life, Sister. I pray to God every night, askin' him to help me."

"Let's hear what you wrote, then."

"I wrote about a message in a bottle. You know what that is, right?"

"Yes. Go ahead."

"It fits in with what we're talkin' about just now, 'cause—" He stopped short and looked at me. "Hold on. Should I read mine from Wednesday instead? The one you typed? It looks more, you know, professional."

"You can show that to her at the end of class. Let's hear the new one."

"Yeah, I see what you're sayin'. This way she gets both."

Dearest Stranger:

This is my last statement on earth. I know people look at me like a criminal and a no-good person. A gang member that's a menace to society because I'm incarcerated, but it's not true. I am a person who is discovering who he really is. I found out that I am a person with many talents.

I know in here sometimes I have to put a mask on and become somebody that I am really not, but that's how you survive in here. I might seem like if I'm big and tough, as if I'm hard as a stone on the outside, but deep inside of me, I am a person with fear, anger, and hurt.

If I was to die today, and you tell people about me, just tell them that I'm finally free, because I don't have to be nobody that I don't want to be.

Francisco beamed at Sister Janet, as if expecting her to throw a parade in his honor, but she merely nodded and smiled and turned to Kevin.

"You're next," she said.

Francisco looked disappointed but kept quiet.

Kevin explained that he was having difficulty remembering his past, and that I had challenged him to write about not remembering. "So I came up with this. I'm not sure it's what he wanted, but it's all I could think of."

As I sit here and think, I really can't remember too many things I've done with my mother. It kind of hurts when I think about how stupid I was for not trying to hold on to those memories, but I was young at the time and felt that if I just forgot about my parents it wouldn't hurt so much. I was wrong. I tried to put my memories aside for almost nine years, and now when I'm all alone I try to bring my memories that I had tucked away back, but I only remember about one-third of the things that happened. I feel depressed sometimes about not being able to remember the most important people in my life, and I try not to let it get me down, but I think it would get anybody down. I guess I just did too much forgetting. Now I regret it.

Sister Janet nodded again, took a breath, then asked Jimmy to read. Jimmy spread several sheets of paper out in front of him, each page crammed with writing, cross-outs, and editing marks. "I've been working on this for a while," he said. "I read a version of it at our play last month. You probably already heard it, Sister Janet."

"I'd like to hear it again."

Jimmy checked the order of the pages, rested his hands on his hips for a moment, then thrust them into his pants pockets.

Here I am
In this lonely place that has become my life,
I am all alone.
My family, my friends, even my dreams are all gone.
Everyone and everything that I've known.
All I do all day is think really hard
about how my life went wrong.
Let me tell you my story. Let me tell you about me.
Don't worry, it won't take very long.
I was born in Taiwan in the year '79
and my father named me Jimmy.
My parents held me in their arms, they gave me a kiss,
they were as proud as any parents could be.
When I was two, we came to the States
and my parents opened up a shop.
We sold some ice cream, we sold some shakes,
but eventually, we had to stop.
From there we moved on, my parents found new jobs,
they began to work for the county.
The hours were long, but the money was good.
Everything went smoothly for all I could see.
When I turned nine, my parents gave me a brother,
and I got to choose his name.
When he entered this world, when he entered our lives,

I knew nothing would ever be the same.
For the next few years, everything was fine,
and my bond with my brother grew.
Then something terrible happened. It caught me by
    surprise.
It hurt me like a hurt I never knew.
When my brother was three, my parents divorced,
they said it was for the best.
The yelling, the screaming, the physical blows,
had finally all come to a rest.
I moved out with Mom, little brother stayed with Dad,
but we'd still see each other on the weekends.
I became a loner, I became withdrawn.
It seemed so hard to make a single friend.
Two years pass, and my brother turns five.
He has grown into an adorable little boy.
He is full of life. He is full of love.
And in his heart, he is full of joy.
Then we noticed something, about the way he walked.
He was always moving and walking on his toes.
So we took him to a doctor, to let him be examined,
and slowly, more changes in him started to show.
He was diagnosed with Duchenne muscular dystrophy,
which is a neuromuscular disease.
When I heard the news, my heart was torn apart.
And hurting, I collapsed and fell to my knees.
The doctors say my brother won't live past the age of
    twenty,
and when he goes, it will be full of pain.
His muscles will start to shrink, he will be unable to move.
The only thing left untouched will be his brain.
And so I tried to ignore him. Tried to unattach myself.
'Cause it hurt too much to be around.
I couldn't stand to see him. I would start to cry,

and burning, my tears would fall to the ground.
So I started cursing God for allowing this to happen.
To my sweet, innocent, beloved little brother.
Why did this have to happen? Why did He hurt us so?
I always thought that we'd be together. Forever.
And then my dad got married. To a person that I disliked.
When that happened, he really let me down.
I began to hate my father. My heart was full of anger.
In the sea of rage I began to drown.
I started to hang with gangsters. Gave up on my
*   education.*
I felt that everything was just a waste of time.
One thing led to another, somehow I got pulled under.
The next thing I knew, I was in jail for committing a
*   crime.*
My parents were in shock. They didn't know what to do.
To them, it seemed as if they had lost both their sons.
Many nights were sleepless, my mind was full of questions.
I suddenly realized that having fun isn't always fun.
Now here I am, sitting behind walls.
With nothing to do but think.
About how much I lost. About how much I will lose.
How much further will I be able to sink?
I want my parents to know that I love them. And that I'm
*   really sorry*
for putting them in a situation such as this.
I hope that they'll forgive me. I hope that they'll still
*   love me.*
All the good times that we had I will always miss.

Now you know what happened. Now you know my story.
I hope I'm not just a face for you to see.
I'm a person with a past. I'm a person with a future.
So if I may, can I ask you to please pray for me?

Sister Janet allowed just the right amount of time to pass before looking at each of the boys, congratulating them quietly, then standing up.

"I want you to know," she said, "that what you are doing here is terribly important. This is the kind of writing that can change minds, and can change lives. If you keep writing like this, I promise you, it will make a difference. I thank you for sharing this with me."

She looked each boy in the eye again, her own eyes brimming with tears, then left the unit. The room stayed quiet even after she'd left; no one wanted to break the spell that had been cast over our little gathering. When the boom box started up again, something caught Kevin's attention and he said, "I think our time is up." I looked toward the staff room, where Mr. Sills was pointing at the clock again. This time he made a slicing motion across his throat with the other hand. The boys stood up and handed me their paper and pencils.

"I just want to thank you, sir," Patrick said abruptly, extending his hand toward me. As soon as I'd shaken hands with Patrick, the other boys seemed to want to do the same. After we'd all shaken hands, Kevin said, "Can I ask you something?"

"Sure."

"Why *do* you come here, anyway?"

Over his shoulder I could see Mr. Granillo unlocking the main door to let me out, so I said, "Tell you what. Ask me again when we have more time, and I'll give you as good an answer as I can. OK?"

"No hurry. Just curious."

I shouldered my bag and hurried to the door, but although Mr. Granillo had unlocked it, he wasn't ready to open it just yet.

"Excuse me, *sir*," he said, his eyes round with anger. "Your class is scheduled to go until eleven o'clock, is that correct?"

"Yes . . ."

"That was forty minutes ago."

Payback for Sister Janet and the boom box. I apologized for losing track of the time and promised it wouldn't happen again.

"I just thought I'd tell you, *sir*, that when you do that, it affects our whole program. It means that while your group is having its meeting, all the other minors are locked in their cells, missing recreation. They don't like that. There are going to be consequences."

I felt guilty immediately. I imagined the boys in my group being beaten in retaliation for causing the others to miss recreation, all because I hadn't paid attention to the clock. I apologized to Mr. Granillo again, then asked for his help. I told him if he saw me doing anything stupid in the future, to please tell me right away so that I wouldn't create more problems.

This seemed to catch him off guard. He adjusted the bill of his cap. "I didn't say it was stupid. I'm just letting you know, that's all."

"I appreciate it. Any advice you can give me, I'll be glad to have it."

He adjusted his cap again, then pushed the door open for me. "OK, then. We'll see you next week."

7 / Lockdown

"Bad news," Mr. Jenkins told me and the religious volunteers. "The whole unit's on lockdown this week. No activities tonight." He apologized for the inconvenience, then closed the door.

The volunteers groaned but did not look surprised. "It happens about once a month," one of them told me. "If a fight breaks out, the whole unit gets punished." They turned around as a group and headed back toward the key trailer.

I lingered at the door to the unit, hoping I might at least drop off the boys' work from the previous session. I hated the thought of making the drive to Central for nothing. As I searched through my bag for the pages, I heard the jingle of keys and the clank of a heavy bolt lock, and the door opened once again.

"How many kids you got in your class?" Mr. Jenkins asked quietly.

"Four."

"I doubt I can get four kids out, lockdown and all, but I might be able to bring up one or two. Hold on."

He disappeared into the staff room for a moment, then came out smiling. "Go on ahead into the library," he said. "I'll see what I can do."

He limped down the corridor and returned a few minutes later, with Kevin Jackson and Jimmy Wu on either side of him. "Just these two for tonight," he said. "They're never any trouble."

"I appreciate it."

Mr. Jenkins shrugged. "I might ask you a favor one day, who knows."

As soon as he'd left us, the two boys asked how I'd managed to pull it off. "We've been locked down for days! They wouldn't even let us out of our rooms to go to school. You must have juice around here, Mark."

"It was Mr. Jenkins. He seems to be on our side."

"Yeah, he's into education an' all that." Kevin tilted his head back and breathed deeply. I thought he was going to complain about the smell of disinfectant in the library, which was almost overpowering, but instead he stretched out his arms and said, "Man, it feels good to be out in the open again."

"What happened this week?" I asked.

"Just some stupid racial bullshit," Jimmy Wu said, scowling. "It happens like this: there's a race war goin' on in the adult prisons between the blacks and the Latinos. Whatever happens there trickles down here. If a group of black guys jump a Latino guy up at Corcoran or Folsom, the Mexican Mafia will say that Latino guys got to pick fights with blacks for payback. And if they find out the juveniles didn't carry out the order, they'll be waiting for you when you get sent to the pen.

"So as we were going out of the unit for church on Sunday, this one Latino fool threw his gang sign and jumped this black fool, and before you know it, fools are jumping on other fools, and the staff is goin' nuts and everybody's coughing from pepper spray. Since then we been locked down."

"But how do the people in adult prison keep track of what people here do?" I asked. "How does the information go back and forth?"

"The hard-core people know *everything*," Kevin said. "Since we bein' tried as adults, we get put in the same holding tanks as the guys from the pen. You're there all day, there's not much else to do but talk, and there's nowhere to hide if you wanna keep out of it."

"But the two of you kept out of it."

"I can't afford to get in trouble," Jimmy said. "There's still a chance the judge could send me to Youth Authority or fire camp to do some of my time instead of sending me to the pen. No more screwups for me. If I get called chickenshit, or if I get the shit kicked out of me for it, so be it."

"What about you, Kevin?"

"Me? Oh, I guess I'm just sick of the whole thing." He laid his arms flat on the table and tucked his chin in the crook of one elbow. "So what are we gonna write about today, Mark? I wanna write, but I can't think of anything. Gimme a topic."

"How about describing a time you helped someone? It would make a nice companion to your essay about the teacher who helped you."

He leaned his head over so that his cheek rested on his bicep. "Mm." He picked up one of the pencils I'd set out on the table. "I never did anything that nice for anybody."

"It can be a small thing."

"Mm." He took another deep breath, then straightened up and faced the page. "It's gonna have to be real small, Mark."

"That's not a problem. How about you, Jimmy? Do you have something to work on?"

Jimmy stared out the window. "Not at the moment."

"He's stressin'," Kevin said. "Ain't that right, Wu?"

"Yeah."

"He's stressin'," Kevin repeated, writing his name at the top of his notepad. "The thing is, his situation sounds pretty good to me. He's lookin' at eighteen years with no L. He could be out in twelve if he stays out of trouble. I'd take that deal in a second."

"It's not me that I'm stressing about," Jimmy said angrily. "It's my mother."

"Are you upset because she's worried about you?" I asked.

"That's part of it. She hired a lawyer for my trial, and he charged her sixty thousand dollars up front. She had to mortgage the house to pay him, and the guy didn't do shit. He probably spent an hour on it, total. I lost my case, and now he won't handle the sentencing hearing unless my mother pays him more." Jimmy's eyes welled up. "I'm the one who fucked up, so I know I have to pay the price. But he's ripping off *my mother*— she's gonna lose everything because of me—and I can't do shit about it."

He clenched his fists and swallowed, but would not let himself cry. He kept staring out the window, without blinking, as if trying to will the unscrupulous lawyer to appear before him.

"Maybe you could write a letter to your mom," Kevin suggested.

Jimmy shook his head. "Whenever I see her, I tell her I'm doing fine, that everything is gonna be all right. I have to stay strong for her. I'm gonna write about something else."

This time I offered to write with them, and the hour passed quickly. Just before eight o'clock, Mr. Jenkins gave us a signal: five more minutes. The boys insisted that this time, I read aloud first.

I had chosen to write about my only real-life experience which involved prisoners: while living in mainland China during the early eighties, I found myself on a local train seated next to two young men who had just been released from a forced labor camp. They were drinking hard liquor and celebrating their freedom when one of them began daydreaming aloud about the scene at the railroad station when he and his mother would be reunited. He was going on and on about how much his mother loved him when suddenly his companion struck him hard across the chest and told him to shut up. Pointing at me, the quieter man said, "He's far away from home—he can't see his mother at all. He doesn't need to know how happy you are."

As soon as I began reading the story to the boys I wished I had written something else. Jimmy was upset over his mother's financial troubles and Kevin didn't have a mother; what was I thinking? To my relief, the two boys applauded when I finished and asked if I would make copies of it for them. "When you're locked up, you think about your mother all the time," Jimmy said. "That's true of everybody here."

"It's like it's genetic," Kevin agreed, then he offered to read next.

The only time I can remember helping a complete stranger was about a month ago. I was in here on my way to showers when I recognized a new guy coming out of the shower without any house shoes on. When I went back to my room I debated on if I should give this guy my extra pair. I would have given them to him if he was a dog, but he was from the other side of the unit so I felt I should just let him be. But then I thought about when I first got to jail. I had nothing for about a week until this enemy from a Compton gang gave me some shower shoes and some personals. So I felt some compassion for the fellow and gave them to him after all.

After I was in bed that night about to go to sleep I felt good that I helped somebody out, because I know that someone helped me back when I was struggling.

"Is that person still here?" I asked.

"Naw, he lost his case. He got thirty-five to life."

I asked if two people from enemy gangs could actually become friends in juvenile hall.

They glanced at each other, then both nodded. "It happens a lot, but you can't show it. You definitely have to keep it on the low-pro."

"Low-profile?"

"Right," Jimmy said. "You're supposed to put the gang first, but the truth is, if you could listen to most of us when we're talking in our rooms, when it's just you and your roommate and not in front of everybody else, you'd find out that a lot of guys in here are sick of it. I mean—look where it got us, right?"

Kevin nodded solemnly.

Jimmy tilted his chair back, stopping just at the point of balance. "The problem is, it's hard to get out. It's like this: If you turn your back on the gang, who do you got left? By the time you're locked up, how many people you think still care about you? Your family, maybe, and that's it. And they can't do the time with you. If you leave the gang, you're a buster, and everybody hates you."

Jimmy kicked his feet out and the chair dropped forward. "Bet you never thought you'd end up in a place like this, hanging out with guys like us in your spare time, huh?"

"I sure didn't."

When Mr. Jenkins knocked on the window for us to clear out, Kevin smiled and asked, "So why *do* you come here, Mark?"

"How come you always ask me when it's time to go?"

"That way, you'll have to come back to answer it."

"I can tell you one thing—I enjoy the surprise of it. You guys aren't at all like what I expected."

"What did you expect?"

Even Jimmy smiled now. "Yeah, tell us."

I decided to act it out. I slumped back in my chair, crossed my arms over my chest, snarled at them both, then gave them the finger.

The boys seemed to think this was hilarious, but the person who laughed hardest of all was Mr. Jenkins, who had been standing just outside the library. He stuck his head in and asked me, "So—these clowns finally got on your nerves, huh? You want me to straighten 'em out for you?"

When I explained the context for the rude gesture, he said, "Oh, we don't see anything like that down here, do we Wu? Do we, Jackson?"

The boys shook their heads.

"No, we don't ever have back talk, or bad attitudes, or negativity of any kind," Mr. Jenkins said. "Or minors throwing gang signs during lineup, or disrespecting the staff, or destroying property, or starting fights. It's just nice folks making the most of a bad situation, right?"

"Yep."

"I didn't hear you, Jackson—would you agree?"

"No doubt about it."

"So when I say, 'Take it down to your rooms,' you're going to stand up, thank your teacher for coming, thank me for giving you this little break, stack the chairs, and file out of here without me having to say another word, right?"

"But I didn't get to read yet," Jimmy said. "Give us five more minutes. C'mon, Jenkins."

"I already gave you five more minutes. That was ten minutes ago. I'm in a good mood tonight—don't push your luck."

With the boys on the way to their rooms, Mr. Jenkins unlocked the front door and stepped outside with me. Ribbons of orange and purple crossed the sky, and the scent of a barbecue had somehow drifted its way into the facility. "Somebody's got the right idea," he said.

We debated the virtues of barbecued pork versus beef (pork won in the ribs category; off the bone, though, we agreed that nothing beats a steak), then he asked me how the class was going. I told him I thought it was going well; the boys were writing twice a week, which was more than I had done when I was seventeen.

"It's more writing than I've *ever* done," he said, chuckling. "But don't tell them that. I'd never hear the end of it."

8 / Dream State

On Saturday the lockdown was still in effect, and Mr. Sills would not make an exception for my class. The following Wednesday things were back to normal, and Mr. Jenkins asked me a favor.

"There's a young man I'd like to recommend for your class, if you got room for him. His name's Hall. He's very bright."

"I'd be glad to have him."

"He needs to be challenged. I think this would be good for him."

"Bring him on."

Mr. Jenkins hesitated. "I gotta warn you, though . . . he can be a handful. If he's disruptive, you just let me know, I'll send him right back where he came from."

My regulars were already filing in: Patrick, Kevin, Jimmy, and last of all, Francisco.

"Hey Mark!" Francisco called out, a bit too loudly from halfway across the dayroom, "Whassup?"

I waited until he reached the library before answering. "I understand you guys had a bad week."

He shrugged. "Aw, lockdown don't bother me. I'm used to it. I count the bricks in the wall and shit, I don't trip." He grinned at Kevin. "Whassup, homes?"

"Same ol', same ol'."

"Yeah, you a messenger, lockdown don't make no difference to you anyways."

I asked what a messenger was. "That's a minor who, you know, never gets in trouble," Francisco explained, "so the staff give him stuff to do. Basically he gets out of his room more. Everybody wants to be a messenger, but some of us get discriminated against."

"On what basis?" I asked.

Francisco glared toward the staff room. "Behavior. Fuck that."

"It's so unfair," Patrick said, rolling his eyes.

Francisco seemed oblivious to the sarcasm in Patrick's voice. "It is, man. Judge me by what I say, not by what I do. But these punk-ass motherfuckers get everything backwards." His eyes widened. "Hey! What's goin' on?" He indicated for me to turn around. "What's that fool doin' here? He's not in this class. You gotta be *invited* to be in this class. Mark, tell that fool to get lost."

Nathaniel Hall stood in the doorway with his hands behind his back and an enigmatic smile on his face. He was tall, black, wore his hair teased up into an Afro, and already had a mustache. He looked dashing even in his orange jumpsuit. "May I come in, sir?" he asked, charming me right away.

"Please. Grab a chair."

"Shit," Francisco complained.

The new boy unclasped his hands and rubbed his wrists as if they had just been unshackled. He looked around the room, took a plastic chair off the top of the stack, then sauntered across the room and sat down right next to Francisco.

"Hall, you suck."

Nathaniel ignored him. He raised his elbows to see where they reached on either side. "Just checkin' my clearance." He adjusted his sitting position as carefully as if he were strapping himself into the cockpit of a jet, then lowered his forearms onto the table and nodded a greeting to the other boys.

"Good evening, gentlemen. The moment you've been waiting for has arrived."

"Yeah—time to beat the crap out of Hall," Francisco grumbled.

"Quit fucking around," Jimmy said.

"I prove myself through deeds, not words," Nathaniel boasted. He pointed to the notepads and pencils in front of me. "May I?"

"That's what they're there for."

"Hall, you nothin' but a showboat."

Nathaniel tossed his head back with silent laughter. "Go ahead, get it out of your system now. Because before this hour is through you'll be dazzled by my articulations, stung by my insinuations, envious of my rhymes, and forgettin' your hard times. Ask me to write straight, I'll write twisted. You think you got my number? It ain't listed. I'm an original mind, a face unlined, a close encounter of the criminal kind." He wrote his name at the top of his notepad, then asked me what the topic was for today.

Part of me was annoyed that he had taken charge of the class so easily, but another part of me was fascinated. He was so over the top that I couldn't help feeling amused, and while the other boys made a show of denouncing him, they seemed to be enjoying the show as much as I was.

"You can pretty much write about what you want to," I said, "but if you're stuck, I'll help you with a topic."

"I like a challenge," he said. "Give me one."

"I'll see what I can come up with. In the meantime, I'd like Jimmy to start the class off by reading the essay he wrote last Wednesday. Would you do that for us?"

Jimmy looked uncomfortable. "I'll read it if you want, but some people here might take offense at it."

"Read it," Francisco urged. I had the sense he was anxious to reclaim his status as leader of the class. "What we say in this room stays in this room. It's strictly *confidential*."

Jimmy shrugged. "OK. I don't have a title for it, it's just something that's on my mind these days."

The question of whether there really is a God out there has been bugging me the past couple of months. I used to be a firm believer in the Almighty, but nowadays I ask myself, "Are you out there?" Most of you might be wondering why I am lacking in faith so let me give you a couple of reasons. First of all, my family, as well as many members of our church, have been praying for my little brother. If there really was a God out there, why would he let an innocent child suffer like this? What makes me wonder more is there are so many people praying to this so-called "Creator of All Things." Why hasn't anything happened? Why is my brother now confined to a wheelchair?

. . . People always say that God allows certain things to happen because he's testing our faith. We are only human beings and there is only so much that we can take. Once we reach our breaking point, most of us will just say fuck everything. People also say that the Lord is a jealous one, so if he wants us to rely on him one hundred percent, why does he allow certain things to come into our lives and make us doubt his existence?

I think that if my question of whether there is a man upstairs or not remains unanswered, I will cease to even think about him. To me, everything remains unchanged whether I believe or not believe. It's not like my days go by faster or easier when I pray to him. So until there is solid evidence that someone is watching us, such as a miracle of some sort, please don't try to persuade me into believing.

"I liked that," Nathaniel Hall said, nodding soberly. "I like knowin' I got competition."

Francisco looked aghast. "But he's saying God don't exist!"

Jimmy's face reddened. "I'm not saying that! I'm just saying I can't believe in him anymore. It's not the same thing."

Francisco looked at me for reassurance. "You believe in God, right?"

"I was raised in a nonreligious family," I answered. "I'm neutral."

Even Jimmy looked surprised. "But you work with Sister Janet—don't you have to be Catholic for that?"

"I'm just a writer. Sister Janet brought me here because she believes that writing is important, and she believes in you guys."

Francisco slid back into his chair and rubbed the back of his neck with his hand. "Man, I just assumed you was Catholic and all."

"Do you believe in God?" I asked him.

"When I was on the outs, I didn't believe in nothin'. But now I do. I'm studyin' for confirmation. I know God's watchin' over me, and whatever happens, it's OK because it's in his hands now."

"Have you come up with my topic yet?" Nathaniel asked.

"Yes, I've got one for you. Why don't you try writing about feeling trapped."

He made a face. "I thought you were going to challenge me!"

"I am. Here's the challenge: write it straight, in prose. Put the rhyming aside for a while. I want to see if you can write without all the insinuations and articulations."

He laughed as if he felt sorry for me. "You don't feel the beat of the street the way a young brotha does, I know. That's all right, sir, I can adapt to any situation. A black man has to adapt every day, livin' in a white man's world. Consider it done." Then he put his pencil down, turned his back to me, and began chatting with Kevin about a new kid in the unit.

I decided to ignore Nathaniel for the time being and check up on Patrick, who was talking with Francisco and Jimmy about a girl they had spotted through the cyclone fence separating the female inmates from the males. "Do you have something in mind to write about?" I asked him.

"Not really. We were locked down for so long, I feel like I just need to talk for a little while."

A glance around the room confirmed that he was not alone. Everybody was talking, nobody was writing.

On the one hand, it made perfect sense to me that a group of sixteen- and seventeen-year-old boys, after being kept in their cells for a week with no radio, television, recreation, exercise, or school to keep them stimulated, would have a hard time keeping quiet. On the other hand, I didn't want them to think of our Wednesday night class as simply an hour of recreation. I wanted it to be a time when they actually accomplished something, and built confidence in their ability to express themselves.

I clapped my hands to get everyone's attention. They all quieted down except for Nathaniel, who kept right on talking until Francisco punched him in the arm.

"Oh. Sorry, sir. We were just having a serious intellectual discussion."

"Listen, I realize you all had a rough week, and I don't blame you for being restless. I don't want this class to be something you dread, and I don't want to be a disciplinarian, I'm not built for that. This class is yours, it's your opportunity to make the most or the least out of. But what do you think about us setting aside twenty minutes for writing only—no conversation. Then we'll read aloud, and the rest of the time you can chat or read as you like."

"Sounds good," they said.

"All right," I said. "So let's get the writing out of the way first."

The boys seemed less enthusiastic now. "Just give us a few more minutes," Francisco said. "Then we'll get it together."

"Fine. We'll start writing in five minutes."

The next five minutes were a torment. I felt sure that the staff could see that no work was being done, and that at any moment one of them would step in to call the whole thing off. At 7:20 I clapped my hands again. "OK, time to write."

Patrick, Jimmy, and Kevin dutifully lowered their heads, but Francisco and Nathaniel were arguing about something and they simply would not stop. Neither could allow the other to have the last word. I tapped Francisco on the shoulder, but it had no effect. I waved my hand at Nathaniel and he ignored it.

Finally I stood up and moved my chair between them, and that got their attention. "OK, we're writing for twenty minutes. No talking. I know it's hard—I go through this every day at home, where I want to do anything except write, but that's what you've got to learn to do. To write anyway, even if you don't feel like it."

The room did quiet down, but none of them started writing. They were drumming with their pencils, staring out the window into the dayroom, drawing girls with gigantic breasts in their notepads, mumbling favorite rap lyrics. After ten minutes, Nathaniel leaned forward to look at me. "Let me know when we got five minutes left, would you?"

Jimmy started writing something, but tore the sheet out after a few minutes and crushed it into a ball. "Sorry, Mark," he whispered. "Everybody's too stressed out."

When I announced that we had five minutes left, Nathaniel yawned and stretched conspicuously. He cleared his throat, picked up his pencil, then started writing furiously. Five minutes later he slammed the pencil down and said, "Done. Put it in the books."

"Did anyone else get anything written today?" I asked. "Even a start to something?"

"Naw."

"Sorry, Mark. We'll do better on Saturday."

"Well then, let's have Nathaniel read."

Nathaniel stood up, walked to the head of the table, and said, "I'd like to thank all the little people. Without their support, I would never have cultivated my already impressive natural abilities."

Francisco groaned. "Hall, quit jerking off and just read."

Nathaniel bowed from the waist.

Because of a crime I did I was sentenced to 187 years in Iceberg Prison. I was frozen in a block of ice and placed in cell block 80051. I was eligible for parole in the year 2185.

As the years passed I was in a constant state of dreaming. My eyes were open in the ice and when my dream state was broken, which was rare, I could see the prison workers working around me. But mostly I was dreaming.

Then one day I was unfrozen and brought before the parole board. I was having trouble hanging on to reality after being stuck in a dream state but I was prepared for this day for a long time. I was released a day later and given enough money to keep me fed and housed until I found a method of supporting myself.

I found myself a nice apartment and bought enough food to last me two months. I started looking for a job but I soon found that my limited education and lack of computer skills prohibited me from even being considered for even the most trivial jobs and the ones I did qualify for were already taken by the parolees before me.

I found myself staring into a weapons shop admiring the new guns they have in 2185. I had enough money so I bought one.

Two months later I was still jobless and running out of money. I had no food and the rent was due. I went down to the pawnshop and started to hand over my gun for some money but as I did I realized I could just rob the man and keep my precious gun.

So I turned the gun on him and he didn't move. I got the money out of the cash register and left the building. As soon as I stepped outside I was surrounded by police with their guns drawn.

I instantly put my hands up, then my visions of the workers working outside of my ice block flashed in my mind. I was standing there thinking of how horrible it was to be in that prison. I instantly pointed the gun at the police and started firing. In almost the same instant I felt my body jerking from the impact of bullets. I fell to my knees and I couldn't breathe. My body grew numb and then I fell all the way down. I saw the light leave my eyes and then all was blackness.

My eye caught a glimpse of light and I recognized what I saw. It was the working men of the prison, making their rounds. I realized that I was still frozen and it was all a dream.

This story is an example of the consequences of being incarcerated without being given the education and the skills to make it in the world.

When Nathaniel finished, the boys—who had seemed fed up with him only a few moments before—gave him an ovation. Even Francisco loved the story, and made no attempt to hide it. They stomped their feet, they clapped, they whistled. And Nathaniel, who I expected to strut around the room like a jackass, sat down and acted like the perfect gentleman instead.

When Mr. Jenkins gave us the signal to end class, Nathaniel took his place behind Francisco in line. When he passed through the doorway, Mr. Jenkins put a hand on his shoulder and stopped him.

"Hold on a second, Hall," Mr. Jenkins said. He looked at me and asked, "Did this guy write, or was he just talking the whole time? It looked to me like he was just talking, as usual."

"He talked quite a bit, but he also wrote an excellent essay."

Mr. Jenkins looked unconvinced. "You sure about that? You sure he wasn't disruptive?"

"Let's keep him in the class for a while and see what happens."

Mr. Jenkins put Nathaniel into a playful headlock. "He's covering your back, Hall. But you can't fool me! I saw you in there, you and your motormouth, keepin' everybody from working." He started rubbing Nathaniel's head with his knuckles.

"Ow! That shit hurts, Jenkins!"

"You're a bright kid, Hall, but you waste it with all of your bullshit. I'ma see if I can rub some sense into this thick skull of yours."

"I'ma write a complaint!"

"You go right ahead."

"How's the sense supposed to get through all the fat on your knuckles, huh?"

Mr. Jenkins laughed and released him. "You wanna feel the fat on my knuckles? Come on, tough guy, let's go. Right here. Right now."

Nathaniel put his fists up and started dancing like a teenage Muhammad Ali. "Come on, Jenkins! You can't touch this! I'm too fast for you! You too old to mess with the young bloods."

Mr. Jenkins started walking toward Nathaniel with his hands down at his sides, the smile replaced by a dead stare, and Nathaniel wisely danced backwards toward his cell. "See you on Saturday, sir," he yelled to me before disappearing down the corridor. "And I'd like two copies of my story, please."

9 / Arcana

"Where's Nathaniel?" I asked. Starting late meant finishing late, and I did not want to give the Saturday morning staff any excuses to scold me again.

Francisco tilted his head toward the hallway. "The staff musta forgot to get him. You want me ask 'em to bring him out?" He eased out of his chair and loped toward the staff room. I watched through the window as he talked to Mr. Sills, then returned.

"Sills says Hall ain't comin' today."

"Why not?"

" 'Cause Hall fucked up."

"It wasn't his fault," Patrick said. "Some fool from M/N was talking shit to him in school and Hall talked some shit back. What's he supposed to do?"

Francisco glowered at Patrick. "He's supposed to be smart about it, that's what. He shoulda waited till no staff was around and fucked that punk up good, not just talk shit and burn the spot for the rest of us."

Patrick shook his head, then opened his folder and pulled out a drawing of a teenage prisoner with his hands and feet shackled. Head bowed forward, the figure stood in front of a barred window; outside the window, a flock of birds rose toward the sun. At the top of the drawing he had written the words "Troubled Souls" in decorative script.

"Try to mind your own business in here and you get jumped," Patrick said dryly. "Stick up for yourself and you get locked down. Meanwhile, the ones who start all the shit come out on top. They get all the respect. Fuck everybody, that's my philosophy." He began shading folds in the prisoner's baggy pants.

The drawing was sentimental but technically competent. I complimented him on his work and his mood improved. "I'd like to be an animator someday, that's one of my goals in life. But I don't know if I could make it."

"Man, you gotta have confidence," Francisco advised.

"I don't want to count on something that could get taken away from me. If I lose my case, the animator thing is not gonna happen."

"You gotta think positive, homes."

Patrick rolled his eyes and began erasing most of what he had just done.

"Hey, I'm just tryin'a show support! Fuckin' Chumnikai." Francisco squinted and tucked his lower lip under his upper teeth.

"Fuckin' Javier." Patrick brought his index fingers together over his brow, imitating Francisco's single eyebrow, and crossed his eyes.

I said to Patrick that he had nothing to lose by taking his interest seriously and practicing every day. He nodded and turned his attention back to drawing. "I know. The thing is, I just can't set my mind to it. When other people compliment one of my drawings, I'm happy and it makes me want to do more. But sometimes the person will just look at it and give it back without saying anything. Then I feel so mad I just want to quit. Or I'll see the drawings in magazines and think, I'll never be able to do that. So what's the point?"

I told Patrick that I understood how he felt. I had thought I was going to be a concert cellist until I heard Yo-Yo Ma play; his playing made me quit the cello for fifteen years.

Patrick whistled. "Fifteen years? Either he musta been really good, or you musta been really bad. No offense."

"My point is that we all compare ourselves to others, and we're affected by what others say about our work. But you mustn't let it stop you."

Patrick blew the sheet clean of eraser fragments, then said, "But what if you don't like what you find out? Then you're totally fucked, instead of just halfway fucked." He put the drawing back in his folder and took out his notepad. "What should I write about today? I'm kinda stuck."

I asked if he could remember a time he wanted something, then had to earn it. He stared out the window for a while, then nodded. "Yeah, I can think of a time."

At half past ten, Mr. Sills wandered past the library and looked inside. The boys were all working, but Mr. Sills did not seem impressed. To me, it looked as if he was searching for any excuse to throw us out. He stood motionless in the doorway for two or three minutes, then returned to his office without any comment. My relief must have shown when he left, because Francisco asked, "Wha'chu trippin' about? He can't do nothin' to you!"

"I'm not used to being watched like that."

"Try takin' a shit that way." Francisco slapped his pencil down on the table and looked around the room. "What the fuck's that, Chumnikai? Some kinda bird?"

"It's a penguin."

"What you drawin' a penguin for, fool?"

"In school the other day the teacher asked us what animal we thought we were most like. I said penguin."

"Fuckin' Chumnikai!"

"Fuckin' Javier."

"Why a penguin?" I asked.

Patrick shrugged. "Because a penguin is small, it has wings but it can't fly, and it can withstand cold temperatures. That's me." He began crossing out the drawing, but pressed so hard with the pencil that the tip snapped. He froze, bracing for my angry reaction.

Francisco winced; he also seemed to expect the worst. "Damn, Chumnikai! You fucked up his pencil!" I sensed that this was more of a plea than a reprimand. Francisco seemed to assume that I, as an adult, would naturally go ballistic over a small infraction; he was trying to keep me from taking it out on the whole class.

I handed Patrick a fresh pencil, told him not to worry about the broken one, and asked if he'd finished his essay.

"Yeah—I'll read it if you want." As he had never volunteered to read before, I took this as a gesture of gratitude.

"Go ahead."

It was a Thursday, around mid-October, of '94. It seemed like a normal day, but something happened that day that changed my life forever. I used to be a good kid doing good in school, but that changed. I arrived at my cousin Ryan's house. He was about fifteen at the time, bald-headed, and wore khaki pants and a white shirt. He told me that a group of his friends were coming over to kick it and drink. Ryan's friends were different. They were from a gang. A gang I used to see on the store walls when I was young.

Soon the house was filled up with gang members. It seemed like they were like one happy family having fun, and I wanted to be part of that family. I was sitting on the couch drinking. The air was filled with smoke from the cigarettes, and loud and noisy from the guys who were yelling and singing because we were all drunk from drinking forty ounces, tequila, and vodka. I was a little dazed when I saw a guy who was about twenty, stalky-looking, and had a fade. John was his name. He asked me if I wanted to join. I thought about it for a while. I mean it seemed OK, because we were all talking, dancing, drinking, just having fun. I told him I'd join. So he told me to just hold on tight, and suddenly, two guys just rushed and jumped me. They beat me for about twenty seconds, then they stopped. All of them in the room were watching me. ALL EYEZ ON ME. They shook my hand and gave me a name. Now I was a part of their family. It was about 2:30 p.m. I had to pick up my brother from school. I told John that I was going to walk to the school. But he insisted that he drive me there to pick him up. We went and when I saw my old friends at the school, I felt different. I was from a gang now. I felt like I had power. People would fear me and my friends when we went into places. Little did I know how much trouble I got myself into. I now have enemies I haven't met before, police watching me, endangering my family, and sending me to a place like this. Sure, I thought it was cool three years ago, but I didn't know it could put me in jail. If I had the chance to go back to that day and not join, I would. And maybe I wouldn't be in a place like where I am today.

"I wanted to be in the gang, so I earned it. And now, here I am."

"Negative leads to more negative," Francisco said. "And positive leads to more positive. That's how I changed. It's simple." Francisco looked around the room for support, but Patrick snickered.

"Who was just saying Hall shoulda beat the crap out of somebody instead of just talkin' shit? Who got sent to the Box last month for starting a fight?"

To his credit, Francisco was able to laugh at himself. "Hey, I'm turnin' my life around, but you gotta do it gradually. You try to do that good shit all at once and you could get sick, like tryin'a eat nothin' but nuts and berries all of a sudden. You gotta build up to it. And it's working! Have I shot anybody recently? No!"

"That's so beautiful," Patrick said, wiping away imaginary tears.

"Fuckin' Chumnikai." Francisco made the squinty, buck-toothed face again, and Patrick responded with the fused eyebrow and crossed eyes.

"Francisco, why don't you read next?"

Francisco, who usually jumped at the chance to read, rubbed the back of his neck and declined. "I'll pass this time."

"You're not happy with what you wrote?"

"Naw, it ain't that."

"What is it, then?"

"None of anybody's business, that's what."

"I know what it is," Patrick said.

"You don't know shit, Chumnikai."

"It's a letter to his mom."

"You always peek into other people's shit? Nosy mother-fucker."

"You're the one who doesn't know what a penguin is when he sees it in somebody else's notebook."

"Just read the letter," Jimmy said.

"It's personal, man."

"Oh, like the rest of us don't write anything personal. Come on, Javier, we don't have much time."

"All right, if it makes you happy, I'll read it. But any of you motherfuckers laugh, it's on."

He looked at the sheet of paper and rubbed the back of his neck with his hand again.

Dear Mother,

You don't know how difficult it is to be a youngster. Sometimes I want to throw myself in your arms and cry, but since I'm so big I don't dare to. You know what, Mom? When you lecture or counsel me, even though it doesn't seem like I'm listening, your words stay in my mind. When I go to bed, I reflect on them. I know you think I don't appreciate everything you've done for me, but it's the opposite. I love you more than anybody in this world and I think that there isn't no better mom than you. Sometimes I feel bad at myself and since I don't have the maturity that you have, I often find myself saying things that I really don't want to say. Then I feel worse but you're already mad at me and you make me feel that there isn't anybody that could understand me . . .

You always tell me that I should look more for God. Only if you knew how much I want to feel free from everything that has me tangled. I don't have inspiration to pray, although I try to find the Lord, everything that surrounds me in this world is taking me farther and farther from God. Sometimes I think that there isn't forgiveness for me. How many times I've asked for forgiveness, then I find myself doing the same sin again. I think that God is tired of all this. You tell me that God is wonderful and loving, but don't you think that God has his limits?

None of the boys laughed. I asked Francisco if he planned to send this letter to his mother.

"I don't think so."

"I'm sure it would mean a lot to her."

"You don't know how my family works. You can't say this

kind of stuff directly. Maybe someday, but not now. Right now, I gotta be strong for her."

"I think you oughta send it," Kevin said.

"Somebody else read now. I feel like I'm bein' interrogated and shit."

"I'll read," Kevin said. "Mine's in three parts—see if you can figure out what I'm trying to say."

PART ONE

Sunlight used to be a good thing, and at times it still is. The only problem I have with it now is, it reminds me of all the fun I used to have on sunny days. When I was out there, there was nothing better than a sunny day. Girls dressed in short dresses or shorts showing off their bodies, the water fights with my friends. Going to the beach or a picnic with my homies, and just sitting in my front yard looking at the bees and dragonflies while sipping on a cup of homemade lemonade.

Most of all the good times that I've had during life have been on sunny days, but now that I'm in here I like the night, the darkness. It's like a friend, I can't really explain it but at night when I'm alone it brings me comfort. When I touch down I'll like sunlight again, but until that day comes, the night sky will be my counterpart.

PART TWO

Darkness tries to smother my true being day by day. At times the light shines through all the darkness but that's very seldom. Happiness is very scarce, too. It feels as if more loneliness, hate, and anger comes as every minute passes. It almost seems as if it's hereditary, but I know it's not because I can feel my true being when I'm all alone, thinking about my situation. I can feel freedom when just laying there reminiscing on my past. I believe that I am a good person, I've done good things, but nobody wants to listen to that part of the story, they are too caught up in the darkness.

PART THREE

During difficult times, I think about freedom and what it really is. Some people say that I don't have freedom because I'm in jail but I have freedom and lots of it. I may not have as much as a person on the "outs," but I have enough to make life enjoyable. I can read and write or just sit back and do nothing. Back when black people were slaves they were killed or whipped severely for trying to educate themselves, and that right there helps me to recognize how much freedom I do have. I have spiritual and mental freedom. I can lay on my bed knowing I may never be physically free again, but the Lord allows me to be at peace and have that sense of freedom. Writing also helps me be free. I can create anything with my imagination, pencil, and paper, and before I know it I've created something that was in me the whole time, my pencil and paper just helped me let it out, freely.

"Man," Francisco said, "that says it all! You got everything in there, homes."

"Yeah, but did you get it?" Kevin asked. "Did you get what the meaning is?"

Francisco shrugged. "What's not to get? It sucks being locked up, that's what it means."

Kevin folded his arms across his chest and smiled. "I'm not giving any more hints. Somebody's gotta figure it out."

"It's about opposites," Jimmy said.

"Gettin' warmer."

"It's about how inside every good there's some bad, and inside every bad there's some good."

Kevin's eyes widened. "Damn! I didn't think that shit would work."

"I was thinkin' that," Francisco muttered, "but I didn't say it fast enough."

This seemed the perfect time to ask a question that had been on my mind since I'd first visited Duane's class: Did any of them feel that being locked up had been a good experience? Was there anything positive they could say about it?

They shifted in their chairs and kept their eyes on the table or out the window. At last Kevin said, "I gotta say that, yeah, there's been some good."

Jimmy and Francisco nodded in agreement; Patrick started a new drawing.

"For example, I been doing better in school," Kevin continued. "If my trial keeps getting delayed, I may even get my high school diploma, which I never would have done. And now I talk to people that, on the outs, I wouldn't socialize with unless I was buyin' somethin' from them."

"Yeah, that's true for me too."

"But I also have to say that there's a lot of negatives here. Bein' locked up can make a person feel like they're no longer a person. It makes you feel lower than people on the outside, and that can destroy your will to succeed."

Patrick began erasing vigorously. "I don't think you learn anything in here," he muttered. "It's up to the person. If he or she wants to learn."

"Yeah," Francisco agreed. "How we s'posed to change if we're surrounded by negativity all the time?"

Patrick folded the drawing up and put it in his folder. "I mean, they don't teach you anything in here! They just baby you around. 'No' this, 'no' that, all you can think about is the mistake you made, and 'I can't wait to get out,' and 'I'd do this again, or that again.' The only thing I learned here is how not to be caught next time. I thought this place was supposed to teach you something, but no, it just punishes people. Why should you change your life if all you hear all day is what a worthless piece of shit you are?"

"OK, that's true, but check it out," Francisco argued. "If I hadn't got locked up, I'd most likely be dead by now. Bein' locked up sucks, but it's better than bein' dead."

"I disagree. I wish the cops'd shot me when they busted me. It would've saved everybody a whole lot of trouble."

"Aw, come on! What happens when you get killed? The homies visit your grave and pour some beer on it! Big fuckin' deal—by midnight you're forgotten, you know it's true. The homies don't give a shit about you, that's the bottom line. One takes your clothes, another takes your car, and your best friend fucks your girl the night of the funeral. I don' wanna be no ghost watchin' that shit happen. I wanna live."

"But this isn't living!" Patrick argued. "It's the same as being dead, only you gotta be awake for it. How we supposed to become better people if we can't have any normal friend-ships, any normal conversations, any control over what hap-pens to us? How we supposed to change if we got nothing to look forward to? Everything's abnormal in here, it fucks you up worse than when you got in."

"Institutionalized," Kevin said.

Francisco glared out the window. "Man, now you gettin' me all depressed an' shit." His bad mood didn't last long, how-ever. "Hey—check it out! You see what I see?"

Across the yard, a group of five girls walked single file, hands behind their backs, just ahead of a female staff member.

"They're goin' to the medical module. Damn!"

"Look at the tits on the one to the rear!"

"Fuck that, look at the rear on the one with no tits!"

"Wish I was one a them doctors right now."

"Yeah, I'd tell 'em 'woo-woo heart rate, woo-woo reflexes, now take your pants off.' "

"Time to take your temperature! Don't be afraid or nothin', this is just a meat thermometer."

As soon as the girls disappeared the room fell silent. I had the feeling that the boys either had forgotten our discussion from before or wanted to forget about it.

The library door opened and an inmate I had not seen before stuck his head inside. "Excuse me, sir. I gotta talk to Jackson for a second."

"He's the other messenger," Francisco explained to me.

Kevin stepped over to the door, where the two boys held a whispered conversation. As they talked, I saw something change hands between them. After the messenger left, Kevin handed the mysterious object to me.

"It's from Hall," he said. "It's for you. He says he did the writing for today and wants you to read it aloud since he ain't here."

The object turned out to be a full sheet of paper, folded down to the size of a quarter. When I got it open, I read it once silently, then aloud to the class.

DEEP THOUGHTS

(My Arcane Beginning)
by Nathaniel Hall
Writer
Actor
Producer
Entertainer
Athlete

I stand in the middle of my room staring out of the window, my mind racing from thought to thought only to stop where it started, the field outside. I review my life from the beginning. My mysteriously forgotten childhood which only exists through stories of my chaotic behavior. Stories so clear in my mind it seems as if I really remember living them. Voices flow through my mind like a soothing melody that carries the key to unlock the cryptic code of my past. The words to the song are unattainable to my conscious mind, but echo repetitively in my dreams. The need to know my past causes me to retreat deeper into myself to ascertain the arcane beginning that brought me to where I stand. The only discovery made is bits of a puzzle that escape my grasp as soon as I reach out to embrace them.

Why must things be so unclear to me? I search and search for the answers to my questions but I only find myself in a state of desperation reaching out for what I know is there but only finding burnt ashes left behind by a fire that consumed my history and left me doomed to make the mistakes of my past over and over again.

My dreams are plagued by memories of a time in which I've never been. At least, I don't remember being there.

I return from my expedition into myself only to find I have more questions about my past than I did when I first started. Will I ever find the answer I search for? Will I ever solve the mysteries of my beginning?

"Fuck it, I got the answer for him," Francisco said.

"Let's hear it."

"Conjugal visits. We got too much time on our hands around here, thinkin' 'bout all this depressing shit. We need to get laid, that's what."

10 / Prisoner or Pumpkin

"I've really got to quit," Duane said, leaning against his car to have a cigarette. "But every time I see this place, my willpower disappears." He paused before lighting it; something had caught his attention. I followed his gaze to the row of palm trees growing beside the juvenile court building. "How long do you suppose it's been since those things were trimmed?"

Judging from the number of dead fronds clinging to the trunk of each tree, I guessed fifteen years. Duane guessed twenty.

"So how's your class going?" he asked me.

Delighted by this opportunity to brag, I told him something about each of the boys and even read a few examples of their work aloud. At some point—I think it was when I offered to read one of Jimmy's essays aloud a second time—I realized I sounded like a proud, blathering parent. That stopped me cold.

Duane smoked and I stared at the handful of papers in my hand. "Do you like the kids in your class?" I asked him after an awkward silence.

"Sure. They're likable kids."

He admired the sunset while I tried to figure out what had happened to my common sense. My students were violent criminals, but I no longer thought of them as bad people. In fact, I felt almost no curiosity at all about what they had done to get arrested; all I cared about was what they wrote and what happened during our meetings. Was that healthy? Was it fair?

A familiar voice called to us from the far end of the parking lot. It was Sister Janet, carrying a box full of paperwork. As soon as she caught up with us we offered to carry the box for her, but she declined cheerfully. "I need the exercise! I spend too much time on the phone these days."

She put the box down while Duane finished his cigarette. "I was hoping I'd see you two on the way in. I have good news! But first, tell me how your boys are doing. Is everything OK? Do you need anything?"

"Everything's fine," Duane said.

Sister Janet nodded. "I'm just so grateful for all you're doing. Two more writers have been in touch with me about teaching here. The word is getting out about our program." She pointed down at the box. "Are you ready? A lawyer friend has offered to help establish nonprofit status for us! She'll handle all the paperwork for free. One day we'll have enough money to reimburse you for all the supplies you buy, for your travel, and we might even be able to start a newsletter. I'd like to see the kids stay connected to the program even after they leave here."

Sister Janet savored the thought of this bright future for a moment, then peered at me over the rim of her glasses.

"Is it true what I've heard?" she asked. "That you play the cello?"

"As a hobby, yes."

"Do you think you might play for the children here one day?"

"Sure," I said, confident that this would never actually happen.

"I'm so glad! I hope you won't be angry with me, but I've already mentioned your name to the woman in charge of special events here. She was very excited to hear you would play."

Duane smiled at the palm trees.

"You already told her I'd do it?"

"She's planning an arts festival for Halloween. The holidays are especially depressing for incarcerated children. But if you'd rather not do it, for any reason at all, I'll understand. I'll explain to Mrs. Washington that it was my mistake."

"How many of them would I be playing for?"

"No more than a hundred. That's all they can seat in the chapel at once."

If I played the drums or the electric guitar I might have felt more enthusiastic. Only the accordion is a more uncool instrument than the cello; the last time I played the cello for a group of kids was at a birthday party where the birthday boy kicked my end pin and declared that the cello was stupid.

"Sister Janet, have you ever been to a school assembly where classical music is on the program? It can get ugly."

"Ah," she said, smiling, "but that's *school*. The kids here would *never* behave like that."

"Wha'chu gonna dress up as?" Francisco asked.

Kevin stroked his chin with his thumb and forefinger. "I'm thinking of dressing as . . . a prisoner."

Francisco pouted and tugged at his orange outfit. "I'm gonna be a fuckin' pumpkin. Prisoner or pumpkin, that's the choice this year. I hate these tired-ass county clothes! They oughta let us wear our own clothes, homes. What's the difference? We'd still be locked up."

The boys had been given permission to decorate the library

for Halloween. They had already covered the windows with construction paper, thrown bedsheets over the bookshelves and tables, and sprayed fake cobwebs everywhere—you had to duck to keep from getting them in your hair. "We're turning it into a haunted house," Kevin explained. "The units are having a contest to see who does the best decorations for the season, and we plan to win."

"Yeah, we gonna have live ghosts and everything."

"How we gonna have live ghosts?" Nathaniel asked. "We ain't got any white guys in here—they all in the sex offenders' unit. No offense, Mark."

"Check it out: when the judges come, it's gonna be dark in here, homes. We're gonna play some scary-ass music, and some of us'll take turns hiding behind tables, with sheets over our heads. When the females come through, we'll scream and throw fake blood on 'em."

"They ain't gonna let us throw fake blood, Javier! Get real."

Francisco's eyebrow flatlined. "Then we'll throw spiders an' shit. All I know is, we're winnin' that contest."

"What's the prize?" I asked.

"A lame-ass trophy. That don't matter, it's the pride of the unit on the line."

"I'm surprised," I said. "You're always talking about how much you hate this place. Where does the pride come in?"

Francisco threw up his hands. "Aw, come on! A contest is a contest, you gotta try and win it. Yeah, this place sucks, but we're stuck here. We gotta make the most of it."

"It's human nature," Kevin said. "We know the guys in the other units are the same as us, but a little competition breaks up the monotony."

"It's because we're institutionalized," Nathaniel an-nounced. "They set all this stuff up to turn us into house nig-gers, that's all. It just a way of keepin' us distracted."

"Duh, let's see," Patrick said, slumping his shoulders and

letting his mouth hang open. "Do I want to sit in my room and think about how my life is over, or do I want to have fun building a haunted house? Duhhhh . . ."

"Yeah! If you don' like it, Hall, you don' gotta help. We don' need you."

Nathaniel grinned. "Oh yes you do! If you wanna win, you need me. Wanna know why?"

"Not really."

" 'Cause you need a theme."

"Aw, fuck you, Hall."

"You need a theme, brotha. And I'm the brotha for the job." He slid his chair back until he reached the wall and asked for a beat. Kevin obliged him, pounding out a rhythm on the table with his left palm and right fist.

> *Screams of terror echo through the night*
> *Silhouettes in the sky of birds in flight*
> *Kids walk the streets oblivious to danger*
> *Things unheard of lurk in the shadows, enveloped*
> *   in anger*

> *The streets are dark in spite of the full moon*
> *Police are on standby, knowing someone will die soon*
> *Mothers herd their kids from door to door*
> *While some kids eat candy, never to breathe no more!*

The boys approved of Nathaniel's theme. I tried to get them to settle down and write, but between the excitement over the contest and the contagious beat Nathaniel and Kevin had set in motion (by now most of the boys were drumming on the table and making boom box noises with their mouths), I met with little success.

"I can't concentrate, Mark!"

"Yeah, me neither. We're all restless tonight."

"Do you think it would help if you guys stopped the drumming?"

"It's the beat of the street," Nathaniel explained gleefully. "You can't stop it, any more than you can stop our hearts from pumping!"

"But your hearts pump inside your bodies, not outside. Can't you drum in your heads, and maybe write something while you're at it?"

"He burned you there, Hall! Ha!"

Nathaniel made a bowing, salaaming gesture—the kind Bugs Bunny would make when appearing to defer to Elmer Fudd—and said, "The beat shall be internalized. The pen shall be activized. The truth shall be realized. The—"

"Shut up, Hall, I can't concentrate."

"Look, guys—let's try to write for just fifteen minutes. And I have a topic for you."

"What's that?"

"Since Halloween is on your minds, why don't you write about fear."

"Oh yeah! This is gonna work!"

It did work, but with mixed results. Nathaniel wrote a fictional story about a trio of gangsters named Hitman, T-Bone, and Ric Dog who discover an evil spirit in a haunted crack house and end up shooting each other while trying to kill the ghost. Most of the story was devoted to loving descriptions of the gangsters' weapons.

Jimmy wrote about finding himself in bed with a beautiful woman, only to wake up and realize it had only been a dream. He said that it frightened him to think that this was the only intimacy he could look forward to for the next eighteen years.

Francisco wrote an essay titled, "I Still Remember the Day I Got Shot." Unfortunately, the date was all he seemed to remember about it:

It was December 26, 1994. It was like around 8:30 in the morning. Ever since that day, my life hasn't been the same. The end.

"Did it hurt?" I asked him.

"Naw, it happened so fast. One minute I was standin' on the corner with the homies, the next thing I hear, like, *pop-pop-pop*, and then I was down. I didn't even know I was shot until I tried to get up."

"How long were you in the hospital?"

"Coupla weeks. They don't give you enough food in the hospital, Mark! I kept tellin' 'em, 'I'm a youngster, you gotta feed me more than those old fucks,' but I still got the same fucked-up tray with, like, Jell-O on it."

"Did coming so close to dying make you feel differently about being in a gang?"

"Naw, not really. It was like—all the feelings I had, they got turned into just one. Anger! All I could think about was getting out and finding whoever did it to me." He shrugged. "But instead I got locked up for somethin' else. Pretty sad, huh?"

"Not for the guy who shot you," Nathaniel said. "Think about it: you be prayin' every day, 'God, thy will be done but please help me beat my case.' Meanwhile, that fool must be prayin' every day, 'God, thy will be done, but put that crazy-ass Javier away or he gonna smoke my ass!' God got his hands full with you two."

"Well, at least he don't have to worry about where to send you, Hall."

"How about you, Patrick?" I asked. "What did you write?"

"It's called 'Twenty-four Hours Left.' Just so you know, I had a bad day at court today. My story's kind of twisted. You still want me to read it?"

"If Hall could read his twisted shit every week," Francisco said, "then you could read whatever you want."

1:00 a.m.—I was released from prison. I was sentenced to life in prison and was given twenty-four hours on the streets and then I have to return back to prison. I pack up my stuff and left my TV and radio on cause I'll be back tomorrow.

3:00 a.m.—I'm at home showering.

4:30 a.m.—Finished and dressed up.

5:00 a.m.—Visit my family and tell them I love them. I eat breakfast with them and watch a movie.

7:00 a.m.—Kick it at Citywalk, rob some people, then buy my family a TV and a car. An Accord wagon for my mom.

8:00 a.m.—Go to my homeboy's house. Kick it and tell them to get some guns for tonight.

9:00 a.m.—Go to Magic Mountain. Go on every ride.

10:00 a.m.—Finished. Went to every ride. I cut through lines and put a gun to people's heads to let me go first. I go to Disneyland next.

12:00 p.m—Took longer because I was kickin' it with Minnie Mouse and Daisy Duck.

1:00 p.m.—Eat at Beverly Hills with my mom.

2:00 p.m.—Tired, so I sleep.

9:00 p.m.—Shit! Slept too long! I've only got three hours left. I go to my homie's house.

9:30 p.m.—At homie's house. I get a gun and I go to the enemy's neighborhood.

10:00 p.m.—Shot six gang members, two innocent people, and a dog.

11:00 p.m.—Shot five more enemies and an innocent boy.

11:59 p.m.—Shot by an enemy. I'm paralyzed. I wish I was dead, but the doctors saved me.

12:00 a.m.—Back at the pen, sitting in my wheelchair watching TV. Three guys rush in my cell with knives, but I can't move.

"Damn, that is twisted!" Francisco complained. "How come you put in that stuff about shootin' innocent people? That's cold, Chumnikai."

"Put it in a story, and everybody says it's cold," Patrick said. "It happens for real, and what do people like us say? 'It was an accident.' 'The other guy shot first.' 'Those people shoulda got outta the way.' Which is more twisted?"

No one rushed to answer the question. I asked Patrick what made someone else an "enemy"; what were the gangs really fighting over?

"Nothing at all," he answered immediately. "It's exactly like a video game, where you're just racking up points and trying to end up with a higher score than anybody else. That's your rep. The fact that it's dangerous only makes it a hundred times more fun. An enemy is anybody who's playing against you."

"That's not true!" Francisco objected. "An enemy is somebody who disrespects you, or who disrespects your neighborhood."

Patrick shook his head. "Racking up points."

Francisco shook his head. "Getting respect."

"Think about it! How does a homie get respect? By proving himself. How does he do that? By disrespecting the enemy! You go into his territory, you tag a wall, you mad-dog his homies, you look at his girl like you wanna fuck her. That gives him an excuse to retaliate. When he retaliates, he's dissing you, man! You gotta do something back to represent. I'm telling you, it's a fucked-up game. Now it don't seem fun anymore, so of course we want out, of course we say we want to change. But it's too late! *We fucked up.* And anyhow, we deserve what's coming. They oughta lock us up forever and throw away the key."

"You *did* have a bad day at court today," Jimmy said.

"Fuck it."

"What happened?"

"Nothing."

"It musta been somethin', make you trip like this."

Patrick began rearranging the papers in his folder. "My mom said she was going to be there at the hearing, but she didn't show."

"She musta had a reason, homes. She probably had car trouble or something, or got stuck in traffic an' shit."

"It don't matter anyway, because nothin' happened. I sat in the holding tank all day, got called out to the courtroom, sat down for five minutes, then got told to stand up and come back here."

"You gonna call your mom tonight?"

"What's the point? I'm never goin' home again, why should she care what happens now?"

The talk of mothers had a sobering effect. Several of the boys stared out into the dayroom—most of the religious volunteers were middle-aged women—and Patrick began drawing a clown.

"We haven't heard from Action Jackson yet," Nathaniel pointed out, breaking the silence.

Kevin looked sheepish. "Mine's kinda twisted too."

Francisco buried his head in his hands and groaned.

"I call it 'Plot Gone Bad.' It really happened, though. It's kinda scary, but kinda funny too, except the joke was on me. See what you think."

It was around 9:40 on a humid Tuesday night. Me and my homeboy Tray were on the front porch talking about the day when we came to the idea of going to the store to get something to eat. We had a real bad case of the munchies but the only problem was, we had spent all our money on the weed we had just smoked. I thought about going in the house to cook something but I was kind of high and didn't really feel like it so we just walked around the corner to my brother's house to see if he was there. Due to my luck he wasn't, so I just went in his garage and got two new bikes he had bought about three weeks before. Me and Tray came to the conclusion that we were going to rob the first sucker walking down the street, but before we even finished talking about it, we saw a lady on a bus stop waiting for the bus. Immediately we both gave each other a knowing smile. When we approached her she already knew what was happening because she had her hand tightly clenched on her purse. The homie jumped off the bike and told her, "This can be easy or hard, either way we are gonna get what we want." We were unarmed except for our fists and I wasn't about to hit the lady but I wasn't too sure about my friend. She started to reach in her purse when out of no-where she pulled out a li'l .25 caliber. I was kind of shocked at first, then she said she just wanted us to leave her alone. I thought about snatching the weapon from her but by the time I built up enough courage to do it she jumped on one of my brother's bikes and rode off into the night!

To this day I think her gun was unloaded.

The boys and I laughed so hard Mr. Jenkins came in to check on us. "If somebody told a joke in here, I want to hear it," he said. "No fair you guys having fun in here while I'm working out there."

Francisco explained that we were laughing over a story Kevin had just read aloud, not a joke.

"So read it again, Jackson," Mr. Jenkins said, folding his arms over his chest and leaning against the door. Kevin read the story once more, and the boys enjoyed it as much as they had the first time. Mr. Jenkins shook his head. "I don't see what's so funny about it. That lady could have been my sister. Or one of your mothers."

The laughter died down and the boys looked ashamed; even my face was red.

"What's the moral of that story?" Mr. Jenkins asked.

Silence.

"You know what a moral is, don't you? Come on, I know you boys are smart enough to come up with one. How about you, Hall? You're always telling everybody what a genius you are, why don't you share some of that knowledge with us."

"I don't know what the moral is, sir."

"No? How about you, Wu?"

Jimmy shrugged.

"I didn't hear you, Wu. What was that?"

"I don't know what the moral is either, sir."

"Chumnikai?"

"No sir."

"Uh-huh. Well I *know* Javier knows what the moral is. Let's hear it."

Francisco squirmed in his chair until inspiration came to him. "Don't rob somebody if you don't have a weapon?"

Mr. Jenkins kept silent for a long time, shaking his head, then said, "OK. You clowns clear on outta here. It's eight o'clock." After the boys had returned to the rooms, Mr. Jenkins asked me to follow him into the office. I thought he was going to chew me out, but instead he asked me to read Kevin's piece aloud to the other two guards on duty. When I got to the end of it, where the victim steals Kevin's bicycle, the three of them laughed harder than the boys had.

"Lord help us," Mr. Jenkins said as he walked with me to the door. "What a little family we make."

11 / Feeling Special

"Are you sure this is it?" I asked.

Duane paused in front of the cinder-block fort and looked around. "Only one way to be sure, I guess." He pushed against the door, whose window had wire mesh set in the glass, and it swung open. "If a door around here opens without having to unlock it, it's got to be something special."

We entered a small office and gave our names to a secretary, then sat down to wait on a battered vinyl couch. The cushion under me hissed in protest. The secretary announced our arrival using a small intercom; when the superintendent of Central Juvenile Hall answered through it, we realized he was in the adjacent room and could be heard just as clearly without the device.

"Mr. Burkert will see you now," the secretary said. The couch sucked in air when I stood up.

William Burkert, an Asian-American man in his early fifties, greeted us with a nod when we stepped into his office, but did not get up from behind his desk. "What can I do for you?"

The writing class retreat was Duane's idea, so I let him do the talking. He described our classes and handed several examples of the kids' work across the desk to the superintendent.

"I'm familiar with your program," Mr. Burkert said, putting the writing samples aside. "Believe me, Sister Janet keeps me informed. I'm all for it." He leaned back in his chair. "On the phone you mentioned wanting to arrange something. What did you have in mind?"

As Duane outlined the idea, Mr. Burkert took notes on a yellow legal pad propped on his lap. He winced when Duane mentioned the time frame—all day including lunch—and when Duane mentioned that we had writing classes from five separate units to bring together for the event, he called for a time-out. "Hold on a second. Are we talking about girls here?"

"One of our teachers works with the girls, yes."

"And you want to put them in the same room as the boys? For a whole day?"

"That's right."

Mr. Burkert's jaw set and I saw him write the word "GIRLS" on the legal pad in capital letters, with an exclamation point after it.

When Duane had finished, the superintendent took a deep breath, then said, "OK, here's the situation. We've done retreats here before, mostly with the religious groups. Here's what it involves: I have to hire a team of extra staff, working overtime at overtime pay, to be there. We can't take the regular staff out of their units because the kids who aren't in your classes will still be there. It also means I have to put together a special kitchen crew to bring food to you, set it up, serve it, and clean up. It also means coordinating with movement control, getting the kids to you from all of the different units and then getting them back, making sure that none of them gets 'lost.'" He tossed the pad onto his desk and leaned forward. "All of that I can do, and because I think so highly of your program

I'm willing to give it a try. But having girls and boys in the same room for that long—that's a serious problem."

Mr. Burkert steepled his hands in front of him, as if bracing to hear our complaints, but Duane maintained his customary silence.

"You have to understand," Mr. Burkert explained, "putting girls and boys together in a place like this is a liability nightmare. They're lonely, they're locked up, and they're teenagers. The boys will become overexcited and act out to impress the girls, you can count on it. And the girls will egg them on. Coed activities are very difficult to monitor."

Duane nodded, but a slight tilt of his head suggested that perhaps these difficulties could be overcome. Mr. Burkert became more specific:

"We seat them apart from each other, but even then you have to watch them every second. You wouldn't believe the things that can happen. In the bathrooms, under tables, sometimes right out in the open. You have to understand that these girls are very sophisticated in the sex department. They are experts at using sex to manipulate men—and that includes male staff."

More thoughtful silence. "It's just that it would be a shame to have to leave the girls out," Duane said. "They've worked so hard."

"Couldn't you have a separate retreat for them?" Mr. Burkert suggested.

"The girls only have one writing class. They wouldn't have anyone to meet with."

"That is a problem," Mr. Burkert conceded. "It's because there are so few girls here compared to boys. They don't get as many activities, they tend to get overlooked. But it's getting better." He glanced out the tiny bunker-style window facing the yard. "This place is in better shape than when I first got here, I can tell you that. There were a lot of bad apples on the staff in those days, a lot of physical abuse that went unreported. I got rid of the ones who couldn't handle the job, and now everybody knows what to expect: if you can't act like a professional, you'll be held responsible. I may not be the most popular guy in the world around here sometimes, but nobody's put sugar in my gas tank yet."

I thought that this might be a good time for me to join the discussion. "It must be challenging, trying to run a place like this," I said.

"Oh, it's challenging, all right! Let's just take one example. That boy in your class"— he looked at Duane and pointed at a thick manila file on his desk —"Barreda's his name, right? Sister Janet thinks he's the next Shakespeare. Fine. Sister Janet and I go way back, we've been working together here for years. We may not agree on everything, but we respect each other. But this time, she went too far.

"Barreda is a problem. The staff tell me he gives them lip, he provokes things. They filed a complaint last week, asking me to have him transferred to county jail. It's a standard procedure: if the staff file the complaint, I sign the form and the boy is removed. But guess what happens instead? Sister Janet shows up in my office and throws a fit. She doesn't care what the staff think, she wants Barreda to stay so he can be in your writing class! So she leans across my desk, picks up the transfer form, and tears it into pieces right in front of me. And she says, 'Mr. Burkert, if you do this, it means a divorce for you and me!' I said to her, 'I thought you were married to God!' I like Janet enough that I said I'd do this for her, just this one time, but believe me, the staff don't like it when I don't back them up. I'm going to hear about it, and I'm going to have to smooth things over. These are the kinds of things I have to deal with."

Talking about these problems seemed to make him more comfortable. He and Duane talked about Barreda for a while, then returned to the matter of the girls. "What we were thinking," Duane said, "is that it might be good for the kids to see each other in a different light than what they're used to. A lot of the acting out seems to come from the fact that they know so little about each other. Most of the boys in my class say they've never had a serious conversation with a girl. And the girls feel that boys have never listened to them, never taken them seriously as people. Hearing each other read their work aloud—work that is so personal, that isn't about posturing—might be a good way to start."

Mr. Burkert picked up his yellow notepad again. Duane appeared to be wearing him down. "How many kids are we talking about? Total, if we include the girls?"

"Around thirty."

"And how many volunteers would be present?"

"At least five."

He wrote this information down and sighed. "I suppose if we hired a few extra female staff, sat the girls at a separate table, and watched the bathroom very carefully . . ." He made a few more notes, then said, "When are we talking about? Give me a date."

"How about the first Saturday of November?"

Mr. Burkert leafed through a calendar on his desk and shook his head. "No good. We've got people from Sacramento coming down that day. What about the Saturday after?"

Duane didn't need to check his calendar. "That looks good to us."

"All right, then. A week before that date, I'll need a list of all the kids in the classes so we'll have a precise head count. And I'll need the names of the volunteers or any guest speakers so they'll have clearance to come in. Will you need any special equipment?"

"We bring our own paper and pencils. It would be nice to have a microphone."

"No problem. Anything else?"

"Not that I know of."

"It's a deal, then. There's just one thing I'd like to say before you go, however. It's a comment I'd like to make about your program."

Duane said we welcomed any comments or suggestions.

"I appreciate that. Here's my comment: my staff tell me you make the kids in your classes feel special."

I smiled, assuming that this was a compliment. Mr. Burkert noticed this and focused his attention on me. "You may think that's a good thing, but it isn't. You pay lots of attention to them and they get used to it. They come out of your classes feeling like something special, which makes it hard for them to leave your program and have to go back to our program. It makes them resent being told what to do by the staff, so they resist in subtle ways. This is exactly the problem we're having with Barreda. We can't have it."

Since he was directing his comments to me, I felt obliged to respond. "What do you think we should do?"

"At the end of each class, you might have a little debriefing session. Remind them of where they are, and of who's in charge."

While I tried to picture myself finishing each class by reminding the boys that they were in jail, Duane affirmed that we would have a head count of both students and volunteers ready a week before the retreat.

"And I'll take care of everything else," Mr. Burkert said. He pointed to the writing samples Duane had handed him earlier. "May I keep these?"

"Of course."

He stood up and stretched. "My daughter wants to be a writer. She *is* one already, I guess, but she wants to make a living at it. You guys have any advice?"

"Change professions," Duane suggested.

Mr. Burkert sighed. "I'll pass that on."

12 / Mother's Day

I attracted plenty of attention as I pushed my oversized cello case, which looks exactly like a coffin, through juvenile hall on my way to the chapel. I was assigned to play at two o'clock.

After passing through a maze of cyclone fencing, I reached a building with a cross on its roof surrounded by statuary. The statues were all busts of women, but they did not look like religious figures. They wore wreaths of flowers and necklaces of fruit, like courtesans attending a Roman dinner party.

A group of probation department officers stood outside the front door to the chapel. Over the roar of amplified music coming from inside, I introduced myself to someone with a clipboard and a walkie-talkie, and he leafed through a schedule until he found my name. "Oh yeah, you're up next. Right after this group."

He led me to the chaplain's office, where I could unpack my cello and warm up. "When we call you, you just go through that door and you'll be right on the stage," he explained. After he left, I decided to open the door just enough to peek inside; I was curious to see what kind of act I would be following. The group had eight performers, one playing electric guitar and another playing the organ. The rest played handheld percussion instruments. Their music, which seemed to be a combination of hip-hop and 1960s-style street poetry, was heavily amplified and the audience of prisoners was swaying and clapping along with obvious pleasure. One of the performers was an attractive young woman wearing tight-fitting jeans and a shirt which revealed her belly button. Although she did not sing, and her use of the tambourine suggested a minimum of training, a glance at the all-male audience confirmed that she was the star of the show.

Standing in the aisle between the rows of pews, staring straight ahead and looking none too happy, was Mr. Sills.

I closed the door and slumped into the chaplain's chair. "Am I disturbing you?" a voice asked from behind me. It was Sister Janet, looking radiant as always.

"I don't think having me bring the cello was such a good idea," I said.

"Why not?"

"Listen to what's going on in there! They're all stomping their feet and hooting and working up a sweat, and that's just from watching the girl in the bikini, never mind the music. Can you imagine what a letdown it's going to be when I go out there with a cello?"

"They've got a girl in a bikini?" Sister Janet asked.

"Well, it might as well be a bikini. You watch, this is going to get ugly."

"Have a little faith! You've got friends in the audience. I made sure that K/L unit was invited. The boys from your class are all there."

To kill time, I asked her about the statues planted all around the chapel.

"Oh, those! Somebody donated them to us years ago, after his company ran out of business. He made statues for cemeteries."

. . .

At precisely 2:00, the amplification was unceremoniously turned off and the hip-hop group was led off the stage. They carried their instruments and amplifiers with them. Unlike at most concerts, where the audience cheers and yells for encores at the end of a performance, this audience had to sit quietly, with staff members posted throughout the room to keep an eye on them. No one looked happy about the hip-hop band being sent away.

A man with an ill-fitting toupee shuffled down the aisle between the pews, turned to face the audience, then read aloud from a clipboard: "And now, Mr. Slazman will play the violin." He shuffled back down the aisle and right out of the chapel.

The silence in the room so unnerved me that I failed to see the raised platform on the stage. I walked right into it, stubbing my big toe and careening forward. I narrowly avoided a fall by using the cello as a ski pole, planting the end-pin into the dais and pivoting toward the audience. I hadn't intended to enter like Buster Keaton, but that's how it came across, and the inmates rewarded me with hearty laughter and a round of applause.

Just as I started to feel at ease I caught a glimpse of Mr. Sills and became tense all over again. He looked like a drill sergeant stuck with chaperone duty during a bad USO show. I stalled for time, explaining to my audience that everything they saw on the cello except for the metal strings and end pin had once been part of a living thing. The spruce top, the maple back with its tiger-stripe grain, the ebony fingerboard, the snakewood bow with its hair from a horse's tail, and the pieces of ivory which came not from an elephant but from the tusks of a mammoth preserved in frozen tundra for tens of thousands of years. When we play the instrument, I told them, we bring these pieces to life again by letting them speak to us and affect us and, hopefully, inspire us to live more fully.

When I had run out of little-known facts about the cello, I advised the boys to let the music wash over them and not to feel they had to "understand" it. I encouraged them to daydream. I told them that the first piece I was going to play— "The Swan" by Camille Saint-Saëns—always made me think of my mother. Then I started playing.

With its high ceiling, bare walls, and hard floor, the chapel was as resonant as a giant shower stall. It made the cello sound like several instruments playing at once. The instrument sounded divine in that room, which excited me, but then a rustling from the audience brought me back to reality. The kids were bored, as I had feared.

The rustling grew in intensity, but something about it didn't sound right. It wasn't quite the sound of fidgeting and wasn't quite the sound of whispering either. I glanced at the audience and saw a roomful of boys with tears running down their faces. The rustling that had distracted me was the sound of sniffling and nose-wiping—music to any musician's ears.

I played the rest of the piece better than I had ever played it in my life, and when I finished, Francisco started clapping like a madman. A moment later the applause became deafening. It was a mediocre cellist's dream come true; I had stumbled into the musical version of Shangri-la and been welcomed as a god, and vowed never to play anywhere else.

For my next piece, I chose a saraband from one of the Bach suites. The boys rewarded me with another round of applause, but then someone shouted, "Play the one about mothers again," and a cheer rose up from the crowd. I realized then that it was the invocation of motherhood, not my playing, that had moved the inmates so deeply.

I played "The Swan" again, then more Bach, then "The Swan" a third time. Between pieces I told them stories of cello-related mishaps, like the time I had to go to the bathroom during a lesson but was too embarrassed to tell my teacher. I ended up wetting my pants during the allemande and just had to hope the teacher wouldn't notice since I had a cello between my legs.

At two-thirty sharp the man with the toupee reentered the chapel and signaled that my time was up. The inmates booed, then gave me a final ovation. I packed up my cello and went out the same way the hip-hop band had: down the center aisle, through the silent audience, and out into the garden of funerary statues.

13 / Played

That Saturday as I waited for Mr. Granillo to open the door, I heard pounding on the windows. I could see boys in silhouette through the tinted glass waving at me and giving me the thumbs-up sign, but I could not make out the faces. I waved back; I was no longer the writing teacher guy, I was now the guy who'd played the Song About Mom. The heavy lock on the door turned and the door swung partly open. I greeted Mr. Granillo as usual and he said, "Sills wants to see you in his office before you start your class."

I crossed the dayroom and stood in the doorway to the office. Mr. Sills was sitting in his chair in the center of the room, snacking from a plate of corn chips with melted cheese on them. He looked at me, but his face offered no clue as to what he was thinking.

"These kids don't accept much," he said. "But they liked what you did yesterday."

"I think tripping over the platform helped."

"Lots of people trip over things around here, it doesn't mean they can hold the kids' attention for half an hour. It was the way you talked to them that made the difference. I just thought you should know. The kids liked it."

"Thanks."

He straightened a pile of manila envelopes on the desk in front of him. "I want to know what's the emphasis in your class? Are you improving their skills?"

"I try to correct the obvious problems, but that's not the main thing. I'm trying to build their confidence by giving them topics they want to write about."

"Like what?"

Remembering that I had an extra copy of Kevin's "Trip to the Museum" in my bag, I took it out and handed it to Mr. Sills. He read it slowly. When he finished, he looked behind me toward the hallway.

"Granillo!"

"Yeah, Sills?"

"Get Jackson in here."

A few moments later Kevin appeared in the doorway to the office.

"Come over here," Mr. Sills ordered.

Kevin walked to the side of the desk. Mr. Sills held the essay up so Kevin could see it. "Did you write this?"

"Yeah."

"By yourself? This is in your own words?"

Kevin nodded.

Mr. Sills put it back down on his desk, looked it over one more time, then turned in his chair to face Kevin with his whole body.

"This is a fine piece of writing right here," he said, stabbing the page with his index finger.

Kevin looked toward his feet.

"I'm serious. Look at me when I'm talking to you, boy."

Kevin obeyed. With their eyes locked, Mr. Sills said, "You always know you had this kind of talent?"

"No sir."

"Well, now you know. You stick with this, you understand?"

"Yes sir."

"Is the table in the library set up for your class?"

"Not yet."

Mr. Sills threw his hands up in mock exasperation. "Well, don't just stand there, Jackson—move your ass over there and get it set up."

Kevin smiled. "Yes sir."

Kevin left and Mr. Sills handed the essay back to me. "Well, don't you just stand there either," he said, waving me out of the office. "You got kids waitin' on you."

When I entered the library, Francisco greeted me by thumping his chest with his fist, then extended it toward me so we could knock knuckles. "That was tight the other day, Mark! You were the bomb!"

Patrick nodded. "Everybody was saying you were even better than Miss California."

"Miss California was here?"

"Oh yeah," Patrick said, feigning casualness. "She was cool and all, but kinda superficial."

Nathaniel laughed. "You're just sore 'cause you didn't get to touch her ass."

"No, but I did get to touch the singer's ass. I was helping with the equipment and I made like I was moving the microphone and I managed to brush against it."

"What'd it feel like, homes?"

"Kinda bony. I was disappointed, to be honest."

"Never mind about her bony ass, we're talkin' about Mark here. You were funny. Did you really piss your pants during a cello lesson?"

"I'm afraid so."

"Damn, that musta sucked! Why didn't you just tell the teacher you needed to go?"

"I was afraid of grown-ups when I was a kid. Weren't you?"

"Hell no! I used to laugh when teachers would yell at me."

"Weren't you afraid of being punished?"

"Naw, 'cause I knew they couldn't touch me. Only my old man could make me scared."

"Was he strict?"

Francisco gave a hollow laugh. "Strict is when you set rules and shit, right? Naw, my old man wasn't strict or nothin'. He didn't care what we did so long as we were around when he felt like kickin' the shit out of somebody." He looked over my shoulder and made a waving gesture to someone, summoning him to approach. I turned around and saw a heavyset Latino boy with severe acne shaking his head, not wanting to approach.

"Hey Mark, I got a favor to ask," Francisco said. "See that fool over there? His name is Martinez. He wants to join the class, but he's kinda shy about asking. Can he join?"

"Sure. Tell him to come on over."

"Hey fool," Francisco yelled, "he said to get over here."

Martinez winced but stepped toward us. He had an awkward gait—poor kid, there was nothing graceful about him. I offered him my hand and he shook it. His hand was meaty and warm, almost feverish. "What's your first name?" I asked.

"Victor."

"Welcome to the class, Victor. Do you know how it works?"

"You write what you feel, and you don't gotta worry about spelling an' shit?"

"That's right," Francisco said. "In this class, you write from the heart. And you gotta work, homes. No fuckin' around. But it's cool, it ain't like school, we could talk if we want to."

"Sounds good," Victor said, sitting down next to Francisco.

No sooner had I given him a pad of paper and a pencil than Jimmy Wu tapped me on the shoulder. "Somebody else told me he's interested, too. Could I ask Sills to bring him out?"

"What's his name?"

"Benny Wong."

"All right, but I think that's as many as we can take."

"That's cool."

Jimmy went over to the office and presented his request. Mr. Sills looked at me through the glass; I nodded to signal that it was all right by me. Mr. Sills seemed to consider it for a while, then said something to Mr. Granillo, who went to fetch my new student from his cell.

He brought back the youngest-looking person I had ever seen in K/L unit—fifteen years old was my guess. Benny Wong had perfect skin, owlish wire-rimmed glasses, and a heart-breakingly studious expression. If not for the orange high-risk offender suit, I would have taken him for a tenth-grade science whiz.

"You wanted Wong?" Mr. Granillo asked me.

"Yes, please."

"Wong's all right, sir, you won't have any problems with him. I wish I could say the same for Martinez. I don't know how he slipped in here."

Victor tried to look as inconspicuous as possible.

"I'm gonna be watching you, Martinez. If I see you clowning around in here instead of working, I'll yank your ass out."

As soon as Mr. Granillo had returned to the staff room, Victor grumbled, "Man, why's he always riding me like that?"

" 'Cause you piss him off, homes."

"What'd I do? I didn't do nothin' to him."

Francisco laughed. "He seen you the other day, imitating the way that new staff walks. Remember?"

Victor smiled, but his face reddened. "He saw that?"

"Yeah, homes. You're busted!" Francisco laughed again, then turned to me. "Martinez here is a clown. He can imitate anybody, he can crack you up all day."

"It's not that I'm, like, tryin'a be cruel," he said. "It's just that there are some people who, as soon as I hear 'em talk or see 'em walk, I just *know* I can imitate 'em. And then I *have* to."

"Do the staff guy now," Francisco suggested. Victor leapt up from his chair, but when I reminded him that Mr. Granillo was only thirty feet away, and was at that moment staring right at us, Victor blushed again and returned to his seat.

"That's why you're always getting busted," Benny Wong advised. "You don't think before you act."

Victor glared at Benny and the other boys hooted.

"Wooooong!"

"Wong is always wight!"

"Martinez, you gonna let Wong dis you like that?"

"Excuse me, guys," I said, already beginning to regret having admitted new members to the group. "Benny, do you know how the class works?"

"I think so. It's creative writing, right?"

"Right. If there's something you'd like to write about, feel free to do that. Otherwise I'll suggest topics. The main point is to write about things that really interest you."

"Can we use the dictionary?"

"Of course."

"How about the thesaurus?"

More hooting. "Wooooong!"

"Can we use the dictionary? How about spell check?"

"What if I need a sharper pencil?"

It didn't take me long to figure out where Benny Wong stood in the juvenile hall pecking order. Being physically small and having delicate features was bad enough, but being a smarty-pants really doomed him. It was painful to watch him set himself up for hazing. Victor, on the other hand, must have suffered terribly because of his acne and blocky physique—he looked like a Latino version of Fred Flintstone—

but he compensated for it by being a classic troublemaker/ clown.

"Can I ask a question?" Victor asked. "Is your job being a musician or being a writer?"

"I'm a writer by profession. Music is my hobby."

He rubbed the back of his neck with his hand. "So is writing easy for you?"

It was the first time that any of the boys had asked about my life outside of juvenile hall. Delighted by the opportunity to talk about myself, I told him that writing was agony for me most of the time. All of the boys seemed interested by this confession; how could I do something every day that wasn't enjoyable?

"It's enjoyable at the end, when I finish a book," I said.

"How long does it take to finish one?"

"Well, I've been working on the one I'm writing now for three years."

Francisco looked horrified. "Three years? But you're almost finished, right?"

"No. I'm completely stuck."

"Wha'chu mean, stuck?" Kevin asked. "Like as in, you can't think of nothin' to write on?"

"I know what I want to write, but it comes out all wrong. Or I can't concentrate—my mind goes everywhere except where I want it to go."

"I know that feeling. I'm like that every day."

"Me too. Especially in school."

"Whaddya do when you can't concentrate, Mark?"

I shared my latest strategy with them: I had taken to wrapping a bathroom towel around my head and wearing stereo headphones over that to block out all unwanted sound.

"Damn!"

"That's not all. I have two cats at home, and they like to sit on my lap when I work. That distracts me, too. I read somewhere that cats don't like tinfoil, so I made a tinfoil skirt that I wear along with the towel and headphones."

"Oh *shit*!"

"Damn. Do you ever feel like giving up?"

I confessed to them what I had avoided telling even Duane: that for the past two years I had felt like giving up every day. Writing the book about the nun had turned into the worst experience of my life, and I saw no end in sight. I thought the boys would appreciate hearing that even someone like me—a published author, a married man, a free man—could feel discouraged, but it seemed to upset them, Francisco most of all. His eyebrow bunched up, his face darkened, and he said, "You're gonna finish it. You gotta believe that."

"I said I *feel* like giving up, Francisco. But don't worry, I won't."

"You're gonna finish it," he repeated.

"Yes," I said, realizing my mistake. The boys wanted encouraging messages from me, not discouraging ones. "I will. And it will be worth all of the effort."

"OK, then," he said, relaxing his expression.

Kevin asked me what the topic was for the day. I suggested they write about Halloween.

Patrick cursed. "Fuck Halloween! It was bullshit."

"Yeah. Just because some stupid motherfuckers got in a fight at school, they canceled the haunted house contest. We just sat in our rooms like always. Fuck the staff, man."

"I gotta suggestion for a topic," Nathaniel said.

Patrick rolled his eyes. "Let me guess: 'I Am The Greatest—The Nathaniel Hall Story.'"

"Actually, what I was thinking was: 'I Am a Squinty Motherfucker,' by Patrick Chumnikai."

I felt my stomach tighten. I did not want to lose control of the class on the very day Mr. Sills had finally paid me a compliment. "Enough, guys. What's your idea, Nathaniel?"

He reached into my bag and helped himself to a pencil and pad of paper, a clear challenge to my authority.

"We need to write about life on the street," he said. "The way it really is—the hard-core life that got us all here. I'm callin' mine 'That Life I Live.'"

Francisco shook his head. "I don't live that life no more. I don't got nothin' to write on."

"So call it, 'That Life I Lived,' fool. Weren't you just saying your old man used to beat the crap out of you? That may be normal for *us*, but it ain't suppos'ta be—write on that. The way shit really is, not some Brady Bunch bullshit."

"Don't disrespect the Brady Bunch, homes, I liked that shit. I'd fuck Marcia."

"All I'm sayin' is, keep it real."

"I always keep it real, homes."

"So write it down, then."

With ten minutes left, Francisco and Benny were the only two still writing. As soon as Francisco finished, he slapped his pencil down and announced, "OK, I'm ready. Who reads first?"

"Wong's not done yet," Jimmy said.

"So the fuck what?"

"We wait till everybody's finished before we read. That's the rule."

"We got almost no time left today. Wong can keep writing while we read, it's no big deal."

If I made the group wait for Benny, it would only draw more negative attention to him. But if I allowed someone to read before Benny finished, I would appear to be letting Francisco run the class.

"It's OK," Benny said, saving both himself and me. "I'm just checking for mistakes. You can go ahead and read."

"Then I'll go first," Francisco said. "I'm calling this one 'The G-Ride.'"

It was like around 8 p.m. and I was sitting in my house with my girl. All of a sudden my mom pulls up in the driveway, but as she was pulling up the car was making this loud, fucked-up ass noise. I walked to the porch and as I looked to the driveway, I seen my mom's '94 Thunderbird with the front end fucked up! The front lights were busted, the hood was dented from the front like it was a mountain, the whole front end was fiberglass so it was all cracked. All that was going on through my head was, "What the fuck is my dad gonna do to her?"

As she walked towards me, I seen her face with a frown. Her eyes were watery, as if she wanted to cry. She was real shaky. When she got to the porch I asked her if she was OK? Then I asked her what the fuck did she do? It's 'cause my father had just bought her that car. Luckily my father was working. He starts working at 7 p.m. and doesn't get home until 7 a.m. So she was lucky, cause if my dad would have been there, he probably would of killed her.

Well, she replied that she was OK. Then she told me what happened. She said that she was driving down the street and the car in front of her lights didn't work so when he made a stop my mother didn't see so by the time she pressed the brakes it was too late. All I was wondering was if my dad was going to believe her story. Then she said, "What are we going to do?" I replied, "What are YOU going to do, not WE." But I felt bad. Then I told her that it was too late to go buy any parts. But she didn't want my father to find out so I had to think harder. Then I remembered I had seen a few cars the same color as hers in an enemy neighborhood.

> *I told her I would take care of it. She asked me what did*
> *I have in mind. I told her, "I'm going to help you so my dad*
> *won't woop your ass." Then I left and picked up two homies*
> *so they could help me. Half an hour later we returned with*
> *a brand-new car. We drove it to an alley and stripped it.*
> *Then we put my mom's car together and it looked like new.*
> *So when my dad got home he didn't even notice, so we lived*
> *happily ever after.*

Nathaniel scowled. "Happily ever after? What kinda fairy-tale shit is that?"

"We *did* live happily ever after for a while. What the fuck do you know, Hall?"

"You jacked somebody's car and stripped it! Tell me you weren't watchin' your back for weeks after that, wonderin' if you were gonna get busted. There *is* no happy ever after! Everything only gets worse! It's like that thing, they got a word for it . . ." He made a twirling motion with his hand. "What you call that, when a situation goes round and round, like water getting flushed down a toilet?"

"A vicious cycle," Benny said.

"That's it. Wong—just for that, I won't jack your lunch today like I was gonna."

I asked Francisco if he was ever caught for stealing the car.

"No, but I confessed to God and I know he forgives me. Everybody makes mistakes."

"Mistakes?" Nathaniel blurted. "Who said anything about mistakes? You did the *right* thing! What you *suppos'ta* do when you just a boy, and your daddy beats on yo' momma? You did what you had to do, it was no mistake."

"But it's still wrong," Benny said.

Nathaniel looked at Benny as if he had just dropped in through the ceiling. "What is it with you, Wong? Why you always gotta do that?"

"Do what?"

"Disagree with everything a nigga says! Just when I start to like you, you gotta turn into a disagreeable muthafucka all over again."

"I don't disagree with everything. I'm just giving my opinion, that's all. You don't have to accept it."

All at once, everyone in the class needed to voice his opinion regarding whether Benny Wong was a disagreeable muthafucka. It seemed to take forever before I got them all to shut up—it was like trying to blow out trick candles on a birthday cake—and then I reminded them that the class was what they made of it. "I'm here to give you an opportunity to write what you want to write about, and say what's on your mind, and be heard. You have a choice: you can use the opportunity to say things that really matter, or you can turn it into a cafeteria fight. It's up to you. What do *you* want it to be?"

Silence.

Please, I thought, don't let Benny Wong be the first to speak.

Kevin came to the rescue. "Come on, guys, we gotta quit fucking around. Who reads next?"

"One of the new guys," Nathaniel suggested. "How about Martinez?"

"I'll go later."

Francisco gave him the look. "Naw, homes, you gotta go now. When your name's called, you gotta step up."

Victor shrugged. "It's not really about the topic, it's just what was kinda goin' through my mind as I was sittin' here."

Something really beautiful that has always come in my path through life is the birds. They are so beautiful. Their beauty has taught me a lot, almost enough to find out how beautiful being alive is. For example, the birds people have as pets, they never give up on themselves because even though they are in cages they still sing. They have happiness. They are locked up just like us, but they still enjoy their lives just as if they were free.

Birds are so beautiful, because most of the time they travel in bunches and they stick together, not like humans. They have a hidden beauty that most of us never pay attention to, because we are so blocked out of the wonders of nature and other very important things that might help us go through life easier.

"I like that," Francisco announced. "That part about the birds singin' even though they in cages, that's cool. OK, Martinez, you can stay in the class. Wong, let's hear what you wrote."

Benny didn't seem nervous at all. He held up his sheet of paper and read in a matter-of-fact voice:

Who am I really? I am a seventeen-year-old Chinese male that came to the United States five years ago. My name is Benny Wong. That's only a simple description of me. I want to tell you who I really am, but I don't even know who I really am yet.

The "me" before I got locked up wasn't the real me. I just put on a mask so I could be accepted and also to stop people from picking on me.

Now that I'm in jail, I can't show the real me and I really don't even know the real me. I guess I'll just wait until I have freedom; freedom to explore myself—who I really am.

"I can definitely relate to that," Kevin said. He'd been subdued for most of the hour, but now he was rocking in his chair and drumming with his pencil on his thigh. "The part about not even knowing who the real me is. That's my life, right there."

Kevin's response to Benny's essay set the tone for the rest of the group; they refrained from any teasing. Nathaniel looked impatient, however. He wanted to read, obviously, but appeared to be waiting for someone to ask him.

"Who would like to go next?" I asked, watching Nathaniel out of the corner of my eye. He was trying to look disinterested, but the muscles in his jaw twitched.

"How about you, Hall?" Kevin suggested, smiling. "Don't be shy."

Nathaniel went through his usual ritual of checking to make sure he had enough room on either side of him.

"I call this 'That Life I Lived'—and this is the live version, uncut and uncensored."

"Kick it, Hall."

"I'ma kick it right now."

I was supposed to be in school that day but I chose to go to the hood anyway. I was there for a couple of hours getting blowed. I smoke two blunts and drank a forty-ounce to the neck. After a while I was hungry, since I didn't have a dime to my name and it was close to noon. I decided to go to school. . . .

I reach my school with no problems. I got to the door and realized no one was there, only a few staff. I asked what was up. They told me there was no school today. I got mad because they called my house to tell me to come to school but they didn't call my house to tell me I don't have to come. I just told them to give me a bus token so I could get home which I didn't need but I'd sell it to the homie and get something to eat.

I come out of my school and started the short walk back

to the hood. I only walked a block when the whole epi-
sode started. I was walking, not paying attention to my
surroundings even though I knew I had to cross through
Blood territory to get home. When I reached the end of the
block I noticed a car pass. Not looking up but waiting for
the car to pass so I could cross the street when I noticed the
car had stopped. I looked up and saw the people in the car
just looking at me. I noticed that each of the three people
in the car had on at least some red.

I suddenly realized what I had on. A blue sweater with
a blue and gray Charlie Brown shirt on top of that. And if
that didn't convince them of where I was from, I also had
on blue gloves.

Realizing my situation, I say the only thing I could
think of. "What's up, brotha." I didn't see him open the
door. I didn't see him get out but I did feel him hit me.
I made a motion as if to hit him and he stepped back
surprised at my aggressiveness, but right before my hand
would have reached his jaw I took off running towards
my hood.

Not even a half of a block away I turned around,
hopped up in the air, and banged my hood. I also disre-
spected everything they stood for.

The car followed me and ran up on the sidewalk where
I was running. I hopped up on the hood of the car so I
wouldn't get run over. I took that time to throw up my hood
to the people driving. The car almost ran into an electric
pole but it stopped. The man who hit me was out chasing
me. He was kinda tall so every eight steps I take was one of
his. He caught me fairly quick and swung on me and I fell
down. He tried to kick me but I was rolled up.

I got up but I was too tired to swing. It seemed like I was
done for but I heard a siren. The person who I was squared
off with thought it was the police so he ran back to the car

*and was about to leave when the ambulance that was mak-
ing the noise came into view. I thought he was going to
come back after me but he just pointed at me as if to say,
"You're lucky," and I pointed back at him as if to say,
"You're lucky too."*

*They drove off and I looked at myself. My clothes were
torn and so were my gloves. I walked the rest of the way to
the hood thinking, That's just a part of that life I live.*

Nathaniel tossed his writing pad onto the table and waited
for the ovation that usually followed his readings, but this time,
none came. Perhaps they felt that since no guns were fired
in the incident, it was nothing to brag about—or maybe, like
me, they found it more annoying than dramatic. In any case,
the room stayed quiet and Nathaniel fumed. I asked him if
he felt differently about the gangster life now that he was
incarcerated.

"Nope! The day I get released, I'll go right back to bangin'.
Only I'll be better at it, 'cause I'll have had years of advanced
study. Didn't y'all hear? I'm goin' to tha pen—that's graduate
school on full scholarship, for y'all who don't know."

"But aren't you tired of it by now, Nathaniel? Bad enough
that you're locked up now, and you've said yourself that it will
only get worse—what's the point of all that violence if it
doesn't lead to anything?"

"He's right, homes," Francisco said. "We fightin' over
streets we don't even own."

"Streets got nothing to do with it. If it was about streets, a
nigga would fight for *better* streets, not those pot-holed, dirty-
ass alleys in the 'hood. It's about respect. You gotta get it somehow, and you ain't gonna get it by gettin' A's in English or
flippin' burgers. In the 'hood, you only get respect one way: by
bein' fearless, bein' aggressive, and makin' more money than
any other muthafucka out there."

"That's three ways."

"Shut up, Wong."

The room fell silent again. Nathaniel yawned. "Hey, I never said bangin' solved any problems. All I'm sayin' is, it's real for me. Until you walked in my shoes, I don't believe you or anybody else can judge me."

"God can," Francisco said.

"That's right, but God has the whole file, not just the police report. That's a case I'ma win."

"We only got time for one more," Kevin said, "they're setting up for lunch already. Mine's no good, so who's it gonna be—Wu or Chumnikai?"

Jimmy shook his head. "I couldn't think today."

"I guess it's me," Patrick said. "Mine's about the first time I got busted. Do you—"

"Damn!" Nathaniel interrupted, giving Francisco the high-five sign. "I can't even remember the first time I got busted! I musta been like eight."

"Shhh!"

"Same here, homes. The cops threatened to suspend me from school! I was like, 'Go ahead!' So they hauled my ass in here."

Patrick cleared his throat, but Nathaniel pretended not to hear it.

"When I came to the halls, they put me in with the older homies, man, and I was like—'Hey, what the fuck you doin'? I'ma get killed in here.'"

"A little respect, please," Patrick said.

"Nathaniel, Francisco—quiet down please."

"Not me, I *liked* bein' in with the big homies. They made me their little messenger and shit. I was so happy! The older homies were like, 'Don't end up like us.' And I was like, 'Hell yeah, I'ma come back here first chance I get, this is fun.'"

"That's 'cause you—"

"SHUT . . . THE FUCK . . . UP!" Patrick yelled.

"Damn, Chumnikai! The staff gonna hear you! Don't burn the spot!"

"Uh-oh . . . here comes Sills."

Mr. Sills crossed the dayroom, shoved open the door to the library, then said . . . nothing. The look on his face did the talking for him. He stared at each of the boys one at a time, then asked, "What's going on in here?"

The boys kept their eyes on the table.

"I asked a question and I expect an answer. What is going on in here?"

"It's my fault," I said. "I'm not keeping things on track today."

Mr. Sills wouldn't even look at me. "I didn't ask you. I'm asking them. These *writers*."

Kevin was the only one who dared to speak. "Things got a little outta hand."

Mr. Sills nodded. He finally turned to me, and his expression did not soften. "If you can't control your class, we can't let you continue."

"I understand."

"Are you finished for today?"

"We have one more person who's supposed to read."

"Well, let that person read, and that's it." He looked at the boys again. "You think just because I let you meet in this library means you can do whatever you want? Think again. This is a privilege, and if you can't handle it, I'll take it away from you in a second."

He stared everyone down some more for emphasis, then returned to his office.

Part of me was crushed that the good impression I had made on the staff was now ruined, but another part of me was ecstatic: Hooray for Mr. Sills! How I wished I had that kind of presence. The boys were all subdued now, hanging their heads, eager to display their best behavior.

"Should I read now?" Patrick asked.

He was asking my permission! Nathaniel's mouth was still shut! Hooray for Mr. Sills!

"Go ahead."

Patrick had written about the first time he was arrested, when he was fifteen years old. His father had left the family by then and his mother never came home that evening, so he spent the night at the police station.

> . . . I stayed from 11:00 p.m. until 8:30 a.m. They said they would put me in juvenile hall, but my uncle came and picked me up just in time. I got a long lecture from my cousin, but my mom didn't care. She's cool! I vowed that the "first time" I got locked up would be the last . . . but it wasn't.

As soon as Patrick finished, the group rose and filed out silently for lunch. Nathaniel lingered, pretending to search the bookshelves while I gathered the pencils and pads of paper. When only the two of us were left, he muttered, "I gotta find a good book. There's gotta be something good in here."

I paid no attention to him. When I had cleared the table, he waved dismissively toward the collection of books and leaned against the shelves. "So what you gonna do now? Go home for lunch?"

"That's right."

"You ain't mad at us, are ya? 'Cause of all that talking?"

"I didn't enjoy today, Nathaniel."

"We just restless, that's all. It's not 'cause we don' like you, you know that."

I knew he was only flattering me, but I appreciated the fact that he was trying to make amends. "How you feel about me isn't the issue. I don't like sitting there while you guys screw around like that, it's a waste of everybody's time."

"Raggin' on each other is how we keep from goin' crazy in here, that's all. It's a way of releasin' tension."

"You weren't releasing any tension, you were creating it. Why did you have to do that today, of all days? When we had two new guys in the class?"

He looked aggrieved. "Why you puttin' it all on me? Everybody was doin' the same shit."

"Give me a break."

He used his forearm to even out a row of book spines. "OK, I'm immature, I admit it. Why you think I'm in this place?" He brushed the dust off his sleeve. "Anything else you wanna bust on me for? Now's the time, while I got remorse. You think I never been kicked out of something before? Didn't I write about it last week? You think I fuck everything up *on purpose*?"

My resolve to suspend him from the class weakened. "You've got a lot of talent, Nathaniel, but you're wasting it with all of that screwing around. What can I say to convince you to take yourself seriously?"

Nathaniel looked miserable. He stared at the floor as if fighting back tears. "I need encouragement, not criticism," he said.

"All right, then. I'll do my best, I promise. All I ask is that you make an effort, too."

He looked up from the floor, and I saw right away that he had not been fighting back tears at all. He was concealing a grin. "I gotta tell you, man—you're way too nice for a place like this! You gonna get played here, over and over. Only it won't be by somebody like me, who *tells* you you bein' played. It'll be somebody who *really* plays you, for somethin' that matters, and then nobody'll respect you. You *need* me, man. You need the practice."

14 / A Day of Creation

After Mr. Sills' memorable visit to the library, the class ran smoothly for weeks. Nathaniel didn't provoke anyone, Francisco didn't talk out of turn, and no one picked on Benny Wong. Meanwhile, our upcoming retreat gave the boys something to look forward to: a whole day spent outside their cells, the chance to present their work to a wider audience, and the opportunity to be around girls. Preparing for it became a common goal to work toward, and the boys responded with a flood of essays and poems.

At our last class before the big event, I gave them a pep talk. I emphasized the significance of the retreat, and told them to be proud of what they had achieved so far. They received my speech with enthusiasm, but indicated that I had left something important out.

"We'll be the best group, though, right?"

"We won't let you down, Mark!"

"K/L rules! We'll kick everybody else's ass!"

"The *hinas* are gonna want to sit at our table, not with those other fools!"

I reminded them that the retreat was not a competition. It

was to be a gathering of fellow artists, a celebration of creative aspiration, a festival of unity, and so on—but they wouldn't have any of it.

"Hey Wu—you gotta cut my hair on Friday, homes."

"Mine, too."

"Listen up! I figured out a way to crease our pants using the hot plate."

"Jackson, you gotta get some Scotch tape from the pantry. That way we can make cuffs."

"Mark, you got any tricks about what to do if you get, like, nervous up there? I don' wanna get stage fright or nothin'."

"You better not, homes, or you'll make the rest of us look bad."

"That's why I'm askin', fool!"

"Hold on—we ain't even thought about the females. What if they got some, you know, romantic poems and shit? How we gonna deal with that?"

"Wu got his poem about the wet dream, that'll do it."

"It wasn't a wet dream, fool. You're the one who has those."

I suggested we conduct a "dress rehearsal." I had each of the boys stand up at the head of the room and read while imagining a gymnasium full of people staring at him. This gave me the opportunity to offer some advice about how to present themselves to an adult audience:

"Slow down, Nathaniel, it's not a race to get to the end."

"I ain't readin' fast! It's my normal pace!"

"That's how it sounds to you because you know the material so well. You have to remember—everybody on Saturday will be hearing it for the first time, and they need time to let the meaning sink in."

He nodded and looked at me out of the corner of his eye. "I hear you. We wanna make sure everybody can appreciate my philosophy on every possible level."

"Exactly. Don't cheat your audience."

"Careful not to mumble, Victor."

"Louder, Benny."

"Can you look up from the page and make eye contact with us, Francisco?"

"Then I can't see the words."

"Not the whole time, just every few seconds. It makes the audience feel that you're really talking to them."

"I'll try." He read a line, then paused to stare at me as if I had just challenged him to a fight. Then he read another line. "Like that?"

"Never mind, Francisco. You were fine before."

The retreat was scheduled to begin at nine and to end at five. When I arrived in the gym on the girls' side of the facility at 8:30, Sister Janet, Duane, and Karen were already there, collating photocopies of student work to be placed in folders and given to every participant. The writing teachers from E/F and G/H units, Lydia Johnson and Terry Taylor, came in right after me.

Members of the kitchen staff had set up a long table on one side of the room and stocked it with containers of orange juice, plates of blueberry muffins and bagels, and an urn of coffee for the adults. Two custodians and their crew of inmate assistants arrived with a microphone, an amplifier, and a pair of speakers. After plugging it in and testing it, they helped us set up tables and chairs. The gym had one bathroom, the walls of which were scarred with graffiti carved into the paint. The stainless steel sink had graffiti scratched into it, too, as did the ceiling and the mirror; even the toilet seat had been tagged.

At 9:20, with no sign of any kids making their way toward the gym, Sister Janet started pacing. "This is *so* typical," she fumed. "I came here three times this week, making sure that every unit knew what was going on, that every kid's name was on the right list, that every list was in the right office, and that the staff understood how important it was that the kids get here on time. A lot of good it did." She waited another five minutes, then took off to do battle. The rest of us milled around in the empty gym and drank coffee.

At 9:45, Sister Janet returned with the boys from M/N and K/L units. Of the four staff members who led the boys in, Mr. Granillo was the only one I recognized. I waved to the boys in my group, but they could only nod back. While in transit, the rules 'of Movement Control were strictly enforced: hands clasped behind the back at all times, no talking allowed.

"Where do you want 'em?" Mr. Granillo asked.

Sister Janet made a sweeping motion with her arm. "Boys, feel free to spread out. Sit wherever you'd like."

The two units spread out but did not mix. My group occupied several tables on one side of the room, Duane's did the same on the other side of the room. Predictably, the boys divided themselves according to race: Francisco and Victor claiming one table, Kevin and Nathaniel another, with Jimmy, Patrick, and Benny choosing a third. I comforted myself with the thought that at least they had chosen three tables close together.

Since we were going to be together for a whole day, I thought it would be a good idea to say hello to Mr. Granillo. He leaned against the cinder-block wall, arms folded, watching the boys from under the bill of his cap.

"Good morning," I said.

"Hey. How ya doin'?"

"It's the big day."

"Yep. The guys are excited, that's for sure. Which table are the girls going to be sitting at?"

"I think the plan is for the girls to sit at the same tables as the guys."

He rolled his eyes. "This'll be different."

Before sitting down with my own group, I went over to greet the boys from Duane's class. It had been nearly four months since I'd seen them.

"You got your own class now!" Ruben Barreda said, standing up when I approached his table. "That's cool, man. You must be a good teacher."

"I've enjoyed it a lot. And I have you guys to thank for it."

Ruben looked pleased to hear that. "That's nice to know. It feels good to hear something like that around here." He glanced at the podium and microphone just behind him. "Man—I can't believe how *nervous* I feel. I don't know if I'm gonna be able to do this."

"Everybody feels nervous about reading in front of people," I told him. "The hardest part is the waiting. Once you get up there and get past the first sentence, you're going to be fine." He looked doubtful, so I added, "Your writing speaks for you. Being nervous might make you uncomfortable, but it won't take anything away from what you've written. Just go up there and deliver the message."

"I just hope I don't puke."

At last I felt free to join the boys from my class. I pulled up a chair and asked how everyone was doing, but they barely responded.

"Hey Mark."

"Hey."

Something was wrong. When I asked about it, they shrugged and looked around the room. Sensing I could get information out of him more easily than the others, I cornered Benny Wong. "What's up? Something feels wrong."

He leaned in and whispered, "How come you went over to talk with those guys first? They're our *rivals*, man."

I whispered back loud enough for all of the boys to hear, "Strategy."

Francisco blinked a few times, then started nodding. "I get it! He just playin' with their minds!"

"Naw, it's the other way around—he playin' with *our* minds, fool!"

"Damn, now I'm confused!"

"If those fools could hear us now, they'd *laugh* at our sorry asses."

"We'll let it go this time, Mark."

"Yeah, but don't scare us like that, man. We thought you forgot about us or somethin'."

"So where are the girls?"

"Yeah, when are they gonna get here, Mark? This tape ain't gonna last much longer and we wanna make a good first impression." Francisco was referring to the tape holding the bottoms of his pants legs into cuffs. I began to notice other things: their tops looked fresh from the laundry, Francisco, Kevin, and Patrick had clipped their hair almost to the scalp, Benny and Victor had wetted theirs down and combed it back, Jimmy had found some gel and spiked his, while Nathaniel had combed his hair out into a huge 'fro.

"The girls are coming, don't worry. You're looking good, guys. Did everybody remember to bring his work?"

"Don't trip, Mark, we're cool. We won't let you down."

"Hey Mark—that's a coffeemaker over there, right?"

"Yes."

"D'ya think you could get us some coffee? The staff won't let us have any, but if you get it for us, they won't do nothin'."

"Let's wait until everybody gets here and see what the deal is with the food, guys."

"Aw, c'mon, Mark!"

"Yeah, man, a little coffee ain't gonna kill us."

"And some of them muffins, too. Before everybody else gets here and grabs all the blueberries."

"We don' wanna get stuck with the brown ones, Mark. They taste like shit."

"We're going to be here all day, guys. Just relax."

"I thought you said this was gonna be fun?"

"It is. Be patient, you just got here."

"Aw, man."

I looked over at Duane's group and they were leafing quietly through the handouts. They weren't pestering Duane for coffee or muffins. I felt like a failure.

"Hey Mark—where are the bitches?"

"Don't use that word, Nathaniel! Especially not today."

"No problem. Where's the pussy?"

"Nathaniel—"

"Ha! I'm just playin' with you, man, don't trip. Hey—does that mike come off the stand?"

"I'm not sure. Why?"

"You never heard me rap, Mark! Today's your chance. And look! There's a tape player attached to the amp! I was right! I brought a tape, just in case. Can I go check it out?"

He was exhausting me already. "Have a look at it, but don't play the tape yet or start rapping. Let's not do anything until everybody is here."

"No problem."

He leapt up from his chair and strode over to the microphone. One of the staff immediately confronted him and told him to sit down.

"But my teacher said it was OK!" he protested, his face a portrait of innocence.

"What teacher?"

"Him—over there." He pointed me out. The staff member stared at me, then turned and walked away. While Nathaniel examined the audio equipment, two more writing classes filed in and occupied the tables in the middle of the room. It was 10:00 and the girls were nowhere to be seen.

"Mark, this is getting *boring*, man."

"We'll get started soon."

"I need some coffee or I'm gonna fall asleep."

All of a sudden, a window-rattling rhythm thundered out of the speakers. It was the kind of music you hear coming out of cars with miniature tires and darkened windows. Nathaniel had put in his tape and started it. I waved for him to cut it off, but he pretended not to see me. He fiddled with the volume, turning it down at first but then bringing it up even louder than before. The room came alive; every kid was swaying to the beat now, tapping out the rhythm with hands and feet and talking all at once. Not even the kids from Duane's group could resist. Nathaniel picked up the microphone, turned it on and said, "Test! Test! One, two, three—can you feel me?"

"That's it, Hall! Kick one!"

"Yeah, I hear that. How's everybody doin' today?"

Thump, thump, boom. Thumpa-thumpa-boom.

I got over to the stage as quickly as I could without running and told Nathaniel to turn it off.

"Why? It's not bothering anybody? Look—they like it!"

"I know they like it, Nathaniel. But I asked you not to play the tape and you said you wouldn't. You've got to turn it off now, it's not time for this yet."

He delayed, pretending not to know how it worked, but eventually turned it off and returned to his seat. From the look on his face, I had a feeling he would not be speaking to me for the rest of the day. I checked my watch; it was 10:03. Seven hours of this to go, I thought, and already I could feel a tension headache forming just behind my right eye.

The activity in the room that had started when Nathaniel turned on the music didn't stop. Voices and laughter echoed in the gym, along with the squawks of plastic chair legs scraping across the floor. Everybody was in motion, even though they were sitting down. Nothing organized was happening, and the staff looked uneasy.

And then the girls showed up.

A woman nearly the size of Mr. Jenkins sporting a coach's whistle around her neck entered the gym first. She was outraged by what she saw: boys at every table. She took charge immediately and shooed a group away from a table in the center of the room. With a safe haven created, she waved with her hand and a line of five girls, hands behind their backs and heads bowed forward, marched into the room. The room had become so quiet you could hear their footsteps. With thirty or so pairs of adolescent male eyes on them, none of the girls dared to look up. They looked like rabbits being led into a coyote pen.

Two of the girls were black, three were Latina. One of the Latinas, a petite girl not yet old enough to drive, was obviously pregnant.

Sister Janet approached the woman in charge of the girls and explained that we wanted the different groups to mix—especially the boys and girls, since they had built up so many negative stereotypes about each other.

"Oh no," the guard said, shaking her head for emphasis. "Absolutely not. No way I'm putting my girls at those tables. These minors can listen to each other read, but that's as far as it goes."

Sister Janet let the matter rest. She went to the podium, adjusted the microphone for her height, then welcomed everyone to the first Inside Out Writers retreat. After thanking the volunteers, the staff, and the administration for making the event possible, she spoke directly to the kids.

"I want to thank you for making a dream come true. To see young people who feel they have no voices begin to *find* their voices. Your work has impressed us deeply, and it has already touched more people than you know. But this is only the beginning. You must believe me when I say that our world cannot be complete without you, and without hearing what you have to say.

"True justice cannot exist without compassion; compassion cannot exist without understanding. But no one will understand you unless you speak, and are able to speak clearly. And that's exactly what you have been doing in your classes. Everyone in this room is proud of what you've done so far, and looks forward to hearing from you today."

She asked Mario, a serious-looking boy from Duane's group, if he would lead everyone in a prayer. As soon as Mario took the microphone and bowed his head, everyone in the room followed his example. No one snickered, no one squirmed. Mario thanked God for this beautiful day, for bringing light to such a dark place, and for giving everyone in the room the opportunity to do meaningful work. When he finished with the prayer, Duane joined him at the podium and explained that for the next hour the microphone would be open. Whoever wanted to read should feel free to do so. Then he and Mario sat down.

At first, nothing happened. The kids pretended to read their handouts, they doodled in their notepads. Then, at each table, several kids began urging the most extroverted member of their group to stand up. On my side of the room, it was Nathaniel who became the focus of attention.

"Come on, man, you gotta get up there."

"Yeah, homes, you said you would."

"I'll go later."

"Naw, go now."

"Chill, man. I want to scope things out first."

"Somebody's gotta go first, homes."

"Why don't you go, then?"

" 'Cause I don't read as good as you. The first one's gotta be good."

The guys tugged at Nathaniel's shirt, trying to dislodge him from his chair.

"I ain't ready to read yet! Leggo my shirt, man, you wrinklin' it!"

"Get up, Hall."

"We got a volunteer!" Francisco shouted, his hand raised as high as it could go, with the index finger pointing down at Nathaniel. Patrick and Kevin started clapping.

Nathaniel put up a good show of resistance, but he was not about to let anyone beat him to the podium. The moment someone from one of the other groups raised his hand to volunteer, Nathaniel bolted up from his seat, the plastic chair making a loud noise as it skidded backwards.

"If no one else'll do it, I guess I'll have to," he grumbled, making sure his route to the microphone took him past the girls' table.

He read his story about the iceberg prison, rushing at the beginning but eventually settling into a good pace. When he reached the end of it, where he declares the moral ("This story is an example of the consequences of being incarcerated without being given the education and the skills to make it in the world"), the audience gave him an ovation. The retreat had begun! When he returned to his seat, I gave him the thumbs-up signal and he motioned for me to come closer. I leaned in and he asked, "Should I hit 'em with the rap next? They seem ready for it."

The throbbing behind my eyes started again.

"There aren't any cusswords in it!" he reassured me. "I took 'em all out, I know the drill. And it's got a positive message in the end."

"Can you do it without the music?" I asked. "So we can hear the lyrics?"

He made a slicing motion in front of his throat. "It'll sound weak that way. What you got against rap, Mark?"

"I don't have anything against rap," I said, lying. "But once you play that tape, everybody's going to get excited and no one's going to want to sit still and listen to essays or poems anymore. Let's save it for the end of the day, it can be the finale."

"You're just hopin' I'll forget about it."

"Nathaniel, we're going to be here for another seven hours. There'll be plenty of time for you to rap—all I'm asking is that you wait until everybody else has had a chance to read their work first."

He thought about this for a moment, then nodded. "I can do that."

"Thanks. So how did it feel being up there just now, reading to such a large audience?"

"It felt good. How did I sound?"

"You sounded great. I'm proud of you—you made us look good."

"Thanks. So you gonna hook me up with some coffee now? For good behavior?"

"No, but you have my gratitude, which is far more important."

"If I promise not to bug you for the rest of the day, will you get me some coffee?"

"Nope."

He grinned. "So you're sayin' you *want* me to bug you, then?"

"Shhhh!" Francisco signaled, pointing toward the stage. "Somebody else is readin'! Listen up, fool."

Ruben made his way to the podium and read "Clouds," the essay about seeing beyond the graffiti carved into his cell window. His classmate Nicqueos got up next and read about being abandoned by his mother at the age of four, raised by his grandmother for several years, then put into foster care. When he was thirteen the courts returned him to the custody of his mother, but she turned out to be nothing like the woman he had assembled in his dreams. She was arrested within a year, and Nicqueos went back to a group home. "Ever since then," he told us, "I've been in a rebellious stage. I still don't know where I belong."

Nicqueos barely acknowledged the applause he received; the moment he finished reading he went back to his seat, looking more relieved than exhilarated.

"Well, that settles that," Patrick said, stuffing his own work back into his folder. "Good luck, you guys—you're on your own. I ain't readin' my shit in here, these guys are *good.*"

Francisco began fussing with the crease on one of his pant legs. "Damn! That was some fine-ass writing."

"It just means we gotta take it to another level!" Nathaniel insisted. "Look—we got pencils and paper and all day to come up with stuff. This is what it's all about!"

While Nathaniel focused on writing new pieces, the others listened as, one after another, boys from the other classes got up to read. One boy, whose father was incarcerated while he was growing up, described the moment when it dawned on him that his own son, now two years old, would have the same fatherless childhood he'd had. Another described how angry he felt after learning his grandmother had been mugged, in spite of the fact that he had been mugging people for years. Others wrote about lost freedom and the longing for home and family. We heard grievances against society, declarations of innocence, and admissions of guilt. Some claimed to have found God in jail, while others described themselves as utterly alone in the world, abandoned even by God.

So far, however, only boys were reading. I looked over at the girls' table and saw that they were urging the pregnant girl to get up and represent them. Karen whispered some encouragement into her ear, at which point the girl threw up her hands in a gesture of resignation and stood.

Carrying a sheet of paper, and with her other hand resting on her swollen abdomen, she waddled to the podium, took the microphone off the stand, then sat down on the edge of the stage. "Is it OK if I sit?" she asked, looking to Karen for reassurance.

"It's fine, Vivian," Karen told her. "Just make sure to read loudly enough that we can all hear you."

Vivian nodded. Her hair fell across her face, hiding most of it from view. She brought the microphone close to her mouth and began speaking, but no sound came out from the speakers. She must have turned the microphone off with her thumb when she removed it from its cradle.

"Hit the switch, girl!" someone yelled. "We can't hear you!"

She held the mike out in front of her and squinted at it.

"It's on the side!"

She found the switch and turned it on. "Like this?"

"Yeah! We feel you now."

She tucked her hair behind one ear, thanked Karen for encouraging her to write and to believe in herself, then shared with us her dearest childhood memory: receiving letters from her father while he served time in prison. He addressed each letter to "daddy's little girl," told her he loved her and promised that everything would be all right once he got home. When he did come home, Vivian met the man she had adored from afar and experienced a profound disappointment. Like Nicqueos, she felt betrayed and started getting in trouble. She ended her essay with a confession: now that she was locked up, she prayed every night that her daddy would send her a letter and tell her once more that she was daddy's little girl.

Once Vivian had read, the rest of the girls felt braver and soon all of them made the trip to the podium. At noon, with all of us feeling that something magical was going on, we broke for lunch. While the rest of us ate, Sister Janet negotiated with the female guard, arguing that the boys and girls had earned the privilege of sitting together for the afternoon. The woman looked resolute, shaking her head steadily as the nun pled her case. Not even Sister Janet can pull this off, I thought, but I underestimated her. By 12:30 the guard showed signs of wearing down, and not long after that, I watched as Sister Janet and Karen led each of the girls to a different table. Their chaperone, meanwhile, looked like a hen whose chicks had just been pulled out from under her wing. She seemed uncertain of what to do with herself; she read a few handouts, glanced repeatedly at the clock, and wrung her hands. I felt sorry for her, sitting all by herself at the vacated table, so I joined her for coffee.

"It's gone pretty well so far," I said.

"So far, yes."

"The guys in my group have been looking forward to this for weeks. They even creased their pants and used tape to make cuffs."

She flashed me a taut smile. "Young people are the same everywhere."

"The writing's pretty good, don't you think?"

"Oh yes. There's a lot of talent here. People would be amazed."

After all the buildup over what we could expect if we put the boys and girls too close to each other—I was expecting some kind of sexual explosion—the reality was a letdown. The boys and girls weren't even talking to each other; the girls stared down at their hands and the boys were all suddenly talking about cars. I said to the guard that if it weren't for the orange prison uniforms, you might think they were ordinary high school students. She arched one of her eyebrows.

"Don't take offense," she said, "but in my observation, you are a naïve person. You think everything's just like in a storybook. Oh, I wish I could feel that way, yes I do. Unfortunately, I can't. It's my job to see the truth." She picked up one of the pencils we had distributed throughout the room and held it in front of me. "You see a pencil here. Just a nice little pencil. It would never occur to you"—she changed her grip on the pencil so that it was clenched in her fist—"that this could be driven through someone's ear right into their brain! You hand these pencils out but don't pay close attention to how many come back. I bet you don't know how many were on this table when we came in, do you? I do. There were nine."

She returned the pencil to the table and folded her hands on her lap like a Sunday school teacher. "But it's OK. All of us here are like the ingredients to a stew. You volunteers are the spice. So it's OK that you are the way you are."

Out of the corner of my eye I saw Nathaniel moving toward the tape deck, cassette in hand, threatening my storybook vision of a writing retreat without rap music. I excused myself and got to the podium as quickly as I could.

"Not now, Nathaniel." I felt my headache starting to throb again.

"But this is the break! What better time for a musical interlude?"

"Wait until the end of the day, Nathaniel. Please."

"You said I could play it after everybody read," he pouted. "Well? Everybody read, and now you're saying I can't play it until the end of the day. You broke your word."

Remembering how easily he'd manipulated my emotions before, I struggled to think of a way to talk him into sitting down without creating a scene. Instead my mind tied itself into knots.

"Hall! What the fuck you doin' standing up?"

It was Mr. Granillo. He had approached without my noticing.

I marveled at how quickly, and how skillfully, Nathaniel managed to look injured. "I'm just talking with my teacher. What'd I do wrong?"

"Is this where he's supposed to be?" Mr. Granillo asked me.

"We're talking about a song he wrote," I said. "He wants to perform it, but I think it would be better if it came later in the day. What do you think?"

Mr. Granillo grasped the situation immediately. He ignored my question and got right up into Nathaniel's face.

"Gimme that tape, Hall."

"What? It's my tape."

"Give it to me right now."

Nathaniel handed it over.

"This is a writing retreat, not a rap concert. When your teacher decides it's time, he'll tell you. I'll have the tape right here. Now sit down."

Nathaniel didn't budge. The expression on his face couldn't have been practiced, it was such a naked display of frustration. Here it comes, I thought. He's going to blow, Mr. Granillo is going to deck him, then the other boys will start a riot. Chairs will be thrown. Tables will be used as forts. Pencils will be driven into brains. This will be the last writing retreat ever, and all thanks to me not being able to handle one testy kid.

Nathaniel didn't blow, however. He turned around slowly, with just enough insouciance to preserve his dignity but not enough to give Granillo an excuse to throw him out. He returned to his table, but would not look at or speak to anyone there. He also made a point of refusing to look in my direction; he stared at the wall and smoldered.

I felt badly that Nathaniel's day had been spoiled, but mainly I felt grateful that my day had been saved. I decided to sit with Francisco and Victor for a while. Vivian, the first of the girls to read, had been assigned to their table. I complimented her on the piece she'd written, but she kept her eyes on her hands, which were propped on top of her belly. "My baby just kicked!" she said.

"Can I feel it?" Francisco asked.

She moved her hands to one side, indicating that it was OK to touch.

Uh-oh, I thought.

I felt sure the orgy was about to start, but as soon as Francisco felt the baby kick, he yanked his hand back. "Damn," he said, "it's like the movie *Alien*."

"No it isn't," Vivian said, smiling. "It's a little baby, that's all."

"Hey Mark," Francisco said, "this retreat is even better than I thought it would be. We were just talkin' about it."

"You're enjoying it?"

"Hell yeah! It's cool, hearing all this writing. And having so many people listen to what you wrote—it feels good."

"This is the best day I had since I was locked up," Victor said. "By far."

"Hey Mark—you always doin' stuff for us, let us do somethin' for you. You ain't even had time for dessert, I seen you takin' care of business, talkin' to that fat fuck staff lady. Let us get you somethin'. You want the cupcake or the cookie? Or maybe one of each?"

"That's nice of you. I'll take one of each."

"You got it." Instead of jumping up to fetch it for me, however, Francisco merely snapped his fingers. A boy from one of the other writing groups leapt up from his chair and rushed to our table.

"Get my teacher a cupcake and a cookie," Francisco said, as if placing an order in a restaurant, "and another cup of juice for this lady sitting next to me."

The boy hesitated, as if waiting for further instructions. Francisco was quick to point out the flaw in the service. "Don't just stand there, fool—my teacher's hungry." Without a word, the boy hurried off to take care of our order.

"How does that work?" I asked.

"You mean gettin' little homie to put in work? Hey, when I

was a little homie, I had to put in work for the big homies. Now it's his turn. No big thing."

The boy returned with my dessert and Vivian's drink. "That's cool for now," Francisco said, dismissing the little homie with a nod. The pride in the boy's face was unmistakable. I had just witnessed my first authentic gang transaction, but instead of being horrified, I was struck by how strongly I identified with the little homie. When I was his age, I had a kung fu teacher I looked up to, and whose acceptance I longed for. He was an abusive, self-hating thug, but at fourteen I didn't have the experience to realize it. One day, at a martial arts tournament in New York State, he told me—he barked, actually—to run out and buy him coffee. The thrill I felt at being given this honor, and the pleasure it gave me when he sipped the coffee and pronounced it satisfactory, transformed me. I felt as if my body no longer had any weight to it, that my physical self had been replaced by a flame of pure devotion.

I asked Francisco and Victor if, when they had been "little homies," they had enjoyed being ordered around by the older homies.

"Hell yeah! You just dyin'a prove yourself. You wanna show the OGs they can depend on you. You want that homie love."

"Homie love?"

"Aw—I don' even know how to say it, Mark. Some stuff you can't put in words, it's just too strong."

Victor was willing to try. "It's when you know you'd die for somebody, and they'd die for you. No better feeling than that."

"Love from a female is cool an' all, but a female can change her mind. Homie love is for life."

"But Francisco, I thought you said that since you were locked up, none of the homeboys have written or come to visit? That only your family still cares?"

Francisco blushed. "That's different," he stammered. "On the outs, it's for life. We're talkin' 'bout two different things."

"It ain't different," Victor said bitterly. "Homie love is bull-shit, just like everything else. People say one thing but do another. Everybody's just out for themselves."

Francisco shrugged; Vivian's presence seemed to inhibit him. "Hey, look," he said, pointing toward the front of the room. "Somethin's up."

Sister Janet stood at the podium next to a white-haired gentleman wearing a gray business suit. She asked for every-one's attention, then introduced her visitor. "This is Mr. Kelly. He is the head of the probation department for all of Los Angeles County. I've known him for many years, and he is a caring, thoughtful man. He has been with us all morning, lis-tening to your powerful words, and he has something he'd like to say."

Mr. Kelly—who had been a priest before he began his career with the probation department—took the microphone and explained that actually, he had not come prepared to say anything, he only wanted to listen. "But you know Sister Janet. She has ways of making people say yes to things."

He complimented the boys and girls on their fine writing and congratulated them for working so hard to prepare for the retreat. He talked about how important he felt writing was, and what a crucial role it had played in his own life. Then he said, "When I retire, I'll walk away with some very fond mem-ories of things that went right, of people who overcame ob-stacles I never had to face, who showed courage beyond what I've ever had to show. I didn't know what to expect when I drove out here today, but I can tell you that being here, seeing and hearing each of you read, has been one of the high points of my career. Maybe *the* high point. I just wanted to thank you for that."

His speech electrified the kids. When we opened up the mike for readings, so many of them wanted to get to the podium we had to ask them to form a line. Some returned to read four or five times. For two hours the intensity held steady, then it reached a peak when Ruben and Mario, Duane's star students, presented something they had worked on together.

It turned out they had known each other in elementary school and had even been friends, but after they got to junior high school, one of them moved to a different neighborhood. A long-standing rivalry between the neighborhoods meant that the two boys became enemies by default. They did not see each other again until meeting in prison, in Duane's class, and there they discovered their shared interest in writing. For the retreat, they had written a series of letters to each other trying to retrace their steps and figure out how their lives had spiraled out of control. They read those letters aloud now, standing side by side at the front of the room.

It was an extraordinary performance. Unfortunately, it was also an impossible act to follow. By three o'clock we had run into a problem: the kids had read everything they had brought to the retreat, but we still had two hours to go. They were convinced that if they stopped reading, the staff would send them back to their units early. So they began improvising at the mike, and the quality suffered. Curse words appeared more frequently, as did gratuitous references to criminal activity. Each kid pushed the boundaries a little further than the one before him, and before too long, somebody got up and delivered a rap. It went by so quickly I couldn't understand most of it, but from the way the staff fidgeted, I gathered the content was inappropriate.

Nathaniel made his move. He raised his hand and held it there until I could ignore it no longer. I walked over to his table and he said, "Listen. That fool just did a rap, and it was full of gang shit. Mine is about tryin'a do right, it don't even got a cussword in it. Are you gonna let me do this thing or not?"

How could I say no? I gathered the tape from Mr. Granillo,

handed it to Nathaniel, and sat down. After putting in the tape, he took the microphone and said to the audience, "Listen up, y'all. We losin' focus. We gotta stay on track, so I got a little somethin' for y'all to contemplate on. Peace." He pressed the button, and the windows started rattling.

It was all mumbling and posturing to me, but his peers loved it. Even some of the staff applauded when he finished; as promised, he hadn't slipped in any gang references. But sure enough, once the rapping started there was no turning back. Now every boy and even some of the girls wanted to rap, and the experiments with gutter talk resumed. None of the writers, including me, wanted to be the first to censor anyone (didn't we say in our classes that they could write what they wanted?), while the staff seemed unsure of what to do—who was in charge? As we dithered, the kids gained momentum until a boy finally got up and went for the big brass ring:

> Now I'm stuck 'cuz I was born into a life of crime
> Straight killin' at willin' and drug dealin' to my own kind
> And never seemed to realize how fast time flies
> Sittin' off in the halls with a rap sheet a mile high
> Foe counts of murder and premeditated manslaughter
> 25 to life is the deal that the D.A. offered
> but I ain't goin' out like no bitch
> my trigga finga got the itch
> I'm a nigga on a mission
> Bitch, take it doggy-position
> Ain't no sucka in the w—

Just as the boy grabbed his crotch and shook it for emphasis, the room went quiet. The boy's mouth kept moving, but no obscenities could be heard. A glance at the sound system explained why: the female guard had disconnected the microphone cord from the amplifier. She jabbed a finger into the errant boy's chest and shouted, "I have heard *all I need to hear*! You are *done* for today! You are *no longer welcome*!"

Sister Janet somehow convinced the woman to release the boy to her custody. As the nun escorted him outside for a talk, Duane reconnected the microphone and calmly asked if anyone else would like to read. I looked at the clock: it was 3:20. My head felt as if someone were firing a gun inside it. When no one came forward to read, Duane had the fine idea to suggest that we use the rest of the time to write, talk to friends, "or just relax. You've earned it."

I sat with Jimmy, Patrick, and Benny and talked with them about kung fu movies and Japanese manga cartoons; we were all exhausted from the day's effort. Just before five, Sister Janet approached the podium. The boy who had delivered the obscene rap was standing next to her. The female guard stood up to object, her eyes bugging out of her head, but Sister Janet acted too quickly for anyone to stop her. "It's time for us to say goodbye," she announced. "We have had a wonderful day. You have made us so proud—and you should be proud of yourselves. I'm going to ask someone to lead us through a closing prayer, but first, I have someone here who would like to say something."

She handed the microphone to the boy, who apologized to everyone for his inappropriate behavior. "Especially to the females. I'm sorry for the disrespect." Sister Janet touched him gently on the shoulder, then allowed him to sit back down at his table. "Mario gave us such a beautiful opening prayer this morning. Now I'd like to ask Nathaniel Hall to close for us. Would you?"

Nathaniel walked to the podium and accepted the invitation. I crossed my fingers.

"Can I ask that we all bow our heads?" he began. The room fell perfectly silent, just as it had during Mario's invocation. "First of all, we all want to thank God for this wonderful day.

For this opportunity to listen to each other, to learn, and to show that we can do good. For this wonderful day of creation."

He unfolded a sheet of paper and read aloud from it:

"When we came through that door, we found ourselves amongst writers and poets, not just fellow inmates. We had a chance to shed the restraints placed on us by this place and feel free, even if it was for only one day. We want to thank the staff and the administration for letting us do this. Sometimes we make mistakes, sometimes we slip up, but you don't give up on us. We thank you for that.

"Finally, we want to show appreciation to our teachers for what they do for us. They help give us something we never had: a voice that we could use so we would be heard by people that make the decisions that affect us. With our newfound voice, we can give our opinions on the way others are guiding our lives. With that voice we can explain to the people who have never been in our situation who we really are, and why we do the crimes we do. Amen."

After the prayer, the staff instructed the inmates to observe silence and line up by unit. The girls filed out first, followed by my group and then the rest, clutching their folders behind their backs, mementos from their day of creation.

15 / Busted

"The retreat was cool, Mark."

"I'm glad you liked it."

"How'd we do?"

"You did great. I was proud of all of you."

"Yeah, but Rocha and Barreda were the best. Let's face it, they killed with those letters."

Francisco punched Victor in the arm. "We shoulda wrote that shit, homes! Why didn't you think of it?"

Victor punched Francisco back. " 'Cause I grew up in Mexico, fool. I never heard a you till I got here. Those woulda been some short fuckin' letters."

Francisco rested his head on the table. "I'm tired, Mark. I was in the holding tank at court all day today."

"I hate the fucking tank! It smells like piss."

"And all they give you to eat is a damn orange! You can't eat the sandwich they give you, it's all moldy and shit. And you can't get that orange smell off your fingers, it stays there all day. It's fucked up."

Nathaniel didn't look tired. He still looked fired up from the retreat. "When's the next one, Mark?"

"I don't know. It depends if the staff let us do it again, I guess."

"Of course they'll let us do it again! Why wouldn't they?"

"It got a little hairy toward the end."

"Aw, you mean that fool who rapped about killin' and shit? That's nothin'! We went a whole day without a fight, that's what counts." He folded his hands behind his head and stared contentedly out the window. "Bein' around so much creativity, I had to step up on my stories so I could be in the same class as the rest. Since there were so many beautiful women there, especially at my table, I had to stand out so I would be remembered. I don't know if I achieved my goal, but I tried."

"You achieved it, Nathaniel. That was a great closing prayer."

"I know it," he said, grinning. "Sometimes I just want to kiss myself."

"Hold on a second—where's Jimmy?"

Nathaniel drew a finger across his throat. "Wu's gone. You won't be seeing any more of him."

"He'll be back," Patrick corrected, clicking his tongue. "He's just in the Box."

"I heard they sent him to county."

"They're just saying that to fuck with us."

"What's he in the Box for?"

No one seemed to want to tell me. "Did he get in trouble?"

Francisco looked as if he was trying to keep from smiling. "Yeah, you could say that."

"He got cracked."

"Cracked for what?"

"Dope. They caught him with a pipe and a lighter." Francisco started laughing; Patrick swatted him with the back of his hand.

"You can get that kind of stuff in here?" I asked.

"Any drug you want, you can get in here easy," Nathaniel said. "It's pizza we can't get."

"I ain't laughin' at Wu for bein' in the Box," Francisco explained. "It's *how* he got busted, is all."

"Well—is somebody going to tell me how he got busted?"

"It's kind of embarrassing," Patrick said.

"It was a shitty way to go out," Victor deadpanned, drawing a laugh from the others.

Seeing that it was futile trying to keep the secret any longer, Benny explained it in a matter-of-fact way. "The staff smelled the dope after he smoked it in his room, so they called him out. He tried to hide the stuff in his underpants pocket, but the staff saw it. He gave up the pipe but tried to keep the lighter. The staff made him strip naked and told him to squat. That's when the lighter dropped out."

"Of his ass!" Francisco roared, in case I hadn't figured it out.

"His sentencing hearing is just two weeks away," Benny said. "He shoulda waited until after that to get high. Taking the risk now—it wasn't very smart."

"Fuckin' Wong. Everybody's gotta be smart according to you, huh?"

"I think it *is* smart," Kevin argued. "When you stress in here you get desperate, 'cause there's no relief from it. Getting high is a smarter way to deal with it than fighting. How you think I've been here a year without a fight?"

"Either that or the psych meds," Victor said. "The staff'd rather you be fucked up on those than stomping somebody's ass."

"But those psych meds are *nasty*, homes. You take that shit, you'll be a fuckin' zombie."

The irony of it! A group of delinquent teenagers weighing the merits of smoking dope in jail—at the risk of adding more time onto their sentences—as opposed to accepting the psychotropic medications handed out by the nurses. The legal drugs, the boys felt, were too dangerous.

"How'd you like my closing line?" Nathaniel asked, his mind still on the retreat. "*With our newfound voice we can explain to the people who have never been in our situation why we do the crimes we do.* That's real. You can't fake that shit."

Patrick rolled his eyes. "We do the crimes because we're criminals. Duh."

"You're a criminal, Chumnikai. I'm a political prisoner."

"Hall's just sucking up so we can have another retreat soon," Patrick stage-whispered. "He wants more pizza."

"That's all right with me, as long as he does the writing."

"Hall's right," Francisco said. "Writing gives us a way of telling people what it's like, growin' up with violence all around, no positive role models, crazy shit happenin' all the time at home–"

"Knowin' nobody gives a shit whether you live or die!"

"Feeling like there's nothin' to look forward to. So you stir shit up, just to pass the time."

"Yeah," Nathaniel said, his eyes narrowing, "and check it out: the only people you know who get any respect are the guys slangin' and bangin'. They get the best-lookin' girls, they make the most money—fuck it, they got *exciting* lives. They always talkin' about goin' on missions, about representing the 'hood, about outsmarting the cops, about bein' watchful—if you slip, you die. It's like . . . you know it's wrong, but it makes you feel *alive*. Nobody wants to feel like a fuckin' *nobody*."

"But Nathaniel, look where you are now," I said. "Did you ever think that you might end up in a place like this, and lose everything?"

He shook his head emphatically. "Never. You never think it'll happen to you."

"You don't think about it because you can't," Francisco said gravely. "If you did, no way you'd be able to do the shit you gotta do to prove yourself."

"It's the first rule of life on the street: act first, think later. You *never* think first, or you lose your nerve."

"Why you think gangbangers always gettin' high?" Kevin asked me. "It shuts your mind off. You gotta act on instinct."

"On the outs, I never thought about the future. You're just thinking about today, what do I gotta do right now. That's it."

"You guys have to write this down," I said.

"Yeah, we gotta get word out!"

"Yeah!"

The boys picked up their pencils and frowned at their notepads, but then Victor saw something out in the yard that got his attention. "*Mira!*"

A female officer had just stepped out of the building opposite ours. "Oooh, baby! Come on over here!"

"Yeah, that's it! Don't turn around, baby!"

She walked right up to our unit, but then opened the door to M/N, where Duane's class met.

"Aw, shit!"

"Naw, you don't wanna go up there, baby! You want what's down here!"

"Damn! Now those punks upstairs get a look at that ass all day. K/L sucks."

The boys spent the rest of the hour talking about sex. It was as if that brief discussion of their misguided lives was all they could handle, and now, to protect themselves from the reality of it, they had to fantasize for a while. I was annoyed with Victor for spoiling the moment, but at the end of class, he was the only one who had written anything. It was a poem, only two sentences long:

> *I fear that what I'm saying won't be heard till I'm gone.*
> *I fear that what I'm trying to do won't be felt until I'm gone.*

. . .

Jimmy returned to K/L a week later. He looked shaky after his time in the Box. He sat at the far end of the table and stared out the window with a vacant expression. His eyes looked glazed and watery. When Mr. Jenkins stuck his head into the library to ask, "Any nurse regulars?"—meaning boys who wanted the psych meds—Jimmy stood up and joined the line formed outside the staff room.

None of the other boys said anything when he got up, and none said anything when he came back.

I pulled a chair over and asked how he was doing.

"I guess you heard what happened, huh?"

"Sounds like you had a rough week."

He tried to laugh, but it came out sounding like a cough. "You know the way a baby cries? That all-out kind, where it sounds like he's gonna die? I didn't know I could still cry like that, but I did in the Box."

An argument behind us interrupted our conversation. Victor had drawn a picture of a low-rider automobile, and someone had asked him where they were built. When Victor said they were exported from Japan, Benny insisted that this was not the case, that Japanese cars were banned because they had right-side driver's seats.

"They make 'em both ways, ya little fuck," Victor snarled.

"Nope," Benny said calmly. "The steering wheel's gotta be on the right. That's the law in Japan. You just don't know the law."

"Fuck you, Wong! I got a picture of a club in Japan at home, and the steering wheel is on the left!"

"The picture must have been reversed. That happens all the time in magazines."

Victor looked ready to strangle Benny. "Goddammit, Wong! Why you always gotta do that?"

"Do what?"

"Be such a fucking *punk*?"

"So you're saying it's better to be ignorant?"

"It don't matter if you're right about that shit! It's the way you say it!"

"I'm just telling you a fact. I'm trying to help, and you call me a punk. Maybe you're the punk."

Francisco's eyes lit up. "Ooooh! Wong just dissed you, Martinez! You gonna let Wong dis you?"

This was what happened if I spent too long talking to one boy at the expense of the group. By the time I had gotten Victor and Benny to stop arguing, I returned to check on Jimmy and saw that he was writing something, so I left him alone. At the end of class he declined to read it aloud, but let me take it home to be typed up.

ANOTHER SCREW-UP

I just came back from the Box. Upon entering the unit, I felt that everything was somehow . . . different. The kids looked at me funny, I didn't have any personals, and the room that I had occupied housed a different person. I wasn't really surprised 'cause I knew that I had messed up pretty badly.

To cut the story short, I was sent to the Box for two days and I had all of my personals taken away. I am also unable to receive personals from my parents when they come to see me during visiting day for an uncertain amount of time. As for the hygiene equipment, books, and all of my other belongings that had been taken away, I will not see them again until the staff feels that I deserve them. What a bummer, huh? Well, that's not all. When I was in the Box for those two extremely long days, I had my contacts in my eyes the whole time because the staff forgot to bring me my eye equipment and that was not very nice of them. Not only did I have to have my eyes constantly bugging me, but I also cried and had suicidal thoughts for the first time in twenty months. Suicidal thoughts, I'm sure you understand, but for the crying, let me explain to you. I've been in this institution for almost two years and I have met a lot of people that I have become friendly with. This place is like a home to me and I was thinking about how it would be if I was to leave. Do you understand why I shed some tears now? I'm sure you would do the same if you were to really think about it. I mean, come on, I never expected to have a friendship with anyone in here and some of the teachers and staff . . . geez, they surprised the hell out of me by their kindness and good hearts. I'm really gonna miss these people when I shake the spot. But anyways, I don't want to get too sentimental so let me get back to the story.

I came back from the Box, went to school, and found out that not only did all of my material things get taken away from me but I was also now out of the play that I was participating in. The day that I got cracked, the staff gave me an ultimatum. They said that if I was to snitch and tell them who had the dope in my unit, they would just keep my personals for a while and that would be all. If I was to keep my mouth shut, however, I wouldn't be able to use personals for an undetermined amount of time, spend a day or two in the Box, and not be able to participate in conversating with volunteers or attend the writing class. Now, is it just me or is that a really fucked-up choice? Hmmm . . . what a hard decision, huh? I made up my mind not to say shit and now I get all my privileges taken away from me. I personally think that that's really scandalous, but as most people would say, that's the way life goes.

A couple of days have passed already and things are pretty much cooled down by now, which is a good thing. I guess I can't do much about what happened except regret my stupidity and look towards the future. Leave the past in the past. I mean, there's no use stressing now . . . is there? It's not like anything's going to change, right? I think that I'll eventually forget another screw-up in my life. (How many are there going to be, dammit?) For now, I'll have to deal with the jokes that these ignorant fools make. Ha! Ha! Ha! See, it's so damn funny. Damn, I'm so stupid! Ha! Ha! Ha! That thing fell out of my butt! Ha! Ha! Ha! (They don't know how close I am to transforming myself from a nice and decent guy to a multiple murderer.) Ha! Ha! Ha! I'm such a spot burner! Ha! Ha! Ha! I can take their clowning. I could do this. Ha! Ha! Ha! . . .

16 / Happy Birthday

My birthday fell on a Wednesday that year. I should have been in a celebratory mood, having just finished a draft of my novel about the nun. The boys' reaction to my confession of discouragement had shaken me out of my writer's block, and their willingness to bare their souls at the retreat gave me the courage to send the manuscript off to my publisher. Unfortunately, inspiration and courage had not saved me from writing a bad book. My editor's puzzled reaction to the manuscript led me to read it once more, and by page 50 I wanted to slit my wrists. When, at last, the story reached its improbable yet unsatisfying conclusion, I wondered: How could I ever have thought this was good?

My wife, knowing I was inconsolable, did not insist that we celebrate that year. Before I left for juvenile hall that night, she stopped at a bakery and picked up some éclairs for me to bring to the kids. When I got to the unit and the boys had all sat down, I opened the box and saw to my horror that she had spelled out the phrase "Happy Birthday Mark" on one of the éclairs with candy letters.

"It's your *birthday*?" Kevin asked, looking pained. "Wha'chu doin' *here*?"

"You should be out partying, Mark."

"Damn, you shoulda told us." Francisco's eyebrow bunched up. "We woulda got you a card or somethin'. Man, now I feel bad."

I felt an explanation was due, so I told them about the setback with the book. "I'm not discouraged, though—just not in a 'happy birthday' mood, that's all. Don't worry about it."

The boys fell silent. Francisco was beginning to look dangerous; he was staring, red-faced, out the window with a clenched fist pressing into his thigh. Then he let it out:

"Fuck your editor!"

"Yeah, Mark!" Kevin agreed. "Fuck him, you can go somewhere else."

"My editor's a woman."

"Aw, fuck her, then."

"I'm tellin' you for real," Francisco said, his voice shaking, "*she don't know*. She don't know what the *fuck* she's talkin' about!"

"It's OK, Francisco—"

"It's *not* OK!" He bolted upright, sending his chair crashing against the bookshelves. "She don't know you, she don't know you come down here and help us out, she don't know *shit*. Who the fuck is *she* to judge *you*? She's just a *bitch*, what the fuck does she know about anything?"

Mr. Jenkins opened the door and leaned in. "Javier, what's going on?"

"Somebody fucked with my teacher, that's what's wrong!"

"Sit down, Javier."

"I *ain't* sittin' down!"

Mr. Jenkins let the rest of his body into the room. "You heard me. Sit down."

"Some bitch told Mark he wrote a bad book! And it's his fuckin' birthday!"

Mr. Jenkins glanced at me, then at the open box on the table. "Mm," he said. "Éclairs."

"Have one," I said, feeling worse than ever. "There's plenty."

"Don't mind if I do." Mr. Jenkins finished off the éclair in two bites, then asked, "Who said you wrote a bad book?"

I explained the situation, emphasizing that my editor was on my side and was only trying to help me by being honest. It was her professional obligation to be critical, I pointed out. He nodded and asked if there were enough éclairs to give to the other staff on duty that night.

"Yeah, there's a dozen here."

"Thanks." He took a couple out of the box and made toward the door, where he paused and turned around. "Fuck your editor, by the way."

"*Yes!*" Francisco shouted, pumping a fist in the air.

Mr. Jenkins frowned. "The difference, Javier, is that I can say that without jumping up and down like a fool and busting furniture. You got love for your teacher, I see that, but you gotta learn to control your emotions. Otherwise they control you—and you know exactly what I'm talking about. Don't make me come back in here."

"Fat fuck," Francisco muttered when Mr. Jenkins had left.

"So what are we gonna write about on Mark's birthday?" Kevin asked, changing the subject.

"Maybe we should let Wu choose the topic," Benny suggested. "Tonight's his last Wednesday night class."

I looked at Jimmy and he confirmed it with a nod. "I get sentenced next Wednesday, and they'll bring me straight from court to the Box." He practically spat. "If I was gonna kill myself, I would've done it a long time ago. Sending you to the Box is just one more way of breaking you down. You can't even have friends around you on the worst night of your life." He pulled the nub of eraser out of his pencil, then jammed it back in. "Everybody ought to just write what they want. You're always havin' to come up with topics for us. We depend on it too much. If we can't even come up with our own ideas, we can't say we're really writing."

Jimmy stared at the notepad I'd given him, pencil held against paper, determined to "go out" having written something strong.

At 7:30 Mr. Jenkins returned to ask if there were any "nurse regulars." Nathaniel—who I had forgotten was in the room, he had been so uncharacteristically quiet—shuffled out to join the line of boys waiting for psych meds. When he came back, he sat down at the far end of the table and stared out the window.

By 7:45 it was clear that no one was writing anymore, so I asked if Jimmy would read his piece aloud to us.

He didn't answer; he just held up his notepad so I could see that it was blank, then slapped it back down on the table. Part of me wanted to console him, tell him it was OK to be distracted under the circumstances, but another part of me sensed he didn't want to be fussed over. I decided not to vary from my usual response when a boy told me he had not been able to write, which was to nod and move on.

"How about you, Benny?"

"Mine's kinda weak."

"That's all right. Read it anyway."

Yesterday, after the hard rain, while sunlight was leaving the sky, getting ready for the rising moon, a rainbow stood outside our unit. She stood tall, up through the gray clouds. She danced along with the handsome building next to her. They danced and danced until the golden sun-

light started to fade. As the song slowly ended, she walked away from her partner and left him only a memory of their dance.

"I saw that rainbow yesterday!" Francisco said.

"Me too! It was there for like fifteen minutes."

"My room faces the wall. I don't see nothin'," Nathaniel muttered.

"You do so. You see that billboard."

"What—you mean that fuckin' fool with the crown and the cape? 'The King of Beepers'? Fuck that shit."

"I wish I had my old beeper. The cops jacked it when I got busted. Bet he's usin' it now."

"I'd rather have my gun. Adios, incarceration facility."

"Yeah, more like Adios, Hall. They'd need dental records to ID your ass after the SWAT team got ya."

"Better to go out that way than rot in a cell. This is night-of-the-living-dead shit. If I'ma have death, I want *dead* death, not this lame-ass, eyes-wide-open death."

"I'd be happy if I could just make faces when I shit."

"Patrick? How about you?"

One day my mom picked up my younger brother and me from our house to go and stay at her house for the weekend. She was driving through Santa Monica Boulevard and Virgil when she asked, "What should we do today?" I wanted to go somewhere I had never been before, so I said the cemetery. We went to Forest Lawn.

We passed through the black gates into a narrow path that went through the cemetery. There were a couple of graves that had flowers on them because a few days before was Memorial Day. We parked and walked around. There were thousands of graves and a few people visiting their lost ones. My mom called me over to see one particular tombstone. It was for a one-day-old baby. Next to it was the mother.

So many graves. Is it like this, to be dead? Many seem to have been forgotten. I passed by a few graves, reading the tombstones and finding the oldest one. I brushed some twigs off a tomb to keep it nice.

Afterwards, we rested at a large, green, clear area. My brother was running around playing. I watched him, noticed how alive he was, and realized that death doesn't care if you're old or young. It doesn't care about your race, or if you are poor or rich. It will take anyone, and if it does, you'll probably be forgotten like many people in Forest Lawn. But I know that maybe, just maybe—probably once in a decade—I'll get an unknown visitor passing by and reading my tombstone.

"We supposed to be cheerin' Mark up on his birthday, now we talkin' about cemeteries."

"Oh yeah? What did you write, Mr. Cheery-ass motherfucker? Half an hour ago you was ready to smoke his editor."

"I didn't write nothin'. Sorry, Mark. I let you down on your birthday."

"How about you, Nathaniel?"

"Huh?"

"Did you write anything?"

He seemed caught up in his daydream about blasting his way to freedom. Spittle had formed at the corners of his mouth. "Me? Oh yeah. I got somethin' for ya."

In my knowledge quest I search for the secrets of the mind. I start with psychology. With a perfect understanding of the way the mind works and reacts to certain situations I will be able to interpret a person's actions and react in a way that will cause the desired response or cause the person not to respond.

Another prospect of my quest is gaining an understanding of the most arcane being on this planet: females! An education in the field of psychology will help me understand the behavior of women. Understanding their behavior and way of thinking will allow me to seem caring and understanding.

The final prospect is being able to manipulate people into doing what I desire.

"Is that really the final prospect, Nathaniel? Being able to manipulate people?"

"What else is there?"

"How about being respected or loved?"

He shook his head. "Everybody wants to manipulate everybody else. Most people cover it up with nice-sounding shit until you even fooled yourself into believin' it. But underneath all that talk about doin' right and lovin' your neighbor, we're just animals lookin' out for number one. In prison the truth comes out, that's all."

"I disagree," Benny said. "I don't think love is always about manipulating people."

"How would you know, Wong? You were still wearin' pajamas to bed when you got busted."

Benny ignored the teasing. "I'm not cynical, that's all. Just because some people only care about themselves doesn't mean everybody does."

"Fuckin' Wong! This why you always getting your shit jacked! You always gotta say no when a nigga say yes."

"I don't care what you think. I'm gonna get out of this place someday, and when I do, I'm gonna live a normal life. If you tell yourself love is all selfish, then it will be. If you tell yourself it isn't, then it won't be. You make your own reality."

"Jesus H. Christ!"

"Fuckin' Wong!"

"How about you, Victor? Did you write something?"

Victor's face and hands were covered with some sort of medicine; he suffered from persistent rashes in addition to his acne. "Damn, this shit itches," he said, dragging the back of one of his hands against the underside of the table.

"Don't scratch it," Benny advised. "That only makes it spread."

"Wong, I swear—"

"What did you write, Victor?"

"It's shit."

"Will you read it?"

"Yeah."

> *I hate to see someone leave because it feels like my heart goes with them.*
>
> *I hate to see someone leave because I will never know if I will keep in touch with them.*
>
> *I hate to see someone leave because I get so lonely when I'm not with them.*
>
> *I hate to see someone leave because I don't know if it feels the same way for them.*
>
> *I hate to see someone leave because I know it will always happen to me and them.*
>
> *I hate to see someone leave because it always happens in my life, and it happens to them.*
>
> *I hate to see someone leave.*

Mr. Jenkins tapped on the glass, giving us the signal to leave. Kevin held his pencil out like a conductor's baton and said, "OK, guys. You know what we gotta do now."

"You start it."

"This is for you, Mark."

They sang "Happy Birthday" for me. When the song ended, they all cheered and shook my hand and offered advice from the hood about how I should spend the rest of the night. If I followed it, I told them, I would have to have my stomach pumped, my heart defibrillated, and my crotch sprayed with penicillin.

"So? You only live once."

"You deal with that other shit when it comes."

Eventually the revelers filed out of the room, all except for Jimmy. "Thanks for letting me be in your class," he said, pausing at the door. "Sorry I didn't write as much as I wanted to. I guess that's just me, huh?"

"You wrote plenty. You'll be in class on Saturday, won't you?"

"I hope so. But the way things work around here, you never know. So just in case—thanks for everything." He shook my hand once more, then crossed the dayroom without looking back.

17 / Family Life

"Didn't anybody tell you?" Mr. Granillo asked. "There's some kinda play going on this morning. We're just gettin' ready to head over to the chapel."

All of the inmates were sitting against the wall of the dayroom. Jimmy was right; he hadn't been sent to county or to the Box, but wasn't going to have another class with us after all. I saw him sitting beside the water fountain with Patrick and Benny flanking him. I nodded at him, and he nodded back.

"I think Sills wants to talk to you about something. He's in the office."

When I stepped into the office Mr. Sills waved and gestured for me to sit down. While he finished a conversation with a new member of the staff, I noticed an oversized ledger on his desk containing the names of all the boys in the unit. Next to each name was a three-digit number. Virtually all of the numbers were the same: 187. I knew from watching cop shows that this was law enforcement code for murder.

"You nosing around in my books?" Mr. Sills asked. I had been so fascinated with the ledger I hadn't noticed he was staring at me. I must have blushed, because he laughed. "You know what those numbers mean?"

"Only 187."

"When I first started working here, it was a big deal when they brought in a 187. Hell, we used to go over to processing just to gawk at 'em when they came in. Now, it's a big deal when we get kids in here who *haven't* killed somebody. And that's only 'cause they were lousy shots."

He offered me a cookie from a paper plate on his desk. "I got something to ask you. You got a minute?"

"I've got all morning."

"Good—then you can help me unload some stuff out of my car later." He gestured to Mr. Granillo, who cupped a hand to his ear.

"Bring me Jones," Mr. Sills called out.

Granillo nodded.

"Here's the thing," Mr. Sills said. "I like what you're doing with the kids. I like the results you're getting. I got somebody I want you to have a look at. He won't cause trouble. But hell, you can hardly understand a word he says. The boy mumbles. And the teachers at school tell me when he tries to write, it comes out all mixed up. So I was thinking maybe you could work with him a little. As a favor to me."

As Mr. Granillo brought the boy in, I glanced at the ledger on the desk and found his name: *Jones, Dale. 187.* He was black, stood about medium height, and had a prominent scar on his face. He entered the room but kept his eyes on the floor.

"Jones," Mr. Sills said. "This is the writing teacher."

Jones didn't move.

"Look at me when I talk to you, Jones. Don't stand there like you're stupid or something."

Jones looked up, his face expressionless.

"This is the writing teacher. I'm recommending you for his class, and he says he'll take you. You interested?"

The boy brought a hand up to the back of his neck and rubbed it slowly. "Mm . . . mumble-mumble."

"I can't hear you, Jones, speak clearly."

Jones shook his head and mumbled some more.

Mr. Sills frowned. "What do you mean, *No*? You mean, No, I can't speak clearly, or No, I don't want to be in the class?"

"I . . . don' wanbein . . . de class."

Mr. Sills looked appalled. "I give you an opportunity, and this is what you do with it?"

Jones looked back down at the floor.

Mr. Sills glared at the boy in disgust. "Get out," he said.

Jones glanced up at Sills like a boy whose father has just disowned him.

"You heard me. Get the fuck outta here."

Jones rubbed the back of his neck again, then turned around and shuffled back into the dayroom.

"Sorry to have wasted your time," Mr. Sills said, rearranging some papers on his desk, then returning his attention to the boys out in the dayroom. "Granillo, lead 'em out. But keep Jackson here, I need him to help with lunch."

"Got it. Gentlemen, form a line at the door. Jackson, you stay put."

"Mark, you come with me."

When the unit had emptied out, Mr. Sills led Kevin and me outdoors. We walked around to the side of the unit where Mr. Jenkins was standing next to a barbecue grill fashioned from a fifty-gallon oil drum.

"Jackson, help Jenkins set up while I get supplies. C'mon, Mark. Let's take a walk."

He led me out of the facility to the parking lot. On the way, he apologized again for Dale Jones. "That really has me upset," he said, and I could see that he meant it. "I asked Jones yesterday if he'd be interested in the writing class, and he said yes, he'd be interested. When I go out of my way for a boy, I expect him to follow through. He could at least have given it a try."

"Why do you think he changed his mind?" I asked.

"Oh, fear of making a fool of himself. He hates himself, that's what it boils down to. He needs to find something he can do that he can be proud of. He's not into sports, and he's not like Jackson, he doesn't want to be a messenger. I haven't figured that kid out yet, but I will. First thing, though, is that he has to understand: if he tells me he'll do something, I expect him to follow through. He has to know I'm disappointed if he lets me down. You might think it was cruel of me just now, yelling at him like that, but it's exactly what he needs. It's what he never had growing up. To know that somebody cares enough to get pissed off."

We stopped beside a pickup truck, where he had two giant coolers in the cab buried under a mountain of clothing.

"This is my home, right here," he explained, tossing the clothes aside. "If you ever need me at night, I'm usually parked under the connector where the 10 and the 405 freeways meet."

I tried not to seem shocked. He handed me one of the coolers and took one himself, then started laughing. "I'm just playin' with you, Mark. I run a clothing drive for a homeless shelter. Man, you are too easy to play."

When we returned to the unit he opened the coolers. One contained sodas packed in ice; the other was jammed full of chicken pieces marinating in barbecue sauce. "Homemade," he pointed out. "You can't get this out of no bottle."

"Amen," Mr. Jenkins said.

"These kids don't get a whole lot of real food around here, so I supplement their diet every now and then. You look like you could use a little feed, too. You gonna break bread with us today, Mark."

He handed Kevin a pair of hospital gloves and showed him how to lay the chicken out on trays in preparation for grilling. "No, Jackson! You call that a straight line? Do it like I showed you."

"This is how you showed me."

"Jackson—why would I show you how to do it wrong?"

" 'Cause you don' remember is all. Don' feel bad, that's normal for a man of your age."

Mr. Sills' jaw dropped. "Did you hear that, Jenkins? Did you hear what that minor just said?"

Mr. Jenkins grinned and looked upward. "I'm just lookin' at this beautiful blue sky. I won't see nothin' else for the next—oh, I'd say two or three minutes."

Mr. Sills chased Kevin around the grill, then around a picnic table, where Kevin turned around to stand his ground. They shadowboxed for a few seconds, then Mr. Sills tagged him in the stomach, pulling the punch so that it was no more than a tap. Kevin grunted and fell to his knees on the ground. "Ow!" he complained. "Abuse of a minor! I'm writin' you up."

Sills chuckled. "Yeah, you do that. When you're finished, just hand it in to me and I'll see that it finds its way to the proper authorities. Now get up, Jackson—you're makin' me lose focus here."

He let Kevin pour the lighter fluid over the coals but lit it himself. "No matches for you, Jackson. I don't have time to count 'em." As the coals burned, Mr. Sills sent Kevin into the building to gather supplies. "He seems like a nice kid," I said as the two men watched the fire.

"Oh yes," Mr. Jenkins said. "You'll never have problems with Jackson."

"You see how I sent him in there just now, by himself?" Mr. Sills asked. "I do that for a reason: to show him that I trust him. That builds up his confidence, his pride in himself. It's how you have to work with kids like this. You give 'em a little bit of responsibility, and if they can handle it, you give 'em some more. If they fuck up, you deal with it right away. Jackson may not like it here, but at least when he leaves he'll take something with him. He'll know that if he respects himself, other people will respect him."

"He'll also know how to cook chicken," Mr. Jenkins said, staring at the food.

"Don't stand too close to Jenkins," Mr. Sills warned me. "When he's hungry, he'll take a bite out of anything." He checked his watch, then asked if I had ever seen the unit's kitchen. When I said no, he told me to go inside and have a look. "It's on the right, just after you reach the dayroom. Jackson'll be there. He'll show you around."

I went in through the side entrance, which brought me past the boys' rooms. The doors to the rooms were open, allowing me my first view of where the boys spent most of their time. The tiny cells were identical: two beds neatly made, nothing on the concrete-block walls or the floor, no furniture, no television or radio, and a darkened Plexiglas window etched with graffiti.

"Home sweet home," Kevin said over my shoulder.

"These rooms are awfully small," I said.

"Ten by twelve. I heard they was built for one person, but it's so crowded here now they got two in every room. We even got guys sleepin' on mats near the dayroom. Sills send you in here?"

"He said you'd show me the kitchen."

"Sure. C'mon."

Kevin gave me a tour of the "kitchen," which was really more of a pantry. It featured a sink, some cabinets, a microwave, and a hot plate, but Kevin pointed these features out to me as if we were in the galley of a well-appointed ship. He explained how he helped prepare meals there, showed me the contents of each of the drawers, and reviewed the list of items he kept properly stocked.

"It's all part of being a messenger," he explained. "It's work, but I'd rather work than do nothin'. Anything to get out of that room."

"How many messengers are there in the unit?"

"Two right now."

"Where's the other one today?"

"Sills didn't need him, I guess."

"Hurry up, Jackson!" Sills yelled from outside.

"You want some chips, Mark? We got some nice salsa for it, too."

"No thanks."

"Can I get you a soda? Put one in your bag for the drive home?"

"I'm fine. Shouldn't we be getting outside? We don't want to make Sills mad."

Kevin smiled. "If you hustle too quick he thinks you're kissing ass, and Sills don't like that." He arranged stacks of paper plates, paper napkins, and bags of plastic utensils on a battered metal tray, then leaned against one of the counters. "So Mark—why *do* you come here?"

"*Jackson!*" Sills hollered again. "Let's see some *plates*."

"Can we go outside now, Kevin?"

"Sure, Mark. But you at least gotta let me give you a soda, or Sills'll say I didn't hook you up right. He invited you to the barbecue—you're family now."

18 / Two-Face

"Something's up," Benny said. He was the first to make it into the library that night. "Wu got sentenced today, and it was bad. The staff are letting him come to class tonight instead of going straight to the Box."

"How is he holding up?"

"I don't know, he's been in the office since he got back. You can see him from here."

Jimmy stood with his back to us, speaking to Mr. Jenkins and Mr. Warren.

"There's more," Benny said. "Chumnikai and Hall are gone."

"You mean gone temporarily, or gone for good?"

"For good. I'm not sure about Chumnikai, but Hall got put on the county hit list."

"What's the county hit list?"

"It's for people who cause too much trouble around here, so they send 'em to county jail. That's the worst place to go. Maybe that's why Hall was stressing so much last Wednesday, he might have known something was up."

Francisco had a bounce in his step as he crossed the day-room. "Hey Mark! I'm in a great mood today."

"I can see that."

"I passed the last test we took for confirmation. Man, I never worked so hard for something! That is some *complicated* shit you gotta know if you wanna get close to God. I nailed it, though."

"You still cuss the same as before," Kevin noted.

Francisco shrugged. "Right now I'm workin' on my temp-tation to do evil. Cusswords—that's down the road." He looked at me for reassurance. "I mean, we could use cusswords in our writing, right? How bad could it be if we could use it in class?" Before I could respond, Francisco pointed over my shoulder. "Hey—here comes Wu. He looks like shit."

Jimmy stepped into the room looking pale. He sat down across from me but didn't say hello.

"What happened, Wu?" Francisco asked. "We prayed for you in my confirmation class."

"The judge wouldn't listen to anything my lawyer said."

"Wha'd she give you?"

"Fifteen years and two strikes."

"What kinna shit is that? All you did was rob somebody! One time! Nobody even got hurt! There's *murderers* who get less than that, Wu."

Jimmy looked through me, his eyes fixed in a thousand-yard stare. "It's over. My life is over."

"Don't say that, Wu! It's gonna be OK. You gonna get out soon. Hell, you prob'ly be out in twelve. And you'll only be . . . seventeen plus twelve plus . . . fuck it, how old will he be, Wong?"

"Twenty-nine."

"See? That's *young*, homes! You can have a family an' every-thing. I'd be doin' back flips an' shit if I got fifteen years."

Jimmy's eyes gradually focused on me. "You heard about Hall and Chumnikai?"

"Yes. I'm sorry about your news, Jimmy."

"At least I get to say goodbye. They didn't." He shook his head slowly, then looked around the room. "When I got back just now, I was thinking about how everything in this place, everybody, all of you—this'll be the last time I ever see any of it."

"It's like you die but don't get no funeral," Francisco said.

"I had to say goodbye to my roommate just now and all we could do was shake hands," Jimmy said. "It makes me wonder—if I'm like that now, not even able to hug my friend on the worst day of my life, what am I gonna be like after fifteen years in the pen?"

None of the boys could bring themselves to look at Jimmy now; they were all staring at their folders or at their hands.

"See? We can't even talk about it in here. It's not allowed. That's how fucked up we are." Jimmy asked if he could have a notepad and a pencil. When I gave them to him, he began writing immediately.

The others, seemingly relieved that emotions were no longer being discussed, started bitching about the staff, about the food, and about how society judges young people without knowing the whole story. When I handed out paper and pencils, they either ignored me or practiced writing their names in graffiti-style lettering. I had to pester them for twenty minutes before getting anyone to start writing. "We're stuck, Mark. Give us somethin' to write about."

"How about freedom? Can you write on that?"

Benny said he would try; the others said it was too depressing to think about. I asked Francisco to write about what he was learning for confirmation. "There's too much, Mark. That'd take me days."

"So pick one thing you've learned that has been especially meaningful to you."

I thought he would enjoy this topic, given his enthusiasm for religious matters, but he looked as if I had assigned him to write a term paper about Thomas Jefferson. "You can't think of nothin' else?"

"Try, Francisco."

"What about me?" Victor asked.

"How about this: If you could have one superpower, what would you choose?"

He grimaced. "That's too easy! Everybody here'd pick the same thing—to be invisible so we could sneak the fuck outta here. I need something else."

"How about a time you helped a stranger?"

"I can't remember ever helping a stranger, Mark."

"OK, then," I said, getting exasperated, "how about what Jimmy was just talking about. How you're not allowed to show emotion in here."

Victor grimaced again. "How can I write about it if I can't show it?"

"I don't know, but you'll find a way. That's your topic."

"That leaves me," Kevin said. "I can't write on emotions, Mark. Not now, anyway."

"Could you describe someone who influenced you?"

"You mean like a role model?"

"Yeah."

"I didn't have none."

I threw up my hands. "Have you ever had a pet, Kevin?"

He smiled. "Don't trip, Mark. I'll come up with somethin'."

At ten minutes before eight, all of the boys except Jimmy had finished writing and were getting restless. I didn't want to interrupt Jimmy, but I knew that if we waited too long, none of them would get to read. I asked him how much longer he thought he would need.

"Go ahead and start reading. I'll be finished soon."

"Good enough. Francisco, why don't you begin? Tell us something meaningful that you've learned."

Francisco blushed. "Aw—I couldn't think of any one thing, Mark. It's all meaningful."

"But you seemed to be writing," I said.

"He was drawing," Benny said.

"Shut up, Wong."

"I think he should share the drawing with us," Kevin needled.

"Can we see it?" I asked.

Francisco shrugged and turned his notepad around. He'd drawn an idealized, low-rider-style gangster with a bald head, Ray-Ban sunglasses, handlebar mustache, and tattoos. A woman with bare breasts clung to his arm. For a background, he'd drawn a sunset and some gulls. A clock and a monthly calendar floated in the sky next to the sun; several pages of the calendar had been torn out and were drifting away like clouds. At the bottom of the page, he'd written the words "Good Luck" in an elaborate, decorative script.

"Nice titties," Victor said.

"It's for Wu," Francisco said. "The message is: You do the time. Don't let the time do you."

Jimmy was still writing; he didn't seem aware of anyone else in the room.

"I wanna hear about Jackson's pet," Benny said.

"I bet it was a pussy!" Francisco blurted, guffawing at his own cleverness.

"Can't we be serious even for five minutes?" Benny asked, looking dismayed. "It's Wu's last night."

"Can't we be theriouth even for five minuth?" Victor echoed in a high-pitched voice.

"Some quiet, please," Kevin said, "or you'll miss the show."

Around when I was nine or ten me and my friend Arthur had a puppy named Sparkie. Well, really Sparkie wasn't our dog, he belonged to someone that lived up the street from me. When they would go to work me and my friend would climb the fence and steal their dog for a few hours to play with him and then we would return him before the owners knew he was even gone. But one day when I went over there to get him he wasn't there. I wanted to ask the owners what happened to him but I couldn't do that, they would of got suspicious. So every day for a week I checked, but the dog was never there. Even now I still wonder what happened to the dog. I wonder if Sparkie and I were to cross paths again, would he remember who I am?

"Dogs never forget," Francisco insisted. "I had a pit bull and he remembered me even when I was locked up for six months. When I came home from YA the last time, he was like, all happy and shit, jumpin' up and down."

"Who got the dog now?"

"Nobody. The cops shot him. They did it just to be dicks! My dog wasn't doin' nothin'. He was just in the yard when they came to bust me. I mean, a course he was gonna bark! What's he s'posed to do when all these people show up, yellin' an' shit? But he wouldn't bite nobody. Dicks."

"Sorry about your dog."

Francisco shrugged. "Who's next? Look at Wu—he's still writin'."

"Wong's next. *Woooong.*"

"I wrote about freedom. It starts—"

"I just realized somethin'," Francisco interrupted. "Society can take away our physical freedom, but we still got spiritual freedom. Nobody can take that away from us! You could be in the worst place in the world, but still get as much freedom as you want, as long as you got God in your heart."

"You gotta have both to be free," Kevin said, shaking his head. "Physical and mental."

"I agree with Jackson," Benny said.

"Easy for you to say, Wong. You'll walk outta here with time served."

"Yeah, Wong, shut the fuck up. All I know is, I *am* free 'cause I'm doin' God's will. That's all I need."

Benny would not back down. "I'm happy for you, but most people need more than that. Like Wu said, nothing about life in here is normal. We're like rats in a big lab experiment. 'Let's see what happens if we put all the bad rats in one tiny place. If they get worse or kill each other, well, too bad. They deserved it.' I don't think God would agree with that. In the Bible, Jesus *helps* criminals, he doesn't punish them."

Francisco seemed to be having trouble deciding whether to argue with Benny or agree with him. "Fuck it, Wong. Why is it that even when you say the right thing, it still gets on my nerves?"

"Let the man read," Kevin said.

"OK. Like I was saying, I wrote an argument between my conscience and my mind. The idea is, it's in the future and I'm free, but I can't decide what to do on a Friday night."

"Only Wong would have that problem."

"Shut up, Martinez."

Conscience: *Now that I'm out free, should I read as much as when I was in Central? Or should I go out and have as much fun as I can to make up for the time I was at Central? . . . I think I better stay at home to study more so I can transfer to USC in my junior year . . .*

Mind: *Noooo! Benny, it's Friday night! Go find a date or something. It won't hurt to go out just for a few hours. Plus, you're lonely. Stop being a nerd that stays home "24/7" for once and have a little fun!*

Conscience: *Aaaaah, but school . . . so many things I should read to prepare for next week. I remember I promised myself to study hard when I get out. I'm supposed to make up for all that time I didn't study in high school. I'm supposed to study hard so I can get to USC in my junior year to study business. . . .*

Mind: *Come on, Benny, you're only going out for a few hours. It ain't gonna hurt you. Don't you know you're smart? Everyone tells you you're smart, don't they? You'll be all right to be out for a few hours. Go now before it's too late! Now Benny, put on some nice clothes too!*

Conscience: *Should I? . . . Nah, if I go today for a few hours, then I might go out a few more tomorrow or next week...eventually, I'll be out for a long time every day.*

Mind: *No you won't, just hurry up, get dressed, and leave before it's too late!*

Conscience: *Nah, I actually don't feel lonely at all and I SHOULD stay home to study! What if I don't make it to USC? What if I fail all my classes? What if . . .*

Mind: *So what if you fail all your classes? So what if you don't make it to USC? Life is short! Now think: What if you die soon and you miss out? Then it'll be too late to regret you didn't enjoy your life, Benny. Go now or you're gonna regret it.*

Conscience: *NOOO! FUCK YOU! I can't waste all the hard work I already did! I can't let down all the people that gave me a second chance! I'm gonna stay home tonight and just leave me the fuck alone!*

"Damn, Wong! Your conscience is even more of a punk than you are."

"Maybe so," Kevin said, "but he's probably the only one in this room's gonna make it. Hell, if I could do my life over again, I'd be a nerd. Like Bill Gates. Nobody jacks his shit now."

"Me too," Francisco said. "Fuck it, I'd wear suspenders and a plastic pocket protector. You know, like—who's that little fucker on TV? Urkel! You *know* he's rich by now. He prob'ly got a different Playboy bunny every night givin' him blow jobs."

"Wu, you almost finished? It's after eight o'clock, they gonna kick us out soon."

"I'll be done in two minutes."

"Martinez, you go."

"I don' wanna read mine tonight."

"Come on. If the staff see we ain't readin', they gonna send Wu to the Box."

"Fuck it, then." Victor took a deep breath.

Two-face. That's how I call myself. I say two-face because in this place that I'm housed in, it is real hard for a person to be himself in here.

Because people might think you are weak and might mess with you, in my own time I sit in my room and I'm a real sentimental person, but once it's time for me to go out of my room I go back to my second face.

It is not a good thing and I know, but I know that you can't do nothing but keep on doing what I'm doing, because if I was the real me around my fellow inmates they will consider me a wimp or a schmuck.

Just as before, the mention of genuine emotion was followed by embarrassed silence. This time, however, Francisco dared to speak out. "Wimp!"

"Schmuck," Jimmy added, handing back the pencil I'd given him.

This broke the tension; once everyone could laugh about it, they were able to admit that this was a universal problem. "It's like crying," Jimmy said. "Everybody cries in their room here, but you can never talk about it. If your roommate is in the room, it's just understood: he pretends not to hear it."

" 'Cause he knows he gonna be cryin' one day."

"No doubt."

I asked them if they could describe the prisoner's "second face" to me.

"Sometimes," Victor said, "it's the face that's like, 'I don't give a shit.' Other times it's the clowning around face. Inside you want to die, but on the outside, you're laughing and joking around like it ain't no big deal."

"Then there's the 'fuck you' face," Kevin said. "You gotta wear that when you first get here. You're nervous inside, 'cause you walkin' into a room full a killas. But you can never let that show! You gotta look stone cold."

I asked what would happen if someone came to juvenile hall and would not—or could not—put on the "second face."

"*Woooong!*" four of them said at once, laughing.

"It's true," Benny said. "I take a lot of shit for it, but I'd probably get even more shit if I tried to act tough."

Francisco nodded gravely. "Most normal people, though, they be like—what's that fuckin' lizard called again? You know, the one that changes colors an' shit?"

"Chameleon," Benny said.

"Yeah. Hey—I heard if you put one a them chameleons on a mirror, it'll die. 'Cause it won't know what color to change to—he be, like, all confused an' shit."

"So if you put one on a piece of glass, would it go transparent?" Victor asked.

"Naw, 'cause then you'd see its guts, fool. The guts can't change color, only the skin."

"Uh-oh—here comes Jenkins."

"Staff gonna kick us out."

"No he ain't. Not when he hears Wu's gonna read."

Mr. Jenkins came in the door and pointed to the clock. "Time to go, guys."

"Hey Jenkins, we ain't heard Wu read yet!"

"I already let you go overtime. Don't give me any lip."

"For real, Jenkins—Wu was writin' the whole time and he just finished. Let him read! It's his last class!"

Mr. Jenkins looked at Jimmy, then leaned against the wall. "Read fast, Wu."

Jimmy spread the pages out in front of him and read the way he and the other boys always read, which was without a trace of sentimentality in his voice:

At the sound of the door opening to our holding tank, my conversation with the three other inmates came to an abrupt end. Looking over my shoulder, I saw my lawyer walk into the room. "How are you doing?" he asked. "I'm doing pretty good," I replied. We talked about nothing in particular for a few seconds until I finally popped the question. "So what's going to happen today?" He told me that I would be getting sentenced unless there was some good reason for me not to. We went over what he would present to the judge on my behalf, and when there were no more questions that I needed an answer to, he told me that he was going to go find my codefendant's attorney. "You'll be coming out soon," he said. And with that, he left the room.

Thirty minutes later, the door to the holding tank opened once more. "Gentlemen, step out," a voice called out. My codefendant and I exited the tank and the bailiff that was standing outside the room told us to turn around and put our hands behind our backs. As the cold steel of the handcuffs were snapped onto my wrists, my heart started to pound furiously and I thought to myself, "This is it."

The bailiff led us to the door to the courtroom as I silently said a prayer for everything to go well. Opening the door, he ushered us inside, and when I looked to see who occupied the seats for the public, I saw unfamiliar faces. Feeling depressed, I asked myself, "Where is everybody?" Glancing at my lawyer, I noticed that he was nodding his head towards the door that led to freedom. The bailiff removed the handcuffs and told me to take a seat in the chair that was directly in front of the judge. The sound of a door opening filled my ears, as did the shuffling of several feet. I sneaked a peek to see who had come in and I was amazed by what I saw. Every chair in the room contained someone that had come to court to give me support. People were lined up against the walls smiling whenever I made eye contact with them. The whispering died after everyone settled down and my judgment began.

The judge opened up by acknowledging me and my crime-partner's presence in the courtroom. She informed everyone that if there were no legitimate reason for us not to get sentenced, that would be taking place today. My attorney stood up after we agreed that there didn't seem to be a good excuse, and began pleading to the judge for her to allow me to be housed in Youth Authority until I reached the age of twenty-five. From my viewpoint, he presented a strong statement that should have been taken under serious consideration. Every word that came out of my attorney's mouth seemed to go through one of the judge's ears and out the other. She kept referring to the law book that stated how I would not be eligible to go to YA because of my age and because I would not be able to serve all my time by the age of twenty-five.

As my lawyer continued to argue that this law was passed well after my incarceration, every hope and dream that I had for my sentence to be reduced or for me to be housed in YA slowly vanished. The full realization of what was taking place hit me like a car ramming into a concrete wall at full speed. In a few minutes, I would be a criminal for the rest of my life. In the book that I have to carry for the remainder of my existence, I will be labeled as a convict. A felon. While I was fighting my case, I still had a clean record despite being locked up. Now, my record will forever contain this one mistake that I made when I was a young and naïve adolescent.

I thought about all the people that were sitting in the courtroom giving me their support and love and I lost complete control of my emotions. The tears that I had held in for so long streamed down my face as I cursed myself for letting these people down. Why couldn't the judge see that the young man sitting before her was not the same person that had entered juvenile hall two years ago? Why couldn't she see that I had dreams of getting out and getting my life together, to be somebody?

After a long and hard battle of trying to get me housed in Youth Authority, my attorney finally realized that the judge's mind had already been made up. She was like a tree stump that refused to be moved. Her final decision was to send me to state prison for fifteen years, eight months, and two strikes. We asked if she could recommend fire or work camp, which she did, but that does not seem likely because of the fact that I do not fit the criteria due to the number of years I have to serve. A week or two ago, I thought of fifteen, eight, and two as numbers and nothing but numbers. Sitting in that court with my life in someone else's hands made me open my eyes to the harsh reality of what these numbers really mean. Those numbers that at *one point in my life meant nothing were now representing the number of years that I would be away from my loved ones. The worst of the worst had happened and there was nothing I could do about it.*

Through tear-filled eyes, I looked at the judge and silently asked her, "Why couldn't you give me a chance? Why are you taking away fifteen years of my life for one mistake? I know that I have to pay the penalty for what I did two years ago, but why can't you look at me and see how I have changed?" As I rose to leave the courtroom, the judge looked into my eyes and said, "Good luck, gentlemen." Thank you for that. Thank you for destroying my future, too.

Now a few hours later, I am in some ways relieved that everything's over with. There is no more worrying about how much time I'll get or where I'll be sent. The decisions have been made and I have to live with that. There is only one more thing that I can do, and that is to stay strong. For my parents, for my brother, and most importantly, for myself. Because I have to.

Jimmy handed me the sheets of paper and said, "Guess there's no point in typing that up for me."

"Looks like you got visitors, Wu." Mr. Jenkins pointed to the entrance to the unit, where Sister Janet and Javier Patin, her successor as Catholic chaplain, were letting themselves into the building. As soon as they reached the library, Sister Janet rushed forward to embrace Jimmy, accomplishing in an instant what the six of us boys had talked about for an hour but had not been able to do. She held on to him for a long time, reassuring him in a quiet but firm voice that he was loved and that what had happened to him was a miscarriage of justice. She and Javier offered to help him find a qualified lawyer to handle his appeal, to fight on his behalf to see that he was placed in a facility designed for nonviolent offenders, and promised to help keep his mother informed of his whereabouts at each stage of his transfer to the penitentiary.

"I'm sorry," Mr. Jenkins said, "but it's time."

I knew what I had to do. I went around the table and shook Jimmy's hand, then gave him a hug. What should have been a tender farewell became, instead, a reminder of male awkwardness. We stood there like two forklifts that had bumped into each other, each waiting for the other to back up.

"Let's go, Wu."

Jimmy opened his folder, pulled out a small envelope, which he handed me, then followed Mr. Jenkins out. Francisco, who was gulping down water from the fountain in the dayroom, stopped long enough to watch Jimmy's departure. Water continued to arc out of the fountain as he stared.

"Javier!" someone bellowed from the office. "Either drink your drink or take it down to your room."

I expected Francisco to talk back, or look indignant, or pretend not to have heard the order, but he just lowered his head and gulped some more.

When I got outside I stopped under one of the security lights to open Jimmy's letter. The envelope held a Hallmark card. On the cover was a picture of Snoopy dancing under the word *Thanks*. The printed message inside confirmed Superintendent Burkert's fears about the writing program. It read, *You really made me feel special.*

19 / Send in the Clowns

Christmas Eve fell on a Wednesday that year. To lift the gloom around juvenile hall, I brought a strawberry sheet cake with me large enough to feed everyone in the unit. The staff had not been expecting any volunteers that night, so all of the inmates were in the dayroom watching television when I arrived. I slipped into the library with my odd-sized box, attracting surprisingly little attention, and waited for the members of the writing class to join me. Then I unveiled my surprise.

"*Holy shit!*" Francisco yelped.

I asked Kevin to fetch enough paper plates from the kitchen so we could distribute pieces to the boys in the dayroom.

"Wha—? Hold up, Jackson. Mark, they don' need cake, they're happy watchin' TV."

"This cake's designed to feed fifty, Francisco. Relax."

"I'm tellin' ya, they're cool out there. Let's not disturb 'em."

"We gotta share, Javier."

"Shut up, Wong. Do those fools write? No! Why should they get cake?"

" 'Cause that's what Mark said."

Francisco looked desperate. "Can we at least start first?"

"Sure. There's some forks in the box."

"We don' need forks."

Letting them get an early start was a mistake; letting them eat with their hands was an even bigger one. They fell on the cake like wolves. I soon realized that if there was going to be enough left for the others, I had to act quickly. I waved Mr. Jenkins into the library and invited him to join us.

"Make room," the big man said, reaching into the box.

"I was thinking we might give a piece to everybody," I said. "Including the staff, of course."

Mr. Jenkins sighed. "OK, everybody, time-out. Put that piece back, Javier."

"What piece?"

"The one you just tried to hide on the shelf. Careful, boy—don't get frosting on those Bibles."

When Mr. Jenkins left with the remains of the cake, Francisco wilted. He had so much whipped cream around his mouth that he looked like a gingerbread cookie. "Now fat-ass Jenkins is gonna eat it all by himself," he moaned. He slumped into his chair and searched the folds of his clothing for crumbs.

Our class felt empty without Jimmy, Nathaniel, and Patrick in it. The reality of the situation at last began to sink in: I would never see any of them again. Not only did I miss them, I worried about them. They were somewhere in the adult prison system now, where they would almost surely be targets for abuse and cruelty.

"So what will you guys do tomorrow?" I asked, trying to sound cheerful. "Will your parents visit?"

"Fuck no," Francisco muttered. "No visitors allowed on Christmas. It'll be like any other day in here."

"No presents, no family, no nothin'," Victor said. "And the staff'll be all pissed off that day 'cause they gotta work on Christmas instead a bein' home. It sucks."

Francisco stared out toward the office, where the staff were enjoying their portions of the cake before distributing the rest to the inmates. "This is my fourth Christmas locked up. I hardly even remember what a real fuckin' Christmas is like."

"All I know is, it's when the Grinch comes on TV," Kevin said. "That's my favorite show."

Benny cocked his head to one side. "That's your favorite? How come?"

"I dunno." He had a tennis ball stuffed into the toe of a sock, and was swinging it like a policeman's baton. "What's your favorite?"

"Frosty the Snowman."

"Yeah, but he gets smoked in the end! The sun comes out— and R.I.P. Frosty. It's too sad."

"He comes back, though. That's cool."

"That's why you like it? 'Cause he come back?"

"I dunno."

"See?" Kevin said, swinging the sock until it smacked Benny in the shoulder. "Sometimes you just like somethin', that's all. Don't always gotta be a reason."

"My favorite was Rudolph, the fool with the red nose," Victor said. "An' I got a reason, too. Everybody made fun a the way he looked, but in the end he topped 'em all. Fuckers! I'da left 'em behind. Me and Santa, we could cut costs and split the profit. Gimme a pager and some presents and I'd have my side covered. In five years I'd sell my half back to those punks with the regular fuckin' noses, give 'em a fuckin' flashlight so they don't get lost, then head down to Mexico and buy all the pussy I want."

"Reindeers don't want pussy, fool! They like female reindeers."

"They're called does," Benny said.

"Shut up, Wong."

"Damn," Francisco said, watching the last of the cake disappear as it made its way around the dayroom. "If I lose my case, I'ma spend every Christmas I got left in the pen. You ever think about that shit? We may none of us ever see the inside of a house again."

Victor insisted we talk about something other than holidays or family. "I can't take this shit no more, I gotta think about somethin' else."

"Like what? Tell me somethin' to think about, I'll think about it too."

"Girls."

"Fuck no! That only makes it worse. We may never touch a girl again, homes. Pick somethin' else."

"Cars?"

"We may never *drive* again! Face it, there's nothin' to think about. I just wish I could shut my mind off like a TV, and set it to turn on only if I get released. Otherwise just let it stay off till I die. Fuck it."

"Hey guys, shut up—Sister Janet's comin' this way."

Eager for distraction, the boys watched as the nun crossed the yard, then let herself into the unit with her key. She came straight into the library and asked the boys how the writing class was coming along.

"We just lost three guys," Francisco told her.

"I heard. I'm so sorry. I'm sure you miss them terribly."

"Yeah," Francisco said. "It feels kinda empty in here now."

Sister Janet nodded, then pointed toward the dayroom. "What about them?" she asked. "They're just stuck in front of the TV. Why aren't more of them in this class, boys?"

"They think it's for losers," Benny said.

"They do?"

"Sure. They think anything where you're learning is for losers. It's just ignorance."

"Maybe if they heard some of your work, they'd change their minds," she said.

"That's what changed my mind," Benny said. "I read one of Wu's poems. That's why I'm here today."

"Maybe we could change a few more minds tonight," Sister Janet said. "Would you boys like to choose something for me to read out there?"

None of them wanted his own work read aloud to the entire unit, but Francisco had an idea. "Read Hall's story, Sister Janet! The one about the iceberg prison!"

"Yeah, everybody likes that one."

"Mark, do you happen to have a copy of the story they're talking about?"

I always carried copies of each of the boy's work with me in case they lost their own, and I hadn't removed Nathaniel's work from my bag yet.

"Let's see what happens," Sister Janet said. She went to the office and spoke to the staff, who agreed to shut off the television and let her address the whole unit. She stood at the front of the room and asked how many of them knew about the writing class which met in the library. Two or three raised their hands. One boy muttered something that drew a laugh from the inmates sitting near him.

"Well, let me give you some idea of what kind of writing they're doing," she said. She read Nathaniel's story aloud—the boys cheered when she came to the part where the main character starts shooting at the police—then asked if any of them might be interested in joining the class. More than thirty hands went up. Even Sister Janet looked surprised. "There might not be enough room in the class for all of you right away," she told them, "but I'm going to pass around a notepad and a pencil. Write your name down on it so that Mark can notify you as soon as an opening comes up."

"How long we gotta wait?" one boy asked.

"Yeah, Sister, my trial starts next month, I don't got much time. Take me now."

"Mine starts next week, take me."

"I'm goin to YA soon an' all I did was jack somebody's car. Put me in front of those fools, they killas."

"You can't write, punk! You jus' want in 'cause that teacher brought cake."

"Take me now! I don' wanna watch this bullshit on TV no mo'! I seen this movie ten times!"

"That's enough," Mr. Jenkins said. "If you're interested, put your name down and pass the list around. If you're gonna clown around, you can all take it down to your rooms and I'll watch the rest of the movie myself."

The list made its way around the room. The last boy handed it to me, pointing to his name at the bottom. "Start from there," he whispered.

I thanked the boys for their interest and announced that I would begin taking new members the following week.

"How we gonna know if we in or not?"

"The same way as it works now—I'll give my list to the staff, who will come get you."

Several of the boys groaned. "They ain't *never* gonna come get me."

"Me neither."

"Yes they will," Sister Janet assured them. "This class is for anyone who is serious about writing. The staff won't interfere. Mark is the one who decides who attends and who doesn't."

Mr. Sills took the list of names from me and leaned back in his chair, propping his feet up on his desk. He scanned the page without comment, then reached for a pen. Starting at the top, he began crossing names out.

"Nope. Nope. Nope. OK. Nope."

By the time he was finished, the list had shrunk from an impossible thirty-two to a merely daunting eighteen.

"I hate to see a good thing get spoiled, Mark. Most of the kids I left on here'll still waste your time, you'll see. But it's your class. Who you want first?"

"Might as well start from the bottom, just to be different. How about Sierra, Houston, and Johnson?"

Mr. Sills sighed, "Hey, Granillo?"

"Yeah, Sills?"

"Send in the clowns."

Within a month, the class grew from four to fifteen members. My triage skills proved useless in the face of overwhelming need; each new boy had a roommate or friend who absolutely *had* to get into the class as soon as possible. The constant pestering wore me down, and I felt awful every time I walked into the unit and faced the ones who had not been chosen. Some submitted writing examples, others showed me their drawings, while most simply begged. One boy, after being turned down a fifth week in a row, muttered as I walked away, "Take my name off the list, then. You jus' like all the rest. Get a nigga's hopes up, then take 'em away." After that, I gave up. If a kid with his name on the list made it past the staff and set foot in the library, he was a writer.

Naturally, the class lost focus. I spent all of my energy moving from one clique to another, trying to get them to stop talking, stop teasing each other, stop picking on Wong, stop pulling the erasers out of my pencils, stop drumming on the table. No, I can't give your roommate an extra folder; no I can't give you a pen; no I can't mail that to your crime partner on the outs; no I can't Xerox fifty copies of your poem about your girlfriend's pussy; no I can't bring a cake every week; please stop rapping it's distracting the others; please don't throw that;

please don't bring *Hustler* magazine to class, and how the hell did you get that in here? No I don't want to see a nice pair of titties; no I'm not gay; yes I do have a headache so would you PLEASE stop rapping about blasting on foes and lining up ho's? Enough with the ho's already.

Mr. Sills' prediction that most of the boys on the list would waste my time proved inaccurate. In fact, *all* of the boys on the list wasted my time—only not consistently. One boy, for example, spent his first three sessions in class reciting Tupac Shakur lyrics aloud. Just when I thought I couldn't stand it any longer, he showed up for the fourth session, sat in a far corner of the room, and produced this:

> Which way is home? As I look deep inside I really don't know. I look right, I look left, I look up, I look down. I feel as though I keep running around the world. Perhaps it's one big scattered map. In this life I hold pride and I'm willing to feed knowledge to my mind. I feel as though I run away sometimes from the troubles of the world. Maybe it hurts, maybe I just don't want to face them. Who knows? I just hope that it may one day hit me like a diesel truck, knocking sense into me so that I can finally be free. I would really like to know which way is home so that I may be at peace within my inner soul.

At a low point in February, when I had eighteen boys in the class and it felt as if all anyone wanted to write about was pussy, bullets, and beer, I confessed to Duane that I was getting burned out. "I've got a dozen guys in the class who will write one good paragraph every few weeks but then fuck around for the rest of the time. They're driving me crazy. Do you ever get kids like that?"

"All the time."

"What do you do about it?"

"Nothing. I figure they're probably the ones who need the class most. And sometimes they turn out to be the best writers."

So I persevered, and learned a lot about pussy, bullets, and beer.

Another result of my relaxed admissions policy was that I had to deal with a greater variety of language skills. Up to that point, the boys in my class wrote surprisingly well; the only changes I made to their work when I typed it for them were to correct spelling and punctuation errors. Now I found myself deciphering messages like this:

> 700 Bloc vill life I'm showin muthafuccaz what that WACC life puttin it down 700% Village life real niggaz move in silence after I'm dumpin I'm runnin clearin the scene and I'm outie in gunsmoke bacc to the WxAxCxC out 700 blue and blacc 700 percentage getting in moe shit than denise tha menace Ha! Ha! I got a itchy YAH!YAH! trigga finger chillin wit devious locc from corrigador it's mandatory shit get laid down for grands and indoes

Or this, from a former star athlete at a high school in South Central who was arrested during his junior year:

> One tyme I halpe some one. 1 day me and my lil bother was walk'en down the street. and I sow this old ladey that looc like she need'ed some halpe with her bags. So me and my lil bother halp her with her bag. about 2. day later we saw her a gin and we halp'ed her a gin. and each tyme we halpe her we did not ask for a reword for are halpe. and buy the end of the week I falte good.

I also encountered boys with severe psychological problems. One boy, named Virgil, claimed not to be able to remember anything about his life before being arrested. He was a tall, muscular boy with a complexion so dark it looked blue, like a raven's plumage. He never made eye contact with me, nor did I ever see him make contact with any of the other boys in the class. Each session he would come in, sit down with pencil and paper, then not move until I came over and asked if he needed help.

"Uh-huh."

"Do you need a topic?"

"Uh-huh."

"How about this: a turning point in your life."

"OK."

Forty minutes later he was sitting in the exact same position, having written nothing. It wasn't that he had been chatting during the hour; he didn't talk to anyone, he didn't read magazines, he didn't rap, he didn't join in any of the clowning around. He just sat there the whole time, frozen, staring at the blank piece of paper.

"I couldn't remember no turnin' point," he said. "It all turnin'."

At the next class, I suggested he write about someone who influenced him. Forty minutes later he told me that he couldn't remember anyone who had influenced him. I tried all of the topics that had been successful with kids who felt stuck—describe your mother, a time you felt sad, a time you felt angry, a time you felt afraid—but nothing provoked a memory in Virgil. "It all just a fog," he said. "Maybe it 'cause I been smokin' weed since I was eight years old."

Then one day Virgil woke up. He was sitting as usual, pencil in hand, waiting for me to give him a topic, when I said, "Can you think of a time someone surprised you?"

He looked up from the table, his mouth slightly open.

"Yeah," he said. "I 'member somethin' now. I 'member."

He began writing, and spent the next half hour with his entire upper body leaning over the page, struggling to form each letter. At some point during class I noticed that he had stopped, and was looking at me instead of writing.

"Are you finished, Virgil?"

"No."

"Is something wrong?"

"I need help with somethin'."

"With what?"

He paused. "Spellin' a word."

It was the kind of moment all teachers dream of, a Helen Keller moment, where a young person who has been locked in a box all his life hears you tapping on the outside, and taps back. If you handle the moment right, that kid just might dare to find his way out of the box.

I moved my chair closer so he would not have to say the word loudly and feel embarrassed.

"I'm happy to help, Virgil. That's what I'm here for. What is the word you need help with?"

At last he looked straight at me; his eyes were bloodshot.

"Titties."

I helped him spell it, and this was what he handed in:

It start like this. I woke up to go to school a new school I am a boote in the 10th grade and allraty fucen with to meny girls but a nigga don't think befor he do. I get to school and for some resin I felt werde. All day girls wer loocen at me with a fuc you looc. You know. So most of the day I just stayed by my sister and her homegirls. But it all came out by lunch tyme. My x and a girl I was fucen with big titties was talken the hol tyme. My x was salting me up. That

whole day. But in the end I stell got my pussy so I did not
give a fuc. You know. That surprise me.

It was the kind of moment all teachers dread, a Jack Henry
Abbott moment, when a protégé emerges from the box and
you wonder: How can I get him back in?

Albert, another reticent student, spent his first four sessions
in the class cowering at the far end of the table, unwilling to
write because he was afraid the staff might see his handwriting
and send him to the hospital to be lobotomized.

"What makes you think that?" I asked.

"*One Flew Over the Cuckoo's Nest* was on TV last month,"
Benny said. "Now he thinks they're gonna cut his brain out."

I promised Albert that no one would cut his brain out, but
still he would not write. I asked Sister Janet to look into getting
some help for him, but before she could do anything he was
shipped off to prison.

A more forthcoming boy, Ibrahim, wrote a series of fictional stories about a thug named T-Bone who robbed stores
and shot the helpless clerks for "disrespecting" him. When I
asked the plump, baby-faced inmate what constituted disrespect, he shrugged and said, "Tellin' me to pay for stuff."
When I told him that his stories upset me, he looked confused.

"But why?"

"Because your main character is *mean*, Ibrahim—he kills
people for no reason, he shows no remorse or empathy for
other human beings, and he gets away with it. Why would anyone want to read something like that?"

"But it's not for no reason—I just told you, they disre-
spected him."

"But that's not a reason to kill someone, Ibrahim."

He seemed utterly unaffected by this conversation, as if it
were taking place on a movie screen rather than in real life. I

was hoping, frankly, that he would take offense and not show up for class anymore, but he was the first in the library at our next meeting, greeting me with the same pleasant smile. This time, he wrote an essay rather than a story:

People look at the outside of a person and judge them on that. When society look upon me they see a hoodsta and a madman, lost in the street with no shoes on his feet, but am I really lost and mad or am I free? It's all on your mind state, and what God want you to be. What is mad? Is it me? What I feel inside is all I can be, and that good for me. I guess they call me mad because I killed and robbed but I feel I was just doing my job. Now I see that it was the evil in me.

Ibrahim left for prison a week later. And then there was Jeffrey, one of the few white boys I had seen in K/L unit, who became obsessed with reducing the total experience of his life to one sentence. After weeks of agonized cogitation, he settled on this formula:

If the answer to the all of being stood firm, more bad than good would the puzzle be solved.

Once he'd completed that sentence, he had nothing more to write, and came to class only for the opportunity to stare out the window facing the yard. The window in his cell, he told me, faced a brick wall.

Eventually all of the boys from Sister Janet's wait list made it into the class, but by then I'd learned my lesson: too many clowns spoil the circus. I announced a moratorium on new admissions until the class had dropped back down to a maximum of eight. I told the boys I didn't even want to *hear* about it if someone was interested in joining. Every week we lost someone to either prison, county jail, Youth Authority, or the Box, until finally, in early April, we lost two boys on one day and found ourselves down to seven members. In addition to the original five—Kevin, Francisco, Victor, Benny, and Patrick Chumnikai, who had returned after a two-month stint at YA—the class now included Jose Renteria and Duc Bui.

Duc had arrived as a refugee from Vietnam only two years earlier and had a limited English vocabulary. He was short and squat, with protruding lips and a voice that unfortunately sounded ducklike. As anyone might have predicted, Duc suffered endless torments at juvenile hall.

"*Quack quack quack!* Here comes Duck!"

"Waddle on over here, Duck. I got some pieces a bread for ya. *Quack quack!*"

"Shoddop, assho'."

"It's assHOLE, Duck—*quack quack!*"

But Duc, as the boys say, maintained. He got sent to the Box for fighting every other week or so, but the staff sympathized because it was obvious Duc had no choice. If he was to survive, he had to stick up for himself.

His name had never been on my waiting list; Duc hadn't understood Sister Janet's Christmas Eve recruitment speech. He thought she was giving a sermon. Duc got into the class because Mr. Sills shoved him into the library one day, told him to sit down and shut up, and said to me, "Here's your new student, Mark. Good luck."

At first it was difficult to know what to do with Duc. His small vocabulary prevented him from expressing anything but the simplest facts about his life:

My name is Duc. I'm locked up. I don't like the people, don't like the food. I miss my family.

One day I asked if he owned a Vietnamese-English dictionary. "No way. Don' got nothin' in here." That week I bought
one in a used bookstore for five dollars, then asked Mr. Sills if
Duc could be given special permission to keep it in his room.

"OK," Sills said, "but if Daffy Duck tears out the pages
and stuffs 'em down the toilet, I'm gonna make you pull that
shit out."

When I presented the dictionary to Duc, he pored over it as
if it were the Rosetta stone. At our next class, he handed me
this essay, which he'd completed in his room using the lead
from a pencil hidden under his thumbnail:

> Sometimes I am in the room with the darkness, I could feel
> the light inside my heart. No one could understand how
> light it is. The people just think I am a piece of shit, but
> they never know I feel remorse. And I try to be a good per-
> son without my freedom, I lonely. I need help. Sometimes I
> wonder how can I get back my happiness without help?

From that day on, Duc became the most hardworking student in the class, and his language skills improved at an aston-
ishing rate.

Jose Renteria was Victor's roommate, and the two of them had
become close friends. Jose was a perfect example of what Mr.
Sills called a "clown": he seemed to expect nothing from the
class except an excuse to get out of his room, and made no
effort to take writing seriously. If I left him alone, he talked the
whole hour and brought in pornography to distract the others.
If I got fed up and insisted he write something, he would rein
himself in just enough to prevent himself from being expelled,
but always with a smirk and a few inaudible comments that let
everyone know he wasn't giving in, just making a temporary

concession to strategy. When he did write, I often wished I had let him keep talking instead:

> *one day I woke up in the morning kind of mad cause I didn't have no sex I was very mad but when I got up my girl gave me some so that made me feel really good and also I still remember that when she asked me if I wanted anything to eat I was tripping out because she never did nothing like that before and one day she hooked it up with some good-ass food I was so happy that I gave her some dick*

Jose was a pain in the ass, but the others all agreed that the class worked because it was the one place they knew they could express themselves without fear of being judged, and I was the one adult they could count on not to play the role of authority figure. If I threw Jose out, I worried how this might affect the rest of the class. Also, I couldn't dismiss what Duane had said about the most troubled boys needing the class the most—Francisco, after all, was supposed to have been the biggest clown in the unit. And finally I had managed to survive seven months in that library with as many as a dozen clowns at one time without ever losing my temper; I was determined not to let this one spoil my record.

20 / The Buster

My father passed me the binoculars. "You say they're all bound for prison? Doesn't that depress you, knowing what's going to happen to them once they leave your class?"

We were lying on our backs in a campground in southern Arizona, hoping that the Lyrid meteor shower would turn into a meteor storm. The annual showers tend to be underwhelming events, especially if you've driven for hours to find a dark-sky site and have stayed up all night only to see five or six piddling meteors. Every few decades, however, stargazers are treated to an unforgettable display: meteors tearing through the atmosphere at the rate of hundreds or even thousands per minute. A blizzard of falling stars!

No blizzard for us that night; by 3 a.m. we'd seen eight meteors, a police helicopter, and an owl. To keep myself awake, I had been telling my father about the writing class at juvenile hall.

"It sounds depressing if you think about it," I said, "but that's just it—I *don't* think about it. The boys keep me too busy to think. And I always leave the place feeling good, because I know we've done something worthwhile."

My father sighed. His efforts as a public school social worker had been worthwhile, certainly, but he rarely came home feeling good. There was the day, for example, he saw an unfortunate little girl with two alcoholic parents and only one eye pick up a stone and hurl it right into the face of a boy standing a few feet away. While a teacher rushed the injured boy to the nurse, my father took charge of the girl and demanded to know why she'd done such a terrible thing.

"It wasn't my fault!" she insisted. "I wasn't even throwing it at that kid anyway! He got in the way!" She pointed toward a boy on the swing set and explained, "I was trying to hit *him*— the one with the buck teeth!! Yeah, YOU! *BUCKY BUCK-TEETH!*"

The worst part about it, my father confessed, was having to resist the urge to yell back, "Look who's talking?! You're flunking fourth grade and you've only got ONE DAMNED EYE!"

I passed the binoculars back to him. "I think I just saw one. Over there, near the horizon."

"Nope. That was another satellite."

He swept the sky with the binoculars for a while, then pressed me further. "OK, so you leave the place feeling good. But what's the purpose of the class? Do the kids get into less trouble once they start writing? Do they get credit for it, or time taken off their sentences? State your goals and objectives."

This was an old joke in our family, courtesy of the Greenwich public school system. Every August, my dad had to fill out a form stating his "goals and objectives" for the coming year. These had to be *new* goals and objectives, not just last year's ideals warmed over. He would put the assignment off until the night before it was due, then sit down at the kitchen table with a pencil and a roll of antacids and ask if any of us knew the difference between a goal and an objective. This gave him an opportunity to denounce the inanity of bureaucratic jargon, examples of which he cited from memory until it was our bedtime.

At last, as we marched upstairs to our rooms, he would start writing. Before falling asleep, we usually heard him reading a preliminary draft aloud to our mother: *My goal and objective this year is to not get fired.*

We watched the meteorless sky for another few minutes, then I said, "My goal is to enjoy it." It sounded glib, but I meant it. I had lost two of my favorite students, had survived the Winter of Too Many Clowns, and had sat through Jose Renteria's account of a night in the life of his penis. If I could get through those experiences without losing faith in the value of the class, I could get through anything; enjoying myself seemed as good a reason as any to keep going back.

Dad laughed. "Can you really do that? And not expect some kind of result, or feel it has to lead to something else? More power to you."

I thought of Duane, who obviously expected more of his work with the kids than that it be merely enjoyable, and of Sister Janet, who would be satisfied with nothing less than a complete overhaul of the juvenile justice system. Compared to their goals and objectives, mine seemed shameful. On the other hand, wasn't there something to be said for teaching for the love of it? My favorite teachers, as far as I could tell, had expected only that I learn. What I did with the knowledge after that was my business.

"Enjoyment is its own result," I said, sounding even more glib.

Dad offered me the binoculars again, but I declined. My eyes were closed by then; I had given up.

"So what did these kids do, anyway? It can't be shoplifting if they're all going to prison."

"Most of them are charged with 187s," I said, eager to try out my law-enforcement jargon on someone.

"What does that mean?"

"Murder."

"Oh my GOD!" he gasped. I thought he was reacting to the news that his son was working with violent criminals, but then he jabbed my arm. "Look!"

I opened my eyes, but not in time to see the best meteor of the night. This was how amateur astronomy tended to go for me: long stretches of boredom punctuated by moments of intense disappointment. Teaching at juvenile hall, by comparison, was pure pleasure.

The inmates sat on the floor, legs splayed out in front of them, holding their balled-up shirts in their hands. They had just come in after participating in the semifinals of the annual interunit sports competition. From their exhausted smiles I guessed they had done well. Mr. Sills looked happiest of all; he paced the room, alternating between praising the victorious athletes and taunting the ones who had dropped batons, fallen during the sack race, etc. The boys were enjoying the show, so I was in no hurry to break it up for writing class. I stood in a far corner of the room, trying to draw as little attention to myself as possible, when I bent down to have a drink from the fountain.

"You there!" Sills thundered, pointing at me. "What the hell you think you're doin', takin' a drink without permission? Sit down and shut up!"

When I plopped down to the floor, the boys seemed to think this was the funniest thing they had ever seen—it took Sills a full minute to get their attention back. He picked up where he'd left off, explaining the secret of success at tug-of-war: "You keep your arms locked, like this, and you push with your legs, not your twig-ass arms. Think about it." He pointed to the gangly boy sitting next to me. "What's bigger, Esquivel, your arm or your leg?"

"My leg."

Mr. Sills opened his eyes in mock surprise. "Whoever said we got nothin' but dummies down here? The man's a genius." Now he pointed at Duc Bui. "Hell, Daffy here could beat the whole lot of ya if he used his legs. He'd just put that rope in his bill and take off."

He finished with some hints for the relay team, then sent the boys to the showers. While they cleaned up, I followed Sills and Granillo into the office.

"OK, Mark," Mr. Sills said, "for playin' along with me and bein' a good sport just now, I'm gonna let you sit in my chair for two minutes. Go ahead. You run the place now."

I put my bag down and settled into his chair. Leaning back, I propped my feet on his desk and folded my hands behind my neck.

"It's lonely at the top," I said.

"Don't get too comfortable, there, Mark."

"Where's my soda? And I'd like some chips while you're at it."

Kevin stuck his head in the door to tell Mr. Sills something and saw me sitting with my feet on the boss's desk. He looked at me, then at Sills, then at me again.

"Oh my," he said.

"You never saw nothin', Jackson," Sills said. "Get this clown a soda. But no chips. He won't have time to eat 'em."

All of the boys were in good spirits that day. Spring had arrived, and the combination of fresh air, sunshine, and exercise made everyone giddy. Even Victor and Benny, who typically disagreed with each other on all subjects, bonded over their disdain for action-movie star Steven Seagal.

"He's a fat-ass. He can't even get out of his car—they have a stuntman do it for him."

"You can tell he wears a toupee. Now he says he's a reincarnated Tibetan lama."

"He's a reincarnated fat-ass."

Lately I had been bringing photographs and reproductions of paintings to class to stimulate ideas for writing. One week, for example, I brought in an Annie Leibovitz photograph of the artist Christo, the man who wraps large objects like buildings in fabric. In the photo, Christo has wrapped himself up like a mummy and bound himself with ropes. He is standing in Central Park, with his signature glasses propped on a ridge in the fabric where his nose should be. None of the boys had ever heard of Christo before, so I asked them to come up with stories that might explain how the subject of the photograph had come to be wrapped up that way. They all arrived at the same conclusion: he had gone to a party, been seduced and drugged by a manipulative female, then rolled for his money and left in the park to be humiliated.

This time I'd brought something purely for laughs, and given the boys' mood that day, it seemed the perfect choice. It was the published catalogue for the Museum of Bad Art, an actual collection on permanent display in Massachusetts. The catalogue is subtitled *Art Too Bad to Be Ignored*. The paintings include clowns swimming underwater, Roman athletes wearing shoes and socks, rivers that defy gravity, and beloved poodles. Ironic and/or purposely campy art has no place there; the museum only collects pieces from attics and garage sales which were done in earnest, but were done badly.

I described the concept of the museum to the boys, then pulled the catalogue out of my bag. I anticipated gales of laughter and all sorts of amusing questions about the museum itself: What kind of people would actually take the time to *do* something like this? Where do you *find* things like this, Mark? What *is* it with you white folks, anyway?

The catalogue made its way around the room, but to my disappointment, it failed to elicit a single laugh from anyone. A moment before, they had been guffawing over Steven Seagal's phony CIA background; now they were looking at something genuinely funny and they looked as serious as bankers reviewing a loan application.

Finally one of them spoke out. Pointing at a painting of a nude couple who resembled cadavers (the artist had given them eyes but no other facial features), with the male figure cradling a demented-looking pug, Victor said, "I think that's cool."

"Me too," said Patrick.

"I liked the one of the clown," said Francisco. "With the ghost comin' outta the coral."

"Yeah, that's trippy. I'd hang it in my room."

"I like the battle scene."

Victor handed the catalogue back to me. All of the playfulness in the room had vanished. "I don't know, Mark. I guess we don't get the joke or somethin'. I mean—who are these guys to say what's bad art? These people were just makin' stuff they liked. *We* like it. Why should people laugh at it?"

"Yeah," Francisco said. "What if a bunch a people laughed at our writing?"

I returned the catalogue to my bag, feeling completely ashamed.

"So whatta we gonna write about, Mark?"

"Yeah, what's the topic?"

The topic was supposed to be the Worst Piece of Art I Ever Saw, but now I was ready to suggest that they write on the Worst Example of Judgment Ever Displayed by a Teacher. "I'm out of ideas, guys. Can anybody think of something we should all write on?"

"I can," Jose said, grinning.

I was hoping someone else would come up with something—Jose's last suggestion had been that I allow them to write sexually explicit love letters to the girls in Karen's class—but no one spoke up, so I asked what his idea was.

"Let's write on this: What is a buster?"

The other boys perked up immediately. "Yeah! That's cool, we never wrote on that before!"

"I'm not familiar with that term," I said.

Jose turned to face Benny. "Let's ask Wong. What's a buster?" He snickered. "I'm just foolin' wit' ya, Wong, don't trip. I can't explain what's a buster to ya easy, Mark, I gotta write it down."

Unlike most of the topics I suggested, "The Buster" seemed to appeal to everyone. Still, I had a bad feeling about it. Did it have something to do with humiliating Benny? Should I say something to prevent it? Personal experience settled that question for me: nothing in the savage world of children is worse than having a teacher ask the class bully to stop picking on you.

Fifteen minutes later Jose slapped his pencil down and said, "Finished! Can I read first?"

Everyone else had put their pencils down as well. I held my breath. "Go ahead."

Jose cleared his throat and tugged at the collar of his T-shirt, as if he were loosening a tie.

A buster! Well I think a buster is somebody that be scared of getting down. Just like "Wong" he's a very scared person. Just because he's a little person that's probably why he getting jacked for all his shit. He got his shoes taken by another little guy and didn't do shit about it, that's a trip because some guy name Benny Wong he's a funny-looking guy I mean look at him he's a gay little fool. Well I don't have that much to say so just don't be a buster all right.

Several of the boys laughed nervously; Benny Wong stared at the floor. I refused to give Jose the satisfaction of a response, or even to acknowledge his presence in the room. I turned to Patrick and asked him if he would please be the first to read, as what we had just heard did not count as real writing. Patrick nodded eagerly.

A buster to me is a person who disrespect you. Like if you do something for your former roommate and you know, you expect her to do the same thing to you but she doesn't, and it gets me mad! Or when they are serving food and she grabs both foods, looks at them, and chooses the one that has the most. And if it wasn't bad enough, she grabs the biggest cake, too. What was that?! Then during showers, I put my stuff out and get ready to get in shower #1 (the best shower) and she cuts in front of me and slips in! I just wanted to smack her! But we're all naked, so . . . I will get her back! I won't name any names though . . . Hey, what's up, Wong?

I stood up, prepared to cancel class for the day, but Benny signaled me urgently: *Sit down. Don't say anything.* Without waiting for me to ask, Victor started reading next. His Benny the Buster poem came as no surprise—whenever Jose acted up, Victor followed suit. Francisco lit into Benny next, then even Duc quacked out something about Benny Wong getting his slippers jacked and not doing anything about it. Kevin was the only one to abstain from the feeding frenzy; he'd written about finding himself on a planet where no one has anything to do, no one ages or dies, and no one has any purpose in life.

When Kevin finished, Benny said, "Now it's my turn. You all had your say, now I have mine."

How come people only think others are busters? What about themselves? What's a buster? Is a person who gets picked on all the time a buster? Does the buster have to be a certain size or look a certain way? Are they always small and weak-looking? Or can they be big and mean-looking too?

Well, a lot of people think I'm a buster. Maybe I am, or maybe I just don't feel like doing certain things unless I have to.

Actually, I don't really know the exact definition of a buster either. I can recognize one when I see one though, for example, a person that starts shit only with others that are half his size, and not people his own size. So what if the smaller person gets his ass beat? Does the bigger person, the real buster who never starts shit with people his own size, prove that he ain't no buster? Anyway, maybe I'm a buster, maybe you are too. Who really knows? Yourself.

I applauded Benny's essay and said, "That's real writing. I wish I'd written it myself." I gathered my notebooks and pencils, shook Benny's and Kevin's hands, then left.

I felt so angry—and guilty—over what had happened that I couldn't bring myself to go to juvenile hall that Wednesday night. If my goal and objective as a teacher at juvenile hall was enjoyment, then I couldn't see any reason to go back. For an entire week I played the scene over and over in my head, wondering what I should have done, what I should have said, and most of all, wondering what I would do next. Kick all of them out except for Benny and Kevin? That would be overreacting. What I really wanted was to remove Jose, but how could I justify kicking him out and not the others who had attacked Benny? That Saturday morning I still felt so upset I nearly stayed home again. I decided, however, that the longer I put off facing the boys, the worse it would get. I drove down without a plan, but I did bring a boom box and a recording of the Schubert cello quintet. Not so much for the boys' sake as to keep me calm.

When I got to the library, Benny was already there reading a book.

"Oh, hey," he said. "I have something for you." He handed me an envelope with my name on it. "Don't read it now—wait till you get home."

"I'm sorry about last week, Benny."

"It's not your fault. That stuff happens around here all the time." He pushed his glasses up with the heel of his palm. "Damn, I hate these things! They keep slipping off. My parents bought me new ones, but they're not allowed to bring in any personals during visits."

"It *was* my fault, Benny. I can't undo it, but I can make sure it doesn't happen again. In the meantime, would you like to hear a beautiful piece of music?"

He pushed his glasses up again. "Jackson said you were so mad you weren't ever gonna come back."

"Well, here I am. The thing is, Benny, I used to get picked on like that all the time. Watching it happen all over again made me want to puke."

"*You* got picked on?"

"In junior high school, guys used to fill up squirt guns with piss and use me as a target. Not because they had anything against me. They did it because they knew I wouldn't fight back, and that seemed to egg them on."

"So why didn't you fight back?"

"Because I was too scared to. Is there any other reason?"

"Sure. Not wanting to get in more trouble than you already are."

"You're much less of a buster than me, Benny."

Victor stepped into the room and asked where I had been on Wednesday.

"I didn't feel like coming."

"Oh. Hey, this music is nice."

"It's one of my favorites."

"Yeah, it's cool. Did you hear about Javier?"

"No."

"He started trial last week. He won't be in the class no more, I don't think."

"Why?"

"While he was at the courthouse, he got caught jerking off in the holding tank, so he got transferred to the sex offenders' unit. Now he's with the rapists and queers."

This was disturbing news, but I couldn't dwell on it just then. When everyone was in the room, I turned the music off.

"A couple of things, guys, then we'll get back to work. From now on, there won't be any writing about someone else in the class. I expect better from you than that, and I know you won't let me down again. Second, we're going to have a quiet time for writing during each session. It'll last thirty minutes. There won't be any talking during that time. If you finish writing earlier than that, you're welcome to read or relax as long as you do it silently. If you slip up and start talking, I'll remind you once of the rule, no problem. If you slip up a second time during that class, you're out, because it means you don't really want to be here. I do this because I've seen the kind of work you're able to do, and it makes me feel badly when you waste time goofing around instead. It means I'm not doing my job, which is to help you focus and get something done.

"I brought this tape player today and we'll try listening to music during the writing period. If it works well and you like it, I'll bring it every time. Does anybody have a problem with any of this?"

None of them stirred—except for Jose. He snickered, then raised his hand.

"Yes?"

"My pencil broke. I need another." He held the pencil I'd given him out so I could see it. He'd snapped the tip off.

I gave him a new one.

"All right. The quiet time starts now. In thirty minutes, we'll read aloud and talk."

I started the tape again. All of the boys started writing—except for Jose. He flipped loudly through the pages of a magazine, scraped his chair back and forth on the floor, then raised his hand again.

"This pencil got some kinda problem too. It broke."

I handed him another.

He flipped through another magazine, then broke another pencil. I gave him another. Then he turned to Victor and said, "Man, did you see that fool in school yesterday? He tripped out in the—"

"Jose, I'm reminding you now of the rule about talking. That was your warning."

"Oh yeah, sorry. I forgot about that, Mark. Sorry, Mark." He sighed loudly, then raised his hand. "Can I get a drink of water? I'm thirsty."

"Go ahead."

He got his drink of water, came back to the library, sighed again, glanced at another magazine—then started writing.

I thought time passed slowly when the boys were goofing around, but I died a thousand deaths that morning when they all behaved. My credibility—and the future of the class—was on the line, and I wouldn't know the verdict until they had all read aloud. If they wrote bullshit about Benny Wong now, I would be finished. I caught a glimpse of my reflection in the window and saw that the armpits of my shirt were soaked through. So much for my hopes of appearing calm.

I don't remember who volunteered to read first. I was so tense I couldn't really pay attention to any of their work, but no one wrote bullshit about Benny Wong. Their essays that day were cautious, designed to please, but not particularly memorable. Even Jose retreated to neutral ground, writing about the importance of giving one's mother a hug and a kiss on Mother's Day.

When Mr. Sills gave us the signal to leave I thanked everyone, shook their hands, and said goodbye.

"You comin' on Wednesday?" Kevin asked.

"Yes, I'll be there."

I got a few yards outside the unit when I heard Mr. Sills calling me back. I turned around and saw that he and Mr. Granillo were standing in the doorway with goofy expressions on their faces and enormous wads of toilet paper sticking out of their ears.

"What was that racket comin' outta the library?" Sills asked me. "You don't call that shit *music*, do ya?"

"I'll be bringing it every week from now on."

"Oh yeah? We're tellin' that nun, Sister what's-her-name. She'll straighten your ass out."

They high-fived each other and disappeared back into the unit.

I started across the yard again, only to hear someone thumping on a window to get my attention. Victor was standing on his bed so I could see him. When I waved, he pounded on his chest with his fist, the homeboy salute, then gave me the thumbs-up. Jose was his roommate and had to have been in the room to see that. My credibility had held. But I couldn't really relax until I'd opened the envelope Benny had given me. Inside was a letter he'd written during the week, when he wasn't sure if I would be returning.

Dear Mark,

 Hey, what's up? I'm just writing to let you know something. Yeah, as you probably could tell, I was pretty sad about what some of them wrote. And I could tell you were, too. It was pretty hard for me to get all those negative comments from them all at once in front of the group. I had to do my best to hold in my tears too, but I listened very carefully also. Some of the things they said were true, some weren't.

 If you remember some of the things I wrote, you might remember I told you I learned a lot from this place. When I came here, I didn't know how to get along with people. Maybe because I was brought up as a single child and even when my brothers and sisters visited me, they would treat me too well too. Patrick was my first roommate and some of the things he mentioned were true so I felt very bad. I apologized to him a while ago already but I guess he didn't really accept it.

 A lot of things and people seemed very scary to me when I first came in here because I've never been in jail or know much about the "unwritten rules" here. People punked me and I would just hold in my anger, thinking that I would be out of this place soon. It took a long time for my fear to go away. I started standing up for myself more and more and it seems like it's a little better than before now.

 The reason why I wasn't really that mad at the people that wrote the bad things about me is because I can really understand the way they think. I know I'm not a buster like the way they said I am (yeah, I'm scared sometimes,

*but not that bad or any worse than the real punks here).
The way they think now was once the way I thought about
people too. They judge people but never judge themselves.
Some of them think they are hard just because they're big
or their "group" is "deep" (meaning there are a lot of
them) in this place. I'm not angry at them but I truly feel
sorry for them because they are so ignorant, too ignorant
to understand more about life and too ignorant to change
the way they think. I really have sympathy for them and
wish they can realize their mistakes like I did, before it's
too late.*

*The good thing about having them around is that I
can learn from their negative acts. If it weren't for them I
wouldn't have learned so much in this place. And also
because of them, I will never ever put myself in a situation
to risk my freedom anymore when I get out. I can't
imagine how I can spend days after days for years with
some of the people here. Fortunately, I believe I can get
out this year and I'm going to live happily ever after. I'm
going to go to a community college far away from L.A.
and not look back at the bad part of the past, but plan
and work for my future instead.*

*Mark, I was really sad but it made me feel even worse
when I knew you were feeling sad with me. I really think
you have a nice heart (at least, in front of me, maybe
you're evil too—joke) and I learned a lot from you too, i.e.,
you come all the time to work but you don't get a penny.
That taught me that money is not always people's motive
to do things. Well, got to go now, take care.*

Your student,
Benny

21 / No Mercy Walls

"Hey Jenkins!" Mr. Sills yelled across the yard. "Send me somebody strong, I need a hand."

Mr. Jenkins nodded from the entrance to K/L. A few moments later a dark-skinned boy wearing no shirt jogged out of the unit. Even from two hundred yards away I could see that he had the physique of a professional athlete.

"No, no!" Mr. Sills hollered, waving the boy back. "Not you! I wanted a Crip, not a Blood!"

The boy turned around and started back toward the unit. Mr. Sills shook his head and muttered, "Einstein he ain't. But you oughta see what he can do with a football." He cupped his hands around his mouth and called back across the yard, "I'm just playin' wit' you, boy! Come on out here. Show me some *game* speed."

The young prisoner shrugged and started toward us again. He closed the distance in eight or nine seconds, making it look effortless. The officer in the guardhouse at the edge of the field whistled in admiration.

Mr. Sills looked pleased. "We got the relay race locked up this year, Mark."

The prisoner thundered past us, needing twenty yards to slow himself down. "Don't get any funny ideas," Sills yelled after him, laughing. "Don't make the old man have to take you down." The boy circled around and stopped in front of us, breathing deeply but smoothly.

"OK, Mark," Sills said. "I got business to take care of with the Flash here, but you go on ahead, your table's all set up. Jenkins knows who's in your class."

When I got to the unit, the boys were already in the library, but Mr. Jenkins took me aside for a private conference. "There's a kid who's asking to be in your class. You taking anybody new yet?"

"Do you think he'd be good?"

"Hard to say. He's no clown, but he's no Hemingway neither. His name's Jones."

It sounded familiar, but by then a lot of names at juvenile hall were beginning to sound familiar. "Can't hurt to give him a try."

The boys filed in quietly as I set up the boom box. Francisco was the last to come in.

"Hey Mark." His face looked pale, and his eyes were swollen from crying.

"Francisco—are you OK?"

"I lost my case, Mark. All counts. It's over."

I let him sit next to me and I stayed quiet.

"I hear you bringin' in music now," he said, looking at the boom box. "What we gonna listen to this time?"

"Mozart."

"If you listen to Mozart, your IQ goes up," Benny said.

"Fuckin' Wong," Francisco said, managing a smile.

The door to the library opened behind me. I turned and realized why the name Jones had sounded familiar: the new student was the boy Mr. Sills had recommended, then chewed out for not wanting to join.

"Dale," I said. "Glad to have you."

He rubbed the back of his neck, stared at the floor, and mumbled.

"I'm sorry, Dale, I didn't catch what you just said."

"YouthinkSillsgon'bemad? 'Bout changin' my mind?"

"Will he be mad that you've changed your mind? I don't think so. You're here now, and that's what matters. You know how the class works?"

He nodded.

As they had the previous week, the boys obeyed the rule about not talking during the writing period, but they weren't writing either. They were stretching, sighing, twirling their pencils, and squirming in their chairs. I stayed next to Francisco in case he wanted to talk, but he only stared out the window.

Benny Wong raised his hand. "Can I make a suggestion?" he whispered.

"Sure."

He pointed at the boom box. "This music is too fast. It's making us nervous."

"Is that true?" I asked the group. "Is the music bothering you?"

They all nodded. Mozart got the thumbs-down.

"Could we turn on the radio instead?" Francisco asked. Someone suggested a rap station, but I drew the line there. Instead we compromised on an R&B oldie station. The boys seemed to relax right away, and within a few minutes all of them except Francisco and Dale were writing. I pulled my chair alongside Dale's and asked if he could think of something he'd like to write about.

"Notreallyrightnowsir."

Remembering that Mr. Sills had described Dale as someone with a lot of anger bottled up inside, I asked if I could suggest a topic.

"Mm-hm. OK sir."

I borrowed his notepad and wrote the word "anger" at the top. "Can you write on that?"

His eyes widened and he nodded.

When I turned my attention back to the class, I saw that Jose was talking to Victor. I got his attention and wagged my finger, but he looked indignant.

"*You* were talking just now," he said.

"Yes, but I'm helping someone, Jose."

"So am I! Martinez needed something."

"OK. Just go back to writing."

A few minutes later Francisco tapped me on the shoulder. "What is it?" I whispered.

"I can't write, Mark. I feel like I'm goin' crazy."

I signaled for him to join me in the far corner of the library so that we wouldn't disturb the others.

"My lawyer says I gotta have hope for my appeal. I do, but I'm still stressin'. What if I get sentenced before graduation?"

"Graduation?"

"Yeah, didn't nobody tell you? Me and Jackson and Chumnikai—hell, everybody in the class 'cept Renteria—we all gettin' our high school diplomas. There's gonna be a graduation ceremony here an' everything, with gowns an' shit."

"Congratulations, Francisco."

"Thanks. I told my lawyer he gotta find a way to delay the sentencing. I gotta be at that graduation so my mom can see it." He was looking down toward our feet—I thought he was about to cry—when he started laughing. "Damn, Mark—look at your socks! You got two different colors on!"

My wife was always pointing out that my socks didn't match, or that they were turned inside out, and I always argued back that no one on earth but her noticed people's socks. Apparently I was wrong. But now I could say that my sock problem had cheered someone up at a difficult moment, so on balance, I felt vindicated.

"I can't write, Mark, but I *wanna* write. I wanna do *something*."

"Do you want to write about the trial, the way Jimmy did?"

"Naw, I feel like I'm gonna be sick when I think about it. Maybe I could write a letter. To my mom, so she knows I'm OK." He nodded. "Yeah, I'ma try that."

When Francisco and I returned to the table, Jose and Victor were talking again. "OK, guys, this is your warning," I said.

"But *Javier* was just talking! It distracted us."

"Give me a break. Just write."

Toward the end of the hour, a female guard stepped into the library and asked how everything was going. I had seen Ms. Brigade before, but she usually worked on the far side of the unit, so I had fewer opportunities to speak with her than with Jenkins or Sills. She was tall and graceful, with her hair cropped short. She had a surprisingly gentle voice for a correctional officer.

"Everything's fine," I said. "We're just about to start reading aloud."

"Mind if I listen in?" she asked. "I've heard good things about this class." I looked around the room and the boys nodded their assent.

Having a woman present—especially one who had expressed an interest in their writing—breathed life back into the room. The boys all sat straighter in their chairs and I didn't need to ask for volunteers to read.

"I'll start," Francisco declared. His letter began just like the one he had written the previous fall, with apologies for his behavior and promises to change, but this time he ended with a request:

*Please help me, Mom! I don't want to find myself lost. I
want to live a wonderful life for God and for you. Maybe if
you fast and pray for me, God will have mercy on me.
There isn't too much time, but I want you to forgive me for
all the bad things that I have done to you. I need you,
Mom!*

"That's quite a letter," Ms. Brigade said. "I'm sure your
mother will appreciate it."

Francisco nodded.

"But I have a comment. In the end, you ask your mother to
fast and pray for you. You're still asking her to solve your problems. You're a man now, Javier—*you* should be doing the fast-
ing and praying, don't you think?"

All the color returned to Francisco's face—and then some.

"Don't get angry, I still think it's a beautiful letter. I think
you're ready to step up a level, that's all."

Kevin read next, an essay about sunlight and the way it
reminded him of summer days when he was a child. Jose declined to read; my guess was that he had written something
silly and was embarrassed to read it aloud in front of Ms.
Brigade. Patrick had written a poem about the moon, and
Benny had come up with a story about an extraterrestrial sent
to earth to observe human behavior.

"Mine's kinda strange," Victor said. "It's about all the stuff
I forget. It's just a list. Now that I look at it, it looks kinda
stupid."

"Better to write something stupid than to not write at all,"
Ms. Brigade said. "I have to write lots of stupid things before I
get to the stuff that's good."

"You write too?"

"Don't look so shocked, Martinez! Just because I work
here doesn't mean I don't do anything else. I write almost
every day."

All of the boys were interested to hear this. "So how come you don't bring in something and read it to us?" Francisco asked.

" 'Cause you never asked, Javier."

"I'm askin', then."

"All right, I will. Anyway, I want to hear what Martinez wrote."

> *Things I don't remember:*
> *I don't remember to write back to people.*
> *I don't remember to pray over my food.*
> *I don't remember to react to things fast.*
> *I don't remember to fight for my rights.*
> *I don't remember to be kind to people.*
> *I don't remember to introduce myself.*
> *I don't remember to tell Mark thank you.*
> *I don't remember to say good night.*
> *I don't remember to say good morning.*
> *I don't remember to pray at night.*
> *I don't remember to thank God for life.*
> *I don't remember to tell my family I love them.*
> *I don't remember to write slower.*
> *I don't remember to remember things.*

"There's nothing stupid about that," Ms. Brigade said. "It's a poem, really."

"Naw, I could never write poetry."

"Why not?"

"You got to be a certain kinda person to write poetry. You know—kinda . . ."

"Kinda gay," Jose said, snickering.

"That's the ignorant view," Ms. Brigade said. "Most people grow out of it." Jose slumped in his chair and didn't say anything more after that.

"Now me," Duc said. "This about a person who surprise me."

Five months ago when I stepped out of my class and joined the line movement I saw a guy, he is looking like a guy that I know. When we went back to the unit, the staff did a search, I saw his tattoo on his arm and I know that he is my victim's brother. I shot my victim, but he lived. I looked at this guy real mad and I just wanted to take off on him but I know if I take off on him the staff will stop us and send me to the Box. I tried to hold my anger to looking for a better chance to beat his ass. After the search he passed me in the hallway, he looked at me with a scary face and told me with a scary voice, "I'll talk to you later." It made me think of myself when I first got locked up. Scared, worried, and don't know what's gonna happen. I felt sorry for him but I was still mad because his brother is a snitch and came to court to testify against me. I think he talked to me because he was scared and afraid that I would beat his ass.

That day when we were showering in the bathroom, he asked me with a scared voice, "Duc, how are you?" I was afraid of getting locked down because the staff don't let us talk in the bathroom. I didn't say anything to him. After that, every day he tried to talk to me and I was cool with him because I didn't want to beat a scared guy and someone smaller than I am. Then one day I go into my room and there he is. The staff make us roommates. Because we are both from Vietnam, I find out we are almost the same in everything. He surprised me. We became friends.

One day I ask permission to apologize to his brother, and his mother. He said yes, so I apologized. Now I could see his brother, my victim, and his mother every Sunday when they come to visit him.

I looked around the room, wondering if the boys had been as moved by Duc's story as I had, but they looked ready to move on to the next essay. Ms. Brigade and I shared a glance, then I asked Duc if he could tell us how he apologized. "What did you say when you first saw them?"

"I do it Vietnam-way. I gotta go down on the floor, on my knees."

"He did it in front of everybody, out in the dayroom," Benny said. "On Sunday, when all the families come to visit. There's no privacy, it's all in one room."

"That was a long time ago," Victor said. "There's a bunch of people in here who shot at each other on the streets but now they get along. It's not that unusual."

"And what does that tell you?" Ms. Brigade asked.

"That we're not that different," Francisco answered.

"Does that change how you feel about gangbanging?" she asked him.

"Yeah, but that ain't gonna solve anything. What we think in here don't matter to people on the outs. When I was in YA, we had all these guys who did hard time come and talk to us minors about don't do drugs, don't join gangs. But nobody listened. I guess you just gotta live through it to know."

"I don't believe that," Ms. Brigade said. "I think if you tried hard enough, you could change some people's minds. You have a little brother, right?"

Francisco nodded.

"What do you tell him?"

"I tell him to stay in school and not fuck up so he don't end up like me."

"Does he listen to you?"

"He better. I told him if he fucks up, I'll kill his ass."

"Jones, you gotta read," Kevin said. "You're the only one left."

Dale kept his eyes on the table and mumbled.

Ms. Brigade wouldn't let him off the hook. "I hear you rapping in your room all day, Jones, I know you've got things to say. Don't be shy."

Dale rubbed the back of his shaved head with his hand, then rubbed his forehead. "Nobodygon'unnerstan'me. Everybody-sayJones, you a mumblin' muthafucka."

Ms. Brigade waved her finger like a metronome. "So . . . read . . . slowly. Like that. It's a technique, that's all. You break it down and put it together one word at a time."

Dale rubbed his head some more, then shrugged and started reading. He was, in fact, difficult to understand—we had to ask him to read the piece twice—but his writing was surprisingly coherent:

> *Deep down inside, this angry person awakens. Another day facing perpetual incarceration behind no mercy walls, as we are inmates.*
>
> *Deep down inside this angry person there is an image of a rejoiceful person who's facing perpetual incarceration behind no mercy walls. Just like your fellow inmates, as you think about the happiness in the past you'll like to shout out for mercy upon your life. But living in darkness for so long, you're taught not to express certain emotions. The voice no one hears is the voice that yells out for freedom in the mind of a forbidden child. Struggling to survive in an ongoing war that seems to have led me and my fellow troops to a meaningless situation. But as I'm found innocent in God's prison, the light should shine on this voice of mine that people just can't seem to follow and understand and I could say farewell to all my hidden voices. And the loneliness in my life shall run for cover.*

When Dale finished reading, he looked up at me, then seemed to notice something over my shoulder. He winced, then looked back down at the table. I turned around and saw Mr. Sills standing in the doorway, staring at Dale through the window. He came inside, picked up Dale's notebook, then said, "Time to set up for lunch. Everybody take it down. Everybody except for Jones."

The boys filed out in silence. When they were gone, Sills asked, "What are you doin' in here?" When Dale didn't answer, he said, "You look at me when I'm talking to you. What are you doing in this class?"

Dale looked up. "Jus'doin'somewritin'."

Mr. Sills paused, then said, "I asked you if you wanted to be in this class and you said no. You remember that?"

Dale nodded.

"So what happened? Why are you in here now?"

"Changemymind."

"You changed your mind." Sills looked at me and asked, "Did he write?"

"Yes."

"Did he read it aloud?"

"Yes."

"I want to hear it, Jones. Read to me what you wrote."

He handed the notepad back to Dale and sat down. Dale read his piece a third time. When he finished, Sills kept silent for a long time, staring out the window toward the yard, then said, "I *understood* that." He looked at Dale. "I understood that. You know what that means?"

Dale shook his head.

"It means you're not retarded, Jones."

Dale rubbed the back of his neck and smiled.

"You just look that way, that's all. Now get on outta here."

After Dale had left, Mr. Sills leaned back in the plastic chair and smiled. "I like those results," he said.

22 / Window Tappers

"Ms. Brigade brought her poem," Victor said, using *The Truth About Hell*—an evangelical tract popular around juvenile hall— to scratch a rash on his neck. "She said when we start readin' to call her in." He looked out the window and pointed. "Damn, look at that moon. In the daytime an' all."

"It looks fake," Francisco said dreamily. Since his conviction he had become strangely docile.

"It *is* fake," Patrick said. "At least, according to Hall it is."

"What kinna stupid shit is that? A course it's real."

"He said it was something the government put up there to keep everybody's mind off poor people in the ghetto."

Victor rolled his eyes. "Dumb-ass! He said ain't no *astronauts* really gone up there, that *that* was fake. Everybody knows the moon is real, fool."

"I'm not saying I thought it was fake. I was just quoting somebody."

"Mumble-mumble . . . t'sitfor?" Dale asked, squinting upward.

"Huh? Can't hear you, fool."

"What'sit *for*? The moon, know'umsayin'?"

"Ask Mark, he's the teacher. What's it for, Mark?"

"As far as I know, the moon doesn't have a purpose. It's just there, the way the earth is here."

Dale rubbed his head. "Butthesun, itgotapurpose. Mumble-mumble giveoff light sowecanlive."

"Well—that's what the sun *does*, but it doesn't do that on purpose, the way you might decide to do something. Do you see what I mean?"

Dale shrugged. "Whatmakesit shinin', then?"

"The sun?"

"Naw. Sunshine's'causafire mm-hm. I'msayin', howcome-themoonshine?"

"It shines because the sun shines on it. The light gets reflected off it, then comes to us."

Dale looked skeptical. "Howcomeit change*shape*then?"

I asked Kevin if he could go into the office and get the staff to lend me a ball—any kind of ball—and a flashlight. He returned with these items and I gave a little demonstration of the moon's phases, using the flashlight as the sun and a softball as the moon.

"Mmm . . . no shit," Dale said when he made the connection between the model and the actual moon. "Neverlearn-nothin'likethatinschool." He rubbed his head again. "Mm-hm kinda nightsun."

"Talk louder, fool."

"Alwaysthoughtthemoon . . . somekinda *night sun*. Givin'-somekindaorganisms, youknow, energyto*live*offof."

He squinted out the window again and frowned. "Sohow-comeallthe *stars* bemovin'? Like thatone, see? Inanhour, itgon-nabegone. Mm-hm. Iknowfromwatchin'it everydamnnight."

I explained that the apparent movement of the stars was caused by the earth's rotation. Then I asked if any of the boys could explain to me why the North Star alone never moved from its position in the sky. Only Benny knew the answer. Once I had explained the phenomenon to the rest of them, I suggested that they might use it as a topic. "Can you think of some aspect of your lives, or some person, or some idea, that never changes while everything else in your life seems like chaos? Do you have a personal North Star, in other words?"

At the end of the writing period, we invited Ms. Brigade to join us. She sat at the table—the first time any of the staff had done that during class—between Francisco and Kevin. We decided to move clockwise through the room, starting with Kevin and finishing with our guest.

Kevin explained to her what the suggested topic for the evening was, then apologized for not being able to follow it. "There's no North Star for me," he said. "Nothin' in my life ever stayed the same." Instead he had written about his ambition to become a chef.

Patrick, Benny, Victor, Jose, and Duc all wrote about their mothers, who never gave up on them. When it came Dale's turn, he said, "Jus'likeJackson overhere. NoNorthStar. Nothin'butchaos."

"What did you write about, then?"

Dale frowned at his notepad. "Ifeelbadtoday, Mark."

"His roommate got sent to county yesterday," Kevin explained.

"I'd like to hear what you wrote about him," Ms. Brigade said. "I know how close you guys got."

He mumbled a question which I didn't understand but Ms. Brigade did.

"I just know, Jones."

Dale pursed his lips and brushed some eraser fragments off his essay.

When we first met it was an unworthy first-time impression. We exchanged many unlikely words but after a while it was like, whatever. As my time here in K/L was growing, slowly but surely we was speaking to each other but not on a friendly-type conversation level. But once I moved next door to his room, for some reason things changed. It was like, we thought alike, did the same things at the same time, we was just so much alike. Then we became roommates. We adapted to each other's situation right off the bat. I didn't look at him as just a regular person, 'cause neither one of us was. We would stand out from all the rest of the guys here at Central, not just at K/L but throughout the facility. As we talked every day, all day, we found out we WERE each other. He was me and I was him, but I couldn't understand it, I never thought I would share so much, and have so much feeling, emotions for someone I really didn't know. But little did we know we knew each other, but it took us seventeen years to find each other.

Now he's gone. I miss him. Most of all, I wasn't ready to say goodbye.

When Dale finished, he stared at the table and no one said a word until Francisco asked, "Is it my turn?" He hadn't written on the topic and offered no explanation for it; I suspected he had not been paying attention to what we'd been talking about earlier. He read as if he were in a trance:

Every time I look out my window, I see new inmate girls walking by. I just see them waving at us, but we can't be next to them. Then, all of a sudden, I'm next to one one day. She caresses my hand and then it's time for her to go. She stands up, looks at me, blows me a kiss, and she waves at me as she walks away.

*People may think this is ordinary, but in the situation
we are in, it's a miracle to get the chance to kiss a girl,
because we may never get the chance to be with a girl
again.*

"It was at the retreat, Mark," Francisco said. "I'll always
have that memory."

Normally Francisco's essay would have triggered a discussion of male-female relations—and a viewing of Jose's latest
issue of *Hustler*—but Ms. Brigade's presence made everyone
act like a gentleman. Her turn to read had come at last.

"Well," she said, taking a few sheets of paper out of a manila
folder, "I brought something that I wrote one night about
you—not any one of you in particular, but all of you. You may
think that when I and the other staff go home we don't think
about you at all, but it's not true. We think about you a lot. So
listen up."

> *Window tappers*
> > *I hear you tapping for me*
> > *To come see what you need*
> > *So when you hear my steps*
> > *You know I have the key*
>
> > *You stare at the wall*
> > *You wanna take a little walk*
> > > *up the hall*
> > *For a sudden head call*
> > *I know y'all*
> > *Sometimes it's nothin' at all*
>
> *Window tappers*
> > *Still hungry you say*
> > > *Hate to throw food away*

Sometimes it's OK
I'll kick you down with an extra tray
Then you want rec today
And dominoes to play
First, tighten up that room
Take the mop and broom
Sweep out trash like this
Mop up that piss
Stop spittin' on the wall
Like you ain't got no sense
And taggin' the bunk
Then cry like a punk
When you sand that stuff up

Window tappers
Tappin' for attention
Sometimes conversation
Potential rappers
Finger snappers
Three-minute crappers
Teenage nappers (babies sleep at noon)
Slipper-wearin' flappers
Whassup! Whass in
y'all be trippin—need to see the chaplain and
psych
And the man in white (straitjacket)
You tap
For pencils and pens
To pass games to yo' friends
To ask how have I been
Can you go pee again
Would you play Boyz II Men
Can we hear "Kirk Franklin"
We goin' to school when?

You tap
   For the hour
   Like you got somewhere to go
   You and I both know
   That you have lots of time
   So relax your mind
   Practice pullin' yo' pants up
      on yo' behind
   Learn to walk in line
   Without throwin' up your signs, fool

Window tappers
   I see you on Sundays
   As I walk away
   I hear what your hearts say
   Wish I was goin' home too
   What chu gonna do
   When I look back at you
   I see my little brother
   Tapping for my mother

Only now there is no reply

   And all the years she tried
   All the nights she cried
   To God
   For him to straighten up his life
   And the day she died
   He realized
   What was happening
   Shortly thereafter
   He stands at his door window tapping

   I hear you.

The boys cheered her poem. They would not let her leave until she'd given it to me to type up and I'd promised to make copies for each of them to keep in their folders. After she'd gone, Dale mumbled something which only Kevin could understand.

"Translate for us, fool."

Kevin smiled. "He said next time he gotta take a crap, he gonna send a telegram. 'Cause it's harder for the staff to rhyme on."

23 / The Man I Was Supposed to Be

I stood outside the chapel with Sister Janet to watch the forty or so graduates process into the building. Six of my students had earned enough academic credits to finish high school: Kevin, Francisco, Benny, Victor, Duc, and Patrick. Francisco's wish had been granted: his lawyer got his sentencing hearing postponed just long enough for him to attend.

Closely monitored by the staff, the boys and girls formed two lines in the garden of funerary statues and put on their caps and gowns. Then, accompanied by a wrenchingly out-of-tune piano, they marched into the building as their mothers, grandmothers, and younger siblings watched from the pews. I counted only five adult males in the audience.

According to our programs, the ceremony was to begin with a commencement speech delivered by Antonio Villaraigosa, Speaker of the California State Assembly. After several minutes of confusion, the school principal announced that the speaker hadn't arrived yet so we would move ahead to the graduates' remarks.

Nearly half of the boys and girls had prepared speeches for the occasion. They repeated themes heard at just about every high school graduation: we are nervous but excited, we are proud of our accomplishment but sad to be saying goodbye to each other, we are eager to show the world what we can do. The bleak future the graduates were stepping into gave these clichés an unexpected poignancy.

There were no in-jokes delivered from the podium, no goofy grins, no ironic remarks. The adults, on the other hand, brought somewhat less dignity to the moment. Several members of the staff talked loudly during the speeches, and not all of the family members of the graduates were up to the task of paying attention, either.

Mr. Villaraigosa arrived as the last of the graduates stepped down from the podium. The son of a Mexican-American secretary and a Mexican immigrant who abandoned the family when Antonio was five, he grew up in the toughest barrios in East L.A. He was expelled from high school in his junior year for leading student protests and joining in the fistfights that frequently ensued, after having earned an abysmally low GPA of 1.4. Nevertheless, he applied to UCLA and was accepted as an affirmative action student—he described himself as the "poster child" for that program—and thrived there. Now, at age forty-six, he held the second most powerful position in the California state government.

He began by talking about the obstacles facing children growing up in neighborhoods infested with crime, drugs, and violence, then turned to the graduates and said, "But what you've accomplished here makes us feel hopeful. You defy the statistics. You have realized that it is up to you to choose your destiny, and you've taken real steps in that direction." He was an electrifying speaker who hit all the right notes, and by the end of his talk many of the adults were in tears.

Then the principal called each of the graduates by name up to the podium to receive his or her diploma. I sat right behind two of Kevin Jackson's aunts, his older brother, and his wheelchair-bound grandmother, all of whom had come that day by bus. When the principal called out Kevin's name, his relatives whooped, and when he got his diploma his aunts wept freely.

Patrick's name was called out, but he was not present. Only two days before graduation, he'd been transferred to county jail because someone filing paperwork discovered he was too old to be held at Central any longer.

When Francisco's turn came, he turned to face the audience, held the diploma high above his head, and yelled for joy.

When all of the diplomas had been handed out, the graduates filed back out to the garden, where visiting with family members was permitted for a brief period. On my way out, I introduced myself to Kevin's brother, who told me he himself had just been released from prison.

"Kevin was in the wrong place at the wrong time," was his assessment of his younger brother's situation. "Same as me."

He said that Kevin's trial would begin in two weeks, and asked if I would be willing to speak as a character witness. When I said yes, he wrote down Kevin's court-appointed lawyer's name and telephone number for me. "Maybe he'll call you back, since you're white," he said. "We been leavin' messages on his machine for over a year, tellin' him about witnesses he oughta talk to, askin' questions 'bout what he plan to do, but he ain't never called one of us back."

GRADUATE'S DAY
BY DUC BUI

July 10, 1998. That is the day I'll never forget in my life, because it was my high school graduate's day. From the school me and about forty other students took a walk to the chapel, on the way I saw my parents, they were almost crying and waved their hands at me.

When my turn to come up for the speech came I was worried because I know that I have an accent and I was also scared because I had never stood in front of a lot of people to speak, but I was all right. After the speech we went outside and talked to the parents. I talked to my mom, my dad, they almost cried because they're so proud of me. We got food to eat and took pictures, because my parents sneaked the camera in. The staff and principal didn't see it, and we kept taking the pictures until the film ended. Finally, time up and my parents had to leave with happiness and proud of me, and I went back inside the chapel, give back the cap and gown, and go back to the unit, continuing the day of an inmate.

GRADUATION
BY KEVIN JACKSON

The moment I've always been waiting for has passed and now I feel like a whole different person. Every major event of my adolescent life is all happening at once. I feel confused when I think of my near future. It all depends on my upcoming trial. I'm facing a lot of changes in the next few months, and the fact is I'm not sure if I'm ready for so much change all at once. I've been used to doing the same thing for almost two years and it will be hard to adjust to a new setting and a new way of living, but I will be able to do it. Graduating from high school taught me a lot about the courage to keep going. I feel I will make it because the look on my aunt's and my grandma's face made me feel like the man I was supposed to be.

. . .

"Sorry, Mark," Mr. Jenkins said, letting me into the empty day-room. "We're on lockdown again. It's not just us this time, it's all the units."

"What happened?"

"A riot at school. Just a few days after that nice graduation, too. Never a dull moment around here."

I had brought a card for Francisco, which I planned to give him at the end of class. His sentencing hearing was only a few days away, and just in case he disappeared like Patrick, I wanted him to know how much I'd enjoyed knowing him and having him in the class. I asked Mr. Jenkins if he would give the card to Francisco for me, and he said, "Why not have Jackson give it to him? He's on the other side working. I'll tell him to come over."

Kevin appeared a few minutes later with a broom and a garbage bag. "We're back to normal," he said. "Normal as in somebody doin' somethin' stupid."

"Were you at school when it happened?"

"Naw, I was here. Hey Mark—don't nobody ever call you to tell you we on lockdown? To save you the trip?"

"I don't mind. Kevin, do you think you could do me a favor?"

"Anything for you, Mark."

I showed him the card for Francisco. "Could you get this to him tonight? If he gets sentenced this week, I might not see him again."

Kevin took the card and nodded. "It's taken care of, Mark. Anything else?"

"Tell him to write me. My address is inside."

"Got it. But don' worry, those sentencing hearings usually get postponed a bunch of times." He put the card in his pocket. "When I leave, you gonna give me your address, too?"

"You can have it now, if you want."

"Better wait. I'd prob'ly just lose it with so much goin' on."

"Your brother told me you start trial soon."

"Yeah. Part of me just wants to get it over with. It's been almost two years, just waiting."

"I'll call your lawyer this week. What's he like?"

He shrugged. "I haven't met him yet. He's real busy."

"Hasn't he come here to talk to you about your case?"

"I guess he don' need to. Maybe that's a good sign." Kevin glanced toward the office and said, "I better get back to work. You want me to hook you up with a soda or somethin'? I feel bad, you drivin' down for nothin'."

"I'm fine. Tell Francisco . . . you know. That I said good luck."

"It's taken care of."

Kevin passed through the office on his way to the far side of the unit. Mr. Jenkins let me out and stood with me for a while on the concrete steps to get some air.

"I'm a little worried about Kevin," I said. "His lawyer hasn't been in contact with him at all, or with his family."

Mr. Jenkins shook his head. "He won't see his lawyer till the first day of trial. Same thing for most of these kids. No Dream Team for them, they get the scraps."

I asked him, with all of his experience working with juvenile offenders, if he felt that trying teenagers like Kevin as adults was the right thing to do. Did it actually deter other children from committing crimes?

He took a deep breath. "Oh boy. All I can tell you, Mark, is that I know a lot of good folks who thank God we were kids twenty years ago and not now. That's all I can say."

A pounding noise from one of the windows caught his attention. He leaned around the side of the building to investigate, then smiled and said, "I think somebody wants you to look through his window." I stepped around and saw Francisco holding my opened card and nodding to indicate that he'd read the message inside. I had thanked him for being one of the original three to give the class a chance, for bringing so much to it, and for helping to make it such a success. I conveyed my hopes that he would never give up on himself and never stop reading or writing, because he had so much to discover and so much to offer. I thanked him for cheering me up when I felt discouraged over my own writing, and for cursing out my editor when she criticized my manuscript. I finished by saying that I'd enjoyed knowing him and considered him a friend, which was the truth.

He clenched his free hand into a fist and thumped it against his heart. When I waved at him he tried to say something to me, but the window material was too thick for me to hear through it. We communicated with hand signals for a while, then he saluted me and dropped out of view.

I left several messages that week on Kevin's lawyer's answering machine, explaining who I was, how I knew Kevin, and that I would like to help in any way I could. I mentioned that I had spoken about Kevin to a close friend of mine, a former public defender now in private practice, who'd offered to work on the case for free if the attorney could use an extra hand. None of my calls was returned.

That Saturday, as soon as Mr. Granillo opened the door for me, he asked if I'd heard about Javier.

"Did he get sentenced?"

"Yep. They gave him a million years."

The boys were able to give me a more accurate figure: twenty-five years to life for each first-degree murder conviction, adding up to fifty-two years to life. The lawyer had asked that they run concurrently, citing the mitigating factor that Francisco had not been the shooter in either incident, but the judge rejected this suggestion. He did, however, allow the sentences for the two attempted murder convictions—adding up to thirty years to life—to run concurrently with the larger figure.

All of the boys were upset by this news, but Jose, who regularly boasted of being unafraid of prison, seemed to take it hardest of all. He looked as if he hadn't slept in days. He asked me for a pencil and paper, then sat at a far corner of the table by himself and kept silent. He usually liked to sit in the middle of things, with Victor right next to him.

"Homeboy *maintained*," Victor said, scratching at the rash on his neck with a Stephen King novel this time. "I heard he didn't cry or nothin' until he got to the holding tank. So his family wouldn't see."

"Gottabe a man," Dale said.

Benny disagreed. "If I got stuck like that, I'd cry like a baby." For once, no one teased him.

"Everybody cries," Victor said. "But knowin' *when* to cry, that's what makes the man."

"When is the right time to cry?" I asked.

"In the holding tank, just like Javier did it. That way, his family don't gotta go home with a picture in their heads that'll rip their hearts out. Instead they go home with a picture they can live with. An' that's key, 'cause they *gonna* live with it."

"So Mark—what's in your bag?" Kevin asked, changing the subject. On my way into the facility that morning, Sister Janet had given me a gift. Knowing that I was still struggling with my novel about the cloistered nun, she gave me a large, handsome book of photographs taken inside the Trappist monastery of Gethsemane, where the monk and writer Thomas Merton spent most of his life.

The boys huddled around to have a look. The photos were all in black and white, showing the monks at work, praying in the chapel, reading in their cells, having dinner in the refectory. As we leafed through the pages together, it struck me how many of the scenes in the monastery resembled scenes from a detention facility. The monks all wore the same outfit; they had the same close-cropped haircuts; they lived in a walled compound and were forbidden to leave; they spoke only during approved periods of recreation; they lived in cells; intimate relationships were forbidden; personal possessions were limited to books and toiletries; and they observed strict rules of obedience to authority. I pointed these similarities out to the boys, then asked if anyone had a theory to explain it. Monastics describe their life as a journey toward freedom; why, then, would they choose to live like prisoners?

The boys all seemed intrigued by the question, but no one seemed willing to venture an answer. Finally Dale asked for a closer look at the pictures. After gazing for several minutes at a photo of the monks walking single file across the grounds, he asked, "Who'sincharge adisplace?"

"Who's in charge? I guess that would be the abbot."

"Herunsit? Hetheboss?"

"That's right."

Dale ran his fingers over the stubble on his chin, then half smiled. "Hm—deebot airy leperspray?"

Victor winced. "Jones, man, you gotta talk slower, you don't make no sense."

Dale sighed. "Does . . . the abbot . . . carry . . . pepper-spray?"

We all had a good laugh over that. For having illustrated the difference between monks and prisoners so succinctly, Dale was given the honor of stuffing the book of photographs back into my bag.

Taking advantage of the moment, I suggested we begin our writing period. I realized that, having just been released from a week of lockdown, most of them would find it impossible to sit still and concentrate, but I had to try. Jose and Dale were the surprise exceptions to the rule; the two boys from my class who had not graduated from high school were the only ones able to write that morning. After trying to shush the others for fifteen minutes, I gave up and declared it a snow day, explaining that on the East Coast we were allowed a few days each year of school cancellations due to inclement weather. Instead of writing, they talked about which female pop stars they would most like to have sex with.

Before our time was up, I asked Dale and Jose if they wanted to read what they'd written. Jose declined, but Dale seemed willing. "S'a poem," he said, mumbling his way through an account of how the idea had come to him. He had been on the sheriff's department bus on his way to a court appearance when he found himself trying to remember what it felt like driving a car, rather than being a passenger in one.

> I came to a fork in the road
> I took the one that looked right
> It led me left
>   on the wrong path to overcome a journey to a destiny
>   that I wasn't ready for
> Livin' the life I chose
> The only way I know
> Seems to be my downfall on this road
>
> I've ran into and seen so many things that I never would've
>   thought I would
> I lost like everything that was so close to me
> But I guess it's too late now
> I can't go right 'cause I done already went left
> Damn. What can I do, a high-risk offender
> In this pumpkin suit.
> Help me, Lord.

"Renteria, you gotta read now. You hardly never read, fool."

"Naw, it's like a diary."

"Lemme see it," Victor said. Jose handed the page over to his friend, who read it silently, then began reading it aloud without asking. Jose made a halfhearted attempt to grab the page out of Victor's hand, but when this failed, he redirected his anger by flicking eraser shavings at Benny Wong.

> *I once did something that at first made me happy. It felt like I was doing something good for myself. But three weeks later I couldn't even sleep at night. I felt like something was hunting me at night. I would wake up at night in a full sweat, I would even have dreams about it. One thing that would trip me out about is wondering why did I do it? Why did I have to cause other people pain?*
>
> *Now I pray for the people I hurt. I thank God for helping me realize that all that stuff we do on the outs ain't even worth it. Well, I know from now on that I'm going to do better.*

When Victor tried to hand the page back, Jose said he didn't want it. "Fuck it," he said. "Where we goin', we better off bein' the craziest, meanest, ugliest motherfucker on the tier, then at least you don't get punked."

Dale's jaw clenched up. "Anyfool trytopunk me, oneofusdie. Mymindmadeup."

"That scare me most of all," Duc said. "I small, I can't beat everybody's ass. What if somebody try to take my cheeks?"

Benny had to explain the expression to me. "Take somebody's cheeks—it's slang for being raped. That's why nobody wants to go to the pen."

"That's why it's so hard to stay out of the gangs," Victor said. "You jus' wanna be left alone, but you gotta have protection, especially if you the youngest guy there. In return for that, you gotta put in work for the gang, even if you don't wanna be in it no more."

"Like my brother," Jose said. "A month after he got to the pen, the gang slid a shank under the door to his cell and told him to take care of a snitch. He hadda do it, or he'da got sliced."

"We're all gonna face it," Victor said. "That's the reality, no matter how bad we wanna change."

Jose pointed around the room and said, "See this? You got black guys and Asian guys and Martinez and me in here, and we get along fine. As soon as we get to the pen, that's gonna end. It ain't possible there." He slid his notebook and pencil across the table to me, then handed in his folder as well. "You might as well give this to somebody else. I won't be able to take it with me anyway. No personals allowed in the Box."

"Homeboy gets sentenced next week," Victor told me.

"It's all nice," Jose said, "us tryin'a do good in here, goin' to school and takin' writing classes and bein' in plays an' shit. But it don' make no difference. In the end, it all comes out the same."

Jose got up and wandered out into the dayroom, where Mr. Granillo gave him the choice of returning to class or going to his room. He chose his room.

24 / Thanks, Hate

"I'm sure it would mean a great deal if you could be there," Sister Janet called out from her tiny kitchen. "But you're already doing so much for the kids—don't feel you have to do more."

Sister Janet lived in a two-room apartment furnished entirely with purchases from the Salvation Army. Her most extravagant possession hung in a frame on the wall: a sheet of liturgical music dating from the twelfth century. Someone had donated this object to the probation department back in the 1950s to decorate the new chapel at juvenile hall. It was stapled to a velvet panel on the wall, where it languished until the wall had to be torn down to make room for a closet. Realizing it was about to be thrown away, Sister Janet phoned Walt Kelly, the head of the probation department (the former priest who had attended our retreat), and urged that the piece be rescued; she suspected it was much older than anyone realized. Kelly inspected it and came to the same conclusion, but instead of putting it into storage, he arranged for the treasure to be presented to Sister Janet as a gift.

Sister Janet returned from the kitchen with a plate of cookies and a pot of ink black coffee, which she placed on the low table in front of me. I sat on a sofa while she sat on the floor, folding her legs beneath her with the kind of ease that comes from a lifetime of practice.

"I must warn you," she said. "If you do go to watch his trial, it will break your heart. Once you've seen what the legal system does to these children, it becomes far more difficult to stay hopeful."

In fact, I hadn't offered to attend Kevin's trial; I had stopped by Sister Janet's place to discuss my latest draft of the novel about the Carmelite nun which she had been kind enough to read. By then, however, I had grown accustomed to the fact—grown fond of it, even—that conversations with Sister Janet never went the way one expected. Instead they went where the need was greatest.

"Where will the trial be held?" she asked.

"Torrance. Down near Long Beach."

"Ugh—that's an awful drive. And the traffic is impossible. No, it's too much." She looked down at the serving tray and laughed. "Look what I've done! I brought out the coffeepot, but no cups! Hold on." She rose from the floor and glided into the kitchen. "Did you want any cream and sugar? I didn't even think to ask."

"Only if you have it."

I heard her open the refrigerator door. "Is milk OK?"

"Even better."

"I hope you're eating those cookies out there."

She returned with cups and saucers, a creamer filled to the brim with nonfat milk, and a bowl stuffed with at least fifty packets of sugar.

"That poor boy," she said, pouring the coffee for me. "Imagine the kind of pressure he must be under right now. And with no parents to show their support, or make him feel loved. Yet he's always so cheerful and polite when I see him."

"He's been wonderful to have in the class."

"Oh, and *he* has enjoyed it so much. Can I show you something? Do you have a minute?"

She sprang up from the floor again and disappeared into the far room, which doubled as her office and bedroom, returning with a manila folder stuffed with letters. She pulled one out and handed it to me. "I've been asking some of the boys and girls to write down what they feel about the classes. I see changes coming, and none of them good. We may have to fight to keep this program in place; these letters might be what keeps us hanging on."

To Whom It May Concern . . .

Since I joined Mark's writing group I've noticed a lot of changes in my life. Writing has helped me open up to other people and have an open mind to their opinions. Writing has taught me a lot about myself that I never knew I had bottled up inside. Everybody thinks I'm a "hardened criminal" because of the charges against me, but they don't know the real me. For most of my life I didn't even know the real me until writing helped me dig deep down inside and extract my true self. My teacher has helped me, encouraged me, and done everything in his power he can to be more than just a teacher, he's our friend! I'm glad to have been fortunate enough to be in this class. I believe it's been one of my most cherished experiences.

Kevin Jackson
August 5, 1998

"You see?" she said. "You've done so much for him already. Don't worry about the trial; it could go on for weeks. If you could make it to his sentencing hearing, which would only take a day, that would be a wonderful gesture."

·   ·   ·

I went straight from Sister Janet's apartment to the Torrance Superior Court building. After passing through security—the man in front of me refused to submit to the metal detector test and was refused entry—I found the proper courtroom. Kevin's two aunts were there and they told me I hadn't missed a thing; the lawyers were still picking the jury.

The prosecutor, Ms. Rose, dressed conservatively and kept her blond hair pulled back into a tight bun. She had a severe look for someone so young; I guessed her to be in her mid-twenties. Her opponent, alternate public defender Paul Kinion, couldn't have resembled her less. He was overweight and on the far side of middle age, his clothes looked as if he'd slept in them the night before, he needed a haircut, and he gulped water out of an oversized plastic bottle that he kept next to his chair. He seemed relaxed, but not in a way that inspired confidence; he reminded me of a large, friendly basset hound called upon to guard a home.

Kevin sat next to Mr. Kinion, wearing a powder blue suit and a burgundy and yellow tie. It was the first time I had seen him in anything but a prisoner's orange outfit or his underwear. He looked nervous and subdued. During a break, I approached them and introduced myself to his lawyer.

"Oh yes," he said. "I was going to call you back, but I've been so busy preparing this case, there just hasn't been time."

I reiterated my offer to speak as a character witness on Kevin's behalf.

"We would only need that at the sentencing hearing, if he were to lose the case. Right now let's focus on winning."

The trial began with opening statements. Ms. Rose went first, telling the courtroom that the victims—a group of three teenage boys, all black—were leaving a movie theater in a crowded mall complex when the crime occurred. Kevin Jackson, his girlfriend, and another couple approached from the parking lot, on their way to see the same movie the victims had just seen. When the two groups crossed paths, words were exchanged. A scuffle ensued, and a punch was thrown. Mr. Jackson pulled out a gun. One of the victims, Steve Compton, was shot point-blank in the chest, while Brian Webb was shot in the buttocks. They both survived. The third victim, Brandon Stokes, was shot in the back. By the time emergency medics arrived he was already dead.

After the shooting, Mr. Jackson and his friends got into a car and drove away. Rather than dispersing and going into hiding, they went to see the same movie at another theater. Arriving too late, they turned around and continued driving. Moments later their car was spotted by a Torrance police officer who recognized it from witnesses' descriptions of the getaway vehicle. He followed them, pulled them over, and found the murder weapon under the rear passenger seat where Mr. Jackson had been sitting. Later that evening, in an interview with a police detective, Mr. Jackson confessed to firing the gun at the three boys.

The prosecutor told the jury that she would present evidence to show, beyond question, that this was a senseless, cold-blooded murder, not an act of self-defense or manslaughter. And what was it over?

"Words, gang affiliation, wearing red, or wearing blue, bravado, showing off? A punch thrown? Essentially nothing." She promised to demonstrate that the victim was murdered for no reason, and that there was no excuse for the defendant's actions.

When she finished, the judge invited the defense to make its opening statement. Mr. Kinion began by admitting this would be a tough case, but insisted it was one that had to be judged on the basis of evidence, not outrage.

In Mr. Kinion's version of the story, the three victims "approached the defendant—who they *thought* was a Piru Blood gang member from Compton—and said, 'What's up, cuz?'

Now, 'What's up cuz?' seems to us to be innocuous, but it's not. It's a word to gang people that is very confrontational. It's a word from gang people often followed by gunfire and death.

"Kevin Jackson didn't answer. Another of the boys said, 'What's up, loc?' another confrontational term used by Crip gang members, their challenge, which is usually, ladies and gentlemen, in a lot of cases followed by gunfire. To a gang member, it means a very serious challenge. And I told you before it's a challenge that ordinarily results in the death or great bodily injury inflicted upon the person who they asked the question to.

"Jackson ignored the challenges, he tried to avoid the confrontation, but it didn't stop. Mr. Jackson couldn't get away. Mr. Jackson is then hit in the face very hard, and he's stunned, and he pulls out the gun and fires shots. He fired those shots not with the intent to kill or to maim or to hurt anybody, but to get away because he thought his life was threatened.

"This is going to be about a case of self-defense, where a young man shoots a gun to stop himself from being maimed, killed, or hurt by Crips. He had a right to defend himself."

The attorneys approached the judge's bench to settle a procedural issue before going on. Accustomed to watching celebrity trials on television, I expected the courtroom to be filled with observers, but it was practically empty. Besides Kevin's aunts, I counted half a dozen of us in the room. One was a reporter from a local newspaper. The rest, I could only guess, were members of the dead boy's family.

The prosecution began its case by calling one of the two girls who had been with Kevin that night. She testified that after seeing one of the boys punch Kevin, she turned her back and ran, hearing gunfire but not seeing anything. She claimed that when they all got in the car after the shooting, nobody said a word about it and she did not know that Kevin had a gun in the car. The prosecutor pointed out that her testimony contradicted the statement she'd made to the police the night of the killing on several points, but the girl claimed not to know or remember anything about what she'd said that night. She seemed irritated at having to appear in court at all.

After lunch the prosecution called the girl who had been Kevin's date that night to the stand. She told the court that the boy who was killed had said, "What's up, cuz?" and "What's up, loc?" several times to Kevin, and that when Kevin didn't respond, the questions got louder. Soon the boy was yelling them. She said she tried to pull Kevin away so that a fight wouldn't break out, but the boy prevented her from doing so and punched Kevin in the face. Then she, like the other girl, turned around and missed seeing everything else that followed.

After a break, Kevin's male friend took the stand. He had to be reminded continually to speak at an audible level. Like the two girls, he claimed to have seen Kevin being punched, but nothing after that. He did admit, however, to knowing that Kevin had a gun that night. He denied being a Blood gang member, but admitted that many of his friends were gang members. He denied that the red Chicago Bulls T-shirt, black pants, and red Nike sneakers he wore that night—or his cherry red sports car—were signs of gang affiliation. He also wanted it known that it was not his decision to go to the drive-in theater after the shooting—the girls made him drive there because they were annoyed at having missed the screening at the mall.

By the end of the day I understood why the prosecution, and not the defense, had called Kevin's three friends to the stand. They were unappealing, immature, and unreliable—but at least they hadn't shot anyone. Kevin, the jury could only assume, had to have been the worst of the bunch. Their courtroom testimony and police statements did agree on a few points, however. Kevin had been confronted by the three boys, not the other way around. They challenged him several times with the questions "What's up, cuz?" and "What's up, loc?" When Kevin did not respond, one of the boys punched Kevin in the face. Kevin fell backwards, pulled a gun out of his pocket, then opened fire. Did he panic, thinking those boys were armed? Did he have reason to fear for his life? Or was he, as the prosecutor suggested, just a coldhearted thug—a coward who couldn't handle a challenge to a fistfight except by gunning everybody down?

That night I went to bed with a broken heart, just as Sister Janet had predicted—but not because of what the legal system was doing to young people. I had known for a year that Kevin was charged with murder, as were most of the boys in my class. I guess I thought that if I could look at those numbers in Mr. Sills' ledger and go back to the library without flinching, it meant I had faced reality and dealt with it. Now I knew otherwise. One of my students' victims had a name and a family now, and I had to wrap my mind around the fact that someone I had grown so fond of, and who seemed so gentle, had been foolish enough to go to a movie theater carrying a loaded gun, violent enough to shoot three people with it—two of them in the back—and then callous enough to want to go to a movie afterward.

The next day, the prosecutor called several police officers to the stand. They established that the spent cartridges from the crime weapon had been found ten to twenty feet apart, suggesting that the shooter had moved to follow his victims. The defense attorney got them to acknowledge that when a pistol is fired, the empty cartridges are discharged forcefully and sometimes land a good distance away. He also pointed out that the incident took place in front of a crowded movie theater, where the cartridges could easily have been scattered underfoot in all of the chaos that followed the shooting.

The coroner who had performed the autopsy testified next, saying that the entrance and exit wounds on the dead man's body indicated a single shot fired when the victim's back was turned to the shooter. A weapons expert established that the gun found in the car under Kevin's seat was, in fact, the murder weapon.

Toward the end of the afternoon, Robert Lara, a police detective who'd grown up in a gang-infested part of L.A. and who specialized in gang suppression, took the stand as an expert witness for the prosecution. Ms. Rose asked him what the phrase "What's up, cuz?" meant. Detective Lara said it could be a simple greeting between friends, but when delivered by a Crip gang member, it means:

"What are you going to do? The guy will [then] use the term 'Are we boxing or are we gattin',' which is a street term for shoot it out. And the guy will put his hands up, that means it's going to be a physical altercation. If they have a weapon, they're going to retrieve that weapon and the battle will begin. It's like what they perceive as a duel, a representation of masculinity to them."

Ms. Rose asked, "In a situation where 'What's up, cuz?' is followed by a punch, would you expect gunfire to erupt from that situation?"

"No."

On the morning of the third day of the trial, Mr. Kinion called Detective Lara back to the stand for cross-examination.

"[So] if a gang member were to approach someone with the words 'What's up, cuz?' and then hit him in the face, it would mean only a fistfight?"

"Yes."

"Would that testimony change if you knew that on one occasion prior to this night in question that this particular person—"

The prosecutor leapt up from her seat and objected. The judge called the two attorneys to his bench for a lengthy conference. When they finished, the defense lawyer was allowed to finish his question:

"If you knew that on one occasion prior to this incident that this person who hit Kevin had chased him with a gun, would that change your opinion?"

The detective gave it some thought, then answered that, no, it wouldn't necessarily change his opinion.

That afternoon the prosecution called its final witness, Keith Mason, a detective who had been with the Torrance police department for thirty-two years. He had conducted the interview with Kevin the night of the shooting, which was played for the court. As Mr. Kinion claimed, Kevin described being chased by the victim on a prior occasion. The boy had threatened him with a gun at a bus stop, Kevin said, but he escaped by jumping onto the bus.

I expected this piece of testimony to cause more of a stir. Didn't it mean that Kevin had good reason to fear for his life— or at least to be terrified out of his wits—when the boy confronted him at the movie theater? Neither attorney showed much interest in the tape, however. When Ms. Rose announced that she was finished with the witness, Mr. Kinion passed on the opportunity to cross-examine, and the prosecution rested its case.

At last, on the fourth day of the trial, Kevin's defense began. His lawyer called Mr. Steven Strong, a private investigator, to the stand. Mr. Strong had been with the Los Angeles Police Department for over twenty years. Like Detective Lara, his specialty had been to investigate gang-related crimes. Mr. Kinion spent a long time asking him questions about gang activity in the Los Angeles area that didn't seem to have anything to do with Kevin's case; I gathered that this was meant to establish the witness's expertise. At last, he got to the point.

"OK, Mr. Strong, in your experience investigating street gangs, in particular Crips, have you ever heard the expression 'What's up, cuz?' before?"

"Yes."

"And what does that mean to you?"

"Well, it could mean several things. If this particular Crip is in his own neighborhood and he sees one of his fellow gang members, then 'What's up, cuz?' could be just like a greeting, like Hi, how you doing or what's going on. If he were to meet someone he wasn't sure who they were, it's a way of announcing who he is and what area they're in. So depending on what their response is it would be something different.

"It can also be given out as a challenge. If he sees someone he knows of a rival gang or rival neighborhood, that could be a definite challenge that something is going to jump off."

"And what do you mean by 'that something is going to jump off'?"

"If it's somebody he's had trouble with before or somebody he's after and he's confronting them, it's like 'What's up, cuz?' and it would be an immediate gun battle at that point."

"What would it mean if some Crip asks someone he thinks is a Blood, 'What's up, cuz?,' and he had chased him with a gun on another occasion?"

"It would tell me that either he was determined or he meant that he was going to do someone harm, that other person."

"With a gun?"

"Well, I would assume so. Most every gang incident within, Jesus, California and other states is involving a gun. Very seldom it does not."

When it came her turn to cross-examine the witness, Ms. Rose leapt on the key part of his testimony:

"I'm just trying to get this straight. You're saying that between a Crip and a Blood, all assaults involve a firearm?"

"That or a knife. Pretty much all the time, I would say. Yeah."

When she asked him to estimate the percentage of crimes involving gangs in which a weapon was used, he gave her the figure of 90 to 95 percent. She turned to the jury and stared as if she couldn't believe what she had just heard, then promised to show that this claim—along with his claim that the phrase "What's up, cuz?" usually led to gunfire—was ludicrous.

Mr. Kinion kept his redirect examination brief. Referring to a case they had both worked on ten years earlier, when Mr. Strong was the investigating officer, Mr. Kinion asked, "Do you remember whether or not this was a Crip shooting, a Crip shot a Blood in a drive-by?"

"Yes."

"And what was the words that Mr. Johnson used before he shot the victim in that case?"

"What's up, cuz."

Kevin's lawyer turned to face the judge. "That's all I have. Your honor, at this time if the court pleases, the defendant will rest."

Will *rest*? I assumed I must have heard him wrong; he couldn't be finished. He had called only one witness, someone who was not even connected to the case on trial. Wasn't Kevin going to testify?

The prosecutor called Detective Mason back to the stand for a rebuttal. She reminded the jury that he had been with the Torrance police department for over thirty years, and was still working there, unlike Mr. Strong, who had been retired for more than six years. She asked Mason if he had done any gang sweeps, where the police round up suspected gang members and search them, at the very mall where the crime had taken place. Yes, he answered, he had supervised many gang sweeps there.

"Were any guns ever recovered in any of those sweeps?"

"No."

"Have you ever worked crimes against persons, for example, not rising to the level of homicides?"

"Yes, I have." He described a recent incident where a bunch of Crips and Bloods got into an argument, tried to ram each other with their cars, then got out of the cars and fought with their bare hands. Several of the Bloods were beaten so severely they had to be hospitalized, but no guns had been used.

She asked if he knew of any fistfights that had been preceeded by someone using the phrase, "What's up, cuz?"

"Some of them were, yes."

"And those didn't involve shootings?"

"No."

After that, the prosecution rested. The jury was sent home for the day while the judge and the two attorneys debated which instructions to give the jury.

I left for Idaho the next morning to attend a weeklong conference, so I could not go to Torrance to hear closing arguments or wait for the jury's decision. Since the outcome looked gloomy, I did not want to disturb Kevin's family by calling them for updates while I was away. I decided to wait until I got back to Los Angeles to hear the news.

I came home on a Friday night and went to juvenile hall the next morning. As I crossed the dayroom, Kevin waved at me from the kitchen, a spatula in one hand and a jar of salsa in the other. He was back in his orange prisoner's garb. If he had been acquitted, he would have been released. "Want some chips, Mark? I heated 'em up."

"I'll take some, sure."

He put a few onto a paper plate along with a dollop of salsa, handed it to me, then busied himself right away with stirring something on the hot plate.

"What happened?" I asked.

He didn't look up. "Guilty. One count of murder, two attempted murders. I wasn't surprised."

I let him stir for a while, then asked how he was holding up.

"I'm OK. At least it's over."

"I'm sorry, Kevin."

"Yeah. But thanks for bein' there. It was good to see some friendly faces out there." He spooned the mixture from the hot plate into a large plastic bowl, then added, "I'm not supposed to get sentenced till the end of the month, so I'll be around for a while. I gotta stick around to help break in the new guy."

"What new guy?"

"The one in the library. Sills wants him in the class."

I asked if he would like me to speak on his behalf at his sentencing hearing, and he nodded. "My lawyer said you should write it down first and send it to the judge, that way it becomes part of the record. Just in case, you know, somethin' comes up and you can't make it that day." He gave me a few more chips, then shooed me out of the kitchen. As I passed by the staff room, Mr. Sills waved me in.

"You stealin' my chips?" he asked.

I closed the door behind me and sat down in the chair facing his desk. "I went to Kevin's trial last week," I said.

"I heard. I heard his defense lasted half an hour."

"Something like that."

Mr. Sills nodded. "That's a little less than average, but not by much." Then he pointed toward the library. "You got kids waitin' on you in there. Around here, you focus on what you *can* do, and you find a way to live with the rest."

His blasé reaction to Kevin's trial upset me. I had seen the two of them interact many times and I knew that Sills had become like a surrogate father to Kevin. They loved each other. Was this all the man had to say now that Kevin was only a sentencing hearing away from life in prison?

I waited, but Sills said nothing. I stood up from the chair. "Who's the new guy?"

"His name's Toa. If you don't like him, let me know."

The new guy sat at the far end of the table, keeping to himself. When I entered the room, he stood up to show respect, but didn't smile or look directly at me. He was the most intimidating kid I'd ever seen, inside or outside of juvenile hall. He must have weighed close to three hundred pounds, and what wasn't muscle looked like either bone or scar tissue.

"Welcome to the class," I said. "What's your name?"

"Everybody call me Toa."

"Is that a Samoan name?"

"Half of one. You don' wanna try pronouncin' the whole thing."

"What's your first name?"

"Mark. But just Toa's fine."

I greeted the others, who were not teasing Toa the way they usually teased someone new to the class. No one sat too close to him, either; they gave him a wide berth.

"You heard about Jackson?" Benny asked.

"Just now, yes."

"He's not the only one who got stuck. Renteria got sentenced to eighteen to life, and Duc took a twenty-year deal."

I looked at Duc, who nodded.

"How come you still here, then?" Victor asked Duc. "Ain't you s'posed to be at county, or in the Box, like Renteria?"

"They let you stay longer if you take a deal," Benny explained.

"How come?"

" 'Cause guys who take deals don't try to commit suicide."

"Oh."

Since the buster incident, relations between Victor and Benny had improved. They had stopped bickering and sometimes even sat next to each other.

"I wrote poem," Duc said. "Poem how I feel about everything." He handed it to me just as Kevin came into the room. I was still adjusting to the news about Kevin's verdict, and didn't feel like leading a discussion, so I suggested Duc read his poem aloud to start the class off.

THIS IS MY LIFE

Because of my friends, my parents are suffering.
Because of my friends, I joined a gang.
Because of my friends, I shot someone.
Because of my friends, I was sentenced to twenty years.

I call collect, but my friends don't accept.
I write letters, but my friends never write back.
I feel regret, but it is too late.
I confessed, but the judge gave me twenty years.

I write this poem to apologize to my parents.
I write this poem to apologize to the victim.
I write this poem to criticize my friends.
I write this poem to ask for fairness.

"I don't agree with that poem," Toa said, shaking his head.

"Why not?" Victor asked.

"He sayin' it all because of his friends. I say everything you do is done by choice."

"What about peer pressure?" Benny asked.

Toa shrugged. "What about it? He chose his friends. You always got options to choose from."

"Not everyone gets the same options, though," Benny pressed.

"You preachin' to the choir," Toa said. "I got dealt shitty cards just like you, but it's how I played 'em got me in here. Whatever you into, you in it by choice."

"So you sayin' we deserve to get locked up for life for one mistake we made?" Victor asked, getting heated up.

"I'm sayin' if you want the benefit, you gotta face the consequences. Same goes for society. They want the benefit of lockin' kids up and throwin' away the key? They playin' *they* cards wrong. *They* gonna face the consequences."

I asked him what he thought the consequences of adult sentences for juveniles would be.

"Most of us gonna get out someday, right? Teen gangbangers be steppin' out of the pen after twenty, thirty years of livin' like animals, comin' of age in a place where nobody trusts nobody, bein' treated like less than a piece of shit. Wha'chu think they gonna do? Most they family be dead by then. What they got to live for? Revenge. Nothin' else."

Suddenly all of the boys were talking at once. Toa's prediction transformed their frustration into anger. It took me ten minutes to get them to settle down enough to write, but when they wrote, they wrote quickly. Dale, who usually read last and even then had to be prodded, asked to read first.

Amerikkka hasn't been the America we were promised. For centuries Amerikkka has been spitting in our faces and making this world a much better fucked-up place. Instead of colleges, more schools, and programs to help those who need help, they spend all our money on more peniten-tiaries and everything else to keep us away for perpetuity. Instead of dealing with the problem, they figure keep us away in solitary for a long time will solve the problem but it just creates more habits. They have been hiding our his-tory for years and teaching us false information about the past and our ancestors. Fuck Amerikkka. Treat us with dis-respect, switching the situation against the world. Now we hating.

Duc read next. He had written about some of the bad things that had happened to him since coming to this country. Among other humiliations, he described being taunted by a member of the staff at the Sylmar juvenile facility just before coming to Central:

He said, "Are you suck dick?" I was very mad and told him, "You suck my dick," and he locked my ass down for three days. At that time I wanted to take off on him but think about my case and I had to hold my anger.

Victor accused society of judging young people without knowing the circumstances that led them to become criminals:

They don't know what it's like when you come from a fam-ily that didn't have a father there to guide you in the right path. They don't know what it's like when there is nothing to eat when you come home from school. They don't know how it feels when your mother tells you that you need to quit school to get a job, because there ain't enough money for food. They don't know because they come from rich fam-

ilies with parents and money to buy food and pay for their kids' education so they could grow up to go to college to become the judges, lawyers, D.A.'s, prosecutors, politicians, and all them others that are making the laws to put us away for life.

They don't know what it's like to grow up not having a role model in your life.

Even Benny, who usually emphasized the positive in his writing, let some anger show through:

To put it in simple words, jail is a place that separates people who got caught breaking the laws from people that have not gotten caught breaking the laws—the "innocent" people. I agree it's a punishment for those that do care about their freedom, but jail is not a place that makes a person rehabilitate. Jail is just a place that separates people. In it, there are staff that give you rules. It doesn't teach a person anything. It all depends on the person—if he or she wants to learn.

With Kevin's trial still fresh in my mind, I had a hard time listening to these complaints without saying: Yes, you've been hurt—but what about all the damage *you've* done? Are you any better than the people you're blaming? If you think it's unfair that society judges you, what gives you the right to judge society? You say you're just defending yourselves when you shoot at your enemies, you're just trying to survive when you steal cars or rob stores—aren't people like me just defending ourselves by locking people like you up?

When it came Kevin's turn to read, I wondered what his complaint would be. Would he blame the legal system for not providing him with a better attorney? Would he blame society for not taking better care of him after the death of his parents? Would he express a sense of betrayal over the fact that, after being encouraged by adults to improve himself while in juvenile hall and then doing so, it hadn't made any difference to his future at all?

MESSAGE IN A BOTTLE

To the Loser Who Reads This:

I am sitting here on the verge of death, thinking about what purpose I served on this earth, and to tell you the truth I can't think of a good reason for me being created. I wish I could have done more but I was caught up in the wicked ways of the world, and now I'm gonna die by the world. I hope that you read this message and take heed: Be somebody, don't just be an average person, make a difference in the world. I didn't get a chance to because of my ways, but I know that if you try to help others you will have a better life than mine! I would enlighten you on some more things but I'm starting to see bright flashes. I think I'm about to die.

The only reason I addressed this letter to "the loser who reads this" is because only a loser would pick up a bottle on the beach. So I hope you get your life together because—

"Becausewhat?" Dale asked.

"He can't tell you," Toa said.

"Whynot?"

"That where he dies, fool."

Kevin nodded.

Toa tore his sheet out of the notepad, smoothed it out on the table in front of him, and said, "I'm new here, so I kept it simple. I wrote about my partner."

"Your crime partner?" Benny asked.

"You could say that."

"Mark says we're not supposed to write about our cases. For our own protection. It could be used against you."

"My whole life is my case," Toa said. "Don't matter what I write."

Someone who made a big difference in my life was my partner. Well, I should say my ex-partner, hate. Hate was always there for me at night when I was all alone and the air-conditioning was on too high in my room. Hate would keep me warm. I should say he was like my father 'cause for the seven years that my father was gone, hate taught me how to speak, hate taught me how to love, and eventually hate taught me how to hate. My best friend, my mother, my father, hate was all that. Hate helped me grow, or was dat wrong? I asked myself this question one day when I was lookin' into a six-by-nine mirror in my cell. I was wearing somebody else's clothes, underwear, and socks full of holes. Hate had left me to duel with misery and pain. Thanks, hate.

25 / Father's Day

"You teach in K/L, right?" the guard at the key trailer asked. "I don't think you'll be havin' class today. Some kinda rodeo or somethin' goin' on."

I got my visitor's badge anyway and passed by three pickup trucks, each towing a horse trailer, parked in the spots reserved for sheriff's department buses. The boys from E/F, K/L, and M/N—the high-risk offenders' units—sat on the ground as three cowboys, each standing next to a horse, explained the fundamentals of horsemanship. As I got closer, Mr. Granillo waved me over to a shady spot under a tree.

"It's Wild West day," he said. "These guys come every year."

"Do they give a riding show?"

"Better than that. The kids give the riding show. Watch."

The head cowboy asked for three volunteers, who were given permission to stand up and approach the horses. The visitors helped the boys up into the saddles, then led the horses by the reins around the yard. It was obvious from the boys' nervous laughter and the expressions of wonder on their faces that none of them had experienced anything like it before.

"If you still want to run your class, Mark, I could send your kids inside," Mr. Granillo offered. I declined; the boys had writing class twice a week, but this happened only once a year. I leaned against the tree and watched them enjoy themselves.

It was a beautiful day outdoors, not quite eighty degrees and without a cloud in the sky. The sight of animals other than feral cats in the yard made the place look less depressing. One by one, the boys from my class got up and took their turn on the horses: Duc, Dale, Toa, and Benny. Kevin wasn't anywhere to be seen, but when I smelled a barbecue and saw smoke rising from the far side of K/L unit, I guessed he was helping Mr. Sills prepare lunch.

Victor was in the last group of three to ride. When his turn came, he approached the head cowboy and asked a question I couldn't hear. They spoke for about a minute, then the cowboy waved over one of the guards. After another minute or so of discussion, the cowboy nodded and, instead of helping Victor up, simply handed him the reins. Victor put a foot in the stirrup and swung his other leg over with ease. He kept still on top of the horse for a moment and spoke to it in Spanish, then, with a barely visible movement of his hands and feet, got the horse to break into a trot. He rode the horse around the circumference of the yard, patting its neck and speaking to it the whole time. The cowboy, meanwhile, came over to join Granillo and me in the shade of the tree.

Victor put the horse through a series of turns at the far end of the yard, got it to stop and walk backwards, then turned it around and commanded it to run. Throughout all of this I felt as if I was watching a miracle: Victor, with his blocky physique, his acne, and his awkward body language, was transformed.

In the saddle he looked expert, graceful, and handsome. The whole group of boys cheered and laughed as Victor galloped past; I'm sure all of them were hoping he would jump the wall and ride off into jailhouse legend.

"That kid knows what he's doing," the cowboy said.

"He grew up on a ranch in Mexico," Mr. Granillo said proudly.

"Ah. They know their horses down there."

Horse and rider streaked past the guardhouse, drawing another cheer from the inmates. Then they circled the baseball diamond, slowed to a trot, and approached the tree where I was standing.

"Nice horse," Victor said to the cowboy.

"Nice riding," the cowboy responded. "What's your name, son?"

"Martinez." Victor got down from the horse and handed the reins back.

"Ever thought about doing this when you get out? Taking care of horses, teaching people to ride?"

"Not really."

"Maybe you should."

"Thanks. I'll think about it." Victor caressed the horse's nose and thanked the cowboy for bringing him. When he rejoined his fellow inmates out in the sun, they teased him for not making a run for it.

"Seems like a sweet kid," the cowboy said.

"He can be," Mr. Granillo said.

I decided to go around to the far side of K/L unit to visit with Kevin. I had brought along a card for him, like the one I'd given Francisco, with a message encouraging him to keep writing and my mailing address written inside. Mr. Sills seemed too preoccupied to greet me as I approached his homemade grill. A Hispanic boy I didn't recognize stood nearby folding napkins.

"Where's Jackson?" I asked. "I've got something for him."

Mr. Sills turned a piece of the chicken over to check it; it wasn't even singed yet. "Gone. They sent him to county yesterday."

"But he hasn't been sentenced yet . . ."

Sills turned over another piece of chicken, still without looking up at me. "I'm aware of that. This barbecue was supposed to be for him."

"Why did they send him early? He didn't get in trouble, did he?"

"No, he didn't. He was never any trouble to anybody around here. He made people feel good." Sills kept fussing with the chicken until I backed away from the grill. Then he waved the new messenger over. "Now look here—see how I line these up? You get twice as much on at a time this way."

The boy, who looked around fifteen years old, nodded.

"But don't put 'em so close they touch. They need breathin' room." Mr. Sills checked his watch. "It's time. Go inside and see if Jenkins needs help bringing the last of the stuff out."

As soon as the boy started indoors, Mr. Sills barked at him to stop. "What the hell's the matter with you? You haven't even asked this man if he wants something to drink."

Blushing, the boy asked me if I wanted a soda.

"Sure."

"What kind, sir?"

"Anything."

The boy reached into a tub of ice and pulled out a can of root beer. He opened it, handed it to me, then looked at Sills.

"That's right. *Now* you can go help Jenkins."

I drank my soda and rearranged the papers in my bag. If Sills didn't want to talk about Kevin, I wasn't going to force the issue.

. . .

"I know somebody who wants to be in the class," Victor told me. "Could I go get him? Since we lost Jackson an' all."

"Is he a clown?" I asked. Victor's last candidate for admission had been Jose, so I didn't care if I sounded judgmental.

"Naw, he's serious."

"Who you talkin' 'bout?" Toa asked. "Not that fool Ramirez?"

"Naw. Frontuto."

Toa nodded. "Yeah. He's cool. So what's the topic for today, Mark? Everybody feelin' kinda low 'bout what happened to Jackson."

"Haters onthestaff," Dale muttered. "Hateagoodman-'causetheyignorance view."

"Why would the staff hate Kevin?" I asked.

"They don't," Benny told me, lowering his voice to a whisper. "We're pretty sure it's Sills they got a problem with."

"What kind of problem?"

"They think Sills is too friendly to us. He breaks the rules sometimes—like having barbecues and stuff, we're not supposed to get anything like that."

"But what does that have to do with Kevin?"

"Jackson was Sills' favorite. Nobody can fire Sills, so they hurt him by hurting his messenger."

"We gon'write'boutit?" Dale asked.

"No way," Toa said. "Jus' cause more trouble for Sills."

"We could write letter and burn it," Duc suggested.

"Huh?"

"Bible study, remember? What he say 'bout write a letter to your homeboy, then burn it."

"That was if you had something to say to a homeboy who died," Benny explained. "We all wrote letters, then burned them together so the messages would go up to heaven."

"I'd have to flush mine down the toilet," Toa said. "That's where all my friends are."

"This is Frontuto," Victor said, returning to the library with the new boy. "He even brought a poem to show he can write." Victor nudged him. "Go on, fool, don't just stand there. Give it to him."

Frontuto unfolded a piece of paper, shiny from being handled so much, and gave it to me. He had a boyish face but a haunted, distant look—he bore an uncanny resemblance to Montgomery Clift's character in *A Place in the Sun*, after the poor man has been condemned to die. I looked over the poem, then suggested he read it aloud to get the class started. He seemed reluctant, but Toa said, "Read it. That's how you get jumped in."

> *Dad, why weren't you there?*
> *It's not that you didn't care,*
> *But just that you weren't there.*
> *Growing up as a boy*
> *Who was filled with so much joy*
> *I had a mother,*
> *Who had it very rough.*
> *Because she had two boys*
> *And a girl who tried to act so tough.*
> *Not having a manly role model,*
> *But having an older brother*
> *Who can only do so much.*
>
> *So by not having a fatherly figure,*
> *I turned to the streets*
> *And learned how to pull a trigger.*
> *And as I grew older,*
> *My days and nights got colder.*
> *So here I am, sixteen,*
> *And still have not found the right dream.*
> *The dream where I grow old*

And have days and nights that don't feel so cold.
And having kids that I can call my own,
But not having to tell them "I love you" over a phone.

As Frontuto read, Dale became agitated. He grimaced, massaged his neck, and squirmed in his chair. When the poem was finished, he looked relieved.

"I told you he was serious," Victor said.

"What's your first name?" I asked the new boy.

"Sal."

"You know how the class works, Sal?"

"I think so."

"Good. A lot of guys have written about their mothers in this class, but not about fathers. Should we make that the topic today?"

"*Hm!*"

"Dale, are you OK?"

He rubbed his neck again and waved me off. "Nothin' over-here."

"What about me?" Sal asked. "I already wrote on that topic."

"How about a childhood memory? Something you'll never forget. It doesn't have to be anything big, just something that you remember clearly and can describe for us."

"Yeah, I got something."

"Good. Let's go for thirty minutes this time, then read aloud."

The boys settled down to work, but after five minutes I noticed that Dale was squirming and grimacing again. He looked as if he might be suffering from a migraine, so I pulled my chair over and asked once more if he was all right. He stared down at his notepad, which was blank, and said, "Feel-in' bad, Mark."

"Do you want to see a doctor?"

"Not thatkindabad. Bad *here*." He pointed to his heart.

"What do you feel bad about?"

"Feelin' lotta anger. Angrymyfather."

"Was he bad to you?"

Dale nodded. "Never cometoseeme. Neveronce sinceI-beenlockedup."

"Then you have a right to be angry, Dale."

He grimaced again but didn't say anything.

"Can you write about feeling angry?"

He shook his head. "Don' wanna readitaloud."

"You don't have to read it aloud. You could do what Duc was suggesting. Write a letter to your father telling him how disappointed you are in him. When you're finished, you can tear it up. Nobody has to see it. It might make you feel better."

"I'lltryit, Mark."

After another five minutes Dale was squirming again. He had written a few sentences on his notepad but had crossed them all out. When I sat down next to him this time, he looked up at me and said, "Feelin'bad again, Mark."

"What's the problem?"

"Writin' notnicethings. But hestillmyfather."

"Would you rather write about something else?"

He nodded.

"That's fine. How about this: How did it feel to ride that horse the other day?"

"Felt like heaven."

"Good. Write it down."

At the end of the writing period I called on Dale first, hoping it would make him feel better to share a happy memory with the others.

Thanks to the rangers for bringing horses which have never been seen before and spending time with these brokenheart juveniles. Looking at the faces of my peers I saw that they forgot for a moment that they were locked up behind no mercy walls. Everybody had a chance to ride and Martinez had a chance to ride away. We saw a vision to freedom and a cherish mirage.

A few years from now I wonder where would my destination be, dead, roaming free, or in some one penitentiary. Deep down inside there's only a few people in particular that knows and understands the life I would like to achieve as a youngsta. I'm unfigurable and to opponents unfuck-withable but there is time I cry and ask myself, Is there someone who can feel the pain and agony I fail to show but feel. As I leave I'll look back upon this place and chuckle and say

—It was all good and great—

"You got me confused," Toa said. "Is it all good and great, or no mercy walls? Can't have it both ways."

"Can if yo'mind splitintwo."

"Fuck it, Jones, next time write about your pops. Get that shit outta your system, you'll feel better."

Dale rubbed his neck and mumbled.

Duc read next. He hadn't written about his father either; his essay was about the importance of sunlight for life on earth. Benny had written a draft of a letter to the judge on his case that he asked me to look at privately, and Victor wrote about a pair of beloved snakeskin boots.

"None of you fools did the assignment," Toa complained. "Ain't nobody in here got a dad?"

"Maybe we don't got much to say on that subject," Victor said.

"Oh yeah you do. Everybody got somethin' to say on that subject. Thing is, when you hatin' on your dad, you jus' hatin' on yourself. 'Cause in your heart, you believe it all your fault, even if it ain't."

"How could it be my fault if I'm jus' a little kid? Fuck it, the dad suppos'ta be in charge, he the adult."

"I'm talkin' 'bout if he beat you, in your heart you was thinkin' it 'cause you fucked up. If he took off and left, you was thinkin' it 'cause you fucked up. Don' tell me you didn't think it."

"Bullshit!"

"That's right, bullshit. That's why I'm sayin': if you can't write about it, you still believin' it."

"We haven't heard yours yet," Benny pointed out.

"I don't feel like readin' it," Toa said, leaning back in his chair.

"So what are you bitchin' at us for? You ain't even readin'."

"I want Jones to read it for me." Toa tossed the piece of paper across the table to Dale, who picked it up and read it silently. When he finished, he covered his mouth with his hand and laughed.

"OK, I'llreadit. Fuckit."

I seen him for the first time in about seven years. "Hi Daddy. I hate you." Daddy? Pops? More like ghost. My heart raced to find words to say. For years I contemplated this moment. Now here it is. Nothin' but dead silence. He looked into my eyes, I figured he was tryin'a see if I felt anything. "Son, I missed you." My heart froze, like it was stabbed with a ice pick and stuck into a freezer, havin' water poured over it repeatedly, seepin' into the puncture wounds, chemically changing from fluids to solids, cold . . . tha coldest.

Dale tossed the sheet back across the table, still smiling. "Saysitall. Don'gotta saynomore."

"But you only read that side. Turn it over."

Dale turned the page over and glanced at what was written there.

"Nah, nah. Youreadit," he said, tossing the paper back to Toa.

Toa smoothed the page out with his fist.

My mom is the foundation to my family. Without her there ain't no me. When my dad was locked up she was there for us. My mom don't know but that's why I left home so often. 'Cause she had so much on her mind. I felt leaving would lighten the load.

My mom's kind, sensitive, loving, and if you take all that as a sign of weakness fuck you 'cause I ain't nothin' like that and she's my heart so killing you secures somebody I love and that's how much I love her, that I'll kill without remorse. Even though she don't like what I do, my mom's my world. I love her.

"Saysitall," Dale repeated.

"So whad'you write on, Frontuto? You started this shit, after all."

"I already read one today, I don't wanna bore nobody."

"We'll tell you if it's boring. Read it or the staff'll send us down."

"Yeah. Go, Frontuto."

I remember one time when I was living with my dad and we went fishing to the High Sierras. It was a long trip, and on the way over there my dad was so drunk that he fell asleep under the table while we were driving there. So when we got there you could see the mountains and it was a beautiful sight. The mountains were covered with snow, and the air was just so fresh that it felt different to my lungs. I guess my lungs were used to all this bad air out here, so on the way up there we stopped at a store and of course they bought more beer and I made them buy me some beef jerky and a soda and then we got back into the motor home and drove to a lake where we started fishing. So my dad hooked my pole up and I went to cast it out there and it snapped apart. So they made me sit there and watch them fish and it was getting very cold. I got very bored, so I started to throw rocks into the lake, and they all started to yell, "Hey Bill, get Sal's ass and put him in the motor home cause he's scaring all the fish away." So they put me in the motor home and I fell asleep. When I woke up they were drinking again. So we stayed there for a couple of days and then went back home and the funny part is they didn't even catch any fish.

By the end of the story Dale was laughing in snorts, with one hand clapped over his mouth and the other clenched into a fist, pounding his thigh.

"I didn't know it was *that* funny," Sal said.

"Clock say we got five minutes left. What we gonna do till then? Can't just sit here starin' at Jones."

"I dunno."

Benny and Duc shrugged.

"I already read twice," Sal said, "don't look at me."

Toa shook his head. "Too many Indians, not enough chiefs. Mark—what we gonna do?"

I suggested that we each talk about a character from a movie that we really admired or could identify with.

"I know who I'm thinkin' of," Toa said. "Who that little green muthafucka? All hunched over an' shit?"

"Yoda?"

"Yeah."

"Yoda's just a mechanical puppet," Benny pointed out.

"So? He a smart fuckin' mechanical puppet."

"Jones, quit laughin'. You gettin' on my nerves."

"He ain't laughin', he cryin'."

"No he ain't. Show me the tears."

"Damn," Sal said, "I hope I get invited back to this thing."

26 / The Letter

Kevin's sentencing hearing was postponed, first from August to October, then to November, then to December, then to January. Each time, I crept through rush-hour traffic down to Torrance—two hours round-trip from Glendale—only to be told by a representative from the alternate public defender's office that Kevin's lawyer was not feeling well and had asked for a continuance. The hearing finally took place on January 12, five months after Kevin's conviction and expulsion to county jail.

Mr. Kinion did look frail. His face was bloated and pale, and he drank so much bottled water during the hearing I worried he might burst. He began with a motion for a new trial, citing procedural flaws that may have biased the jury against Kevin, but his motion was promptly denied.

Before passing sentence, Judge O'Neill asked the murder victim's mother, who was present, if she wished to address the court. She did. The room went silent as the grieving woman carried a framed photograph of her son, taken at his high school graduation, up to the podium.

"I wanted Kevin to see the person that he murdered," she said, giving each word its full measure. "Brandon was not only our son. He was a brother, a father, an uncle, a grandson, a cousin, a nephew, and a friend."

She held the portrait up so that everyone in the room could see it, then faced Kevin. Without taking her eyes off him, she described the horror of receiving the news of her son's death, and then the despair she felt in the weeks and months afterward.

"I know you know what it feels like to lose someone you love, because I know you lost your mother. But you don't know the pain that a mother feels when she loses her child." She wondered aloud if Kevin could possibly imagine how much damage he had caused, or how many lives he had shattered, then—just as her voice began to shake with emotion—she finished with an admonition: "When you go back to wherever they take you, you need to fall down on your knees and ask the Lord to forgive you for your sin. For you have committed the ultimate sin."

Kevin's aunts spoke next. They each acknowledged the victim's family's grief and expressed remorse on Kevin's behalf, but insisted that justice had not been done. The jury had never heard from Kevin, they had never really heard anything about him. They knew nothing of the obstacles he'd faced in life, or the good things he'd done for others. The police had lost the photos of Kevin taken immediately after the incident, showing the injuries to his face, and had also lost his clothing, which was not gang attire and would have shown that Kevin was not a gang member looking for a fight. They also wanted the court to know that Kevin's attorney had promised to go to juvenile hall to meet with Kevin before the trial to discuss the case, and had promised to set up a meeting with the family members to let them know what he was doing on Kevin's behalf, but had not done either. "To this date, he has never answered any of our phone calls. How do you prepare for a case without taking the time out to discuss the case with your client?"

Kevin's turn to speak came last. Now that he was a convict rather than a defendant, he wore the clothing he would probably wear for the rest of his life: a blue prisoner's jumpsuit and sneakers. He had aged in the half year since I'd seen him; his shoulders had filled out, his face looked more gaunt, and the beginnings of a mustache had formed on his upper lip. He stood up, faced the mother of the dead boy, and said, "I feel remorse for what happened on November 9, 1996. There are no other words I can say to bring back your son, but I'd like to apologize and pray to God to allow you and your family . . ." His voice gave out. He took a few moments to compose himself, then continued:

"I wish the things that I done didn't occur, but unfortunately they did. I wish I could take them back, but I can't. I wasn't really trying to hurt your son or anything like that. I thought I was defending myself. I reacted before I knew what I was doing."

Kevin looked up at the judge. "I would just like to thank you for the chance to speak. I'd like to thank my family and friends for coming to support me and being by my side through this all."

"Anything else, Mr. Jackson?"

"No. Thanks."

After Kevin sat down, Ms. Rose argued for the maximum sentence, citing no mitigating factors and Kevin's juvenile record of four previous arrests. Mr. Kinion disagreed, insisting that there were, in fact, mitigating factors to consider.

"Particularly relevant in that connection," he said, "is a letter by Mr. Joe Sills, a deputy probation officer, dated August 14, 1998, about Kevin. I'd like to read it now."

Your Honor:

I am writing this letter in support of Kevin Jackson.
I am a probation officer at Central Juvenile Hall. I have
been working probation for the past fifteen years.
Throughout my career at Central I have come across
many kids and young men. Out of all the minors that
I have come across I have never met any minor quite
like Mr. Jackson. He stands out in a unique way.

I have known Kevin for almost two years. During
these years he has proven to me that he is trustworthy,
responsible, and sincere. He has also earned position as
a messenger (unit worker), which is a job most of his
peers admire. This is a job that requires intelligence,
dedication, patience, and pride. He has been involved
with the Narcotics Anonymous group, theater group,
writing class, behavior modification courses, college
course, and Bible study classes. Faced with adversity
and peer pressure in a place like this, Kevin Jackson
could have chosen the easy way and given up on himself, but instead he has still maintained a positive
self-image for others and continued to further his
education.

In the beginning when I met Kevin I saw him as a
young kid who has wasted his life. I figured he was like
any other gangbanger that come and go. But as I got to
know him on a personal basis he has shown no signs
of gang involvement.

I believe meeting Kevin was a blessing to me because
he has made me a better person mentally and spiritually.
He has always emphasized to me that his goal was to
become a chef.

I am convinced that if given the chance Kevin has

the tools to become successful in society. I believe Kevin
Jackson is an asset to his culture.
  Sincerely,
  Joe Sills

I looked at Kevin. Tears streamed down his cheeks, but he didn't make a sound or move at all.

"Your honor," Mr. Kinion said, "as a criminal defense lawyer, I have never seen a letter like that from a probation officer on an aggravated murder case like this. I have never seen a criminal defendant in a case like this come before the court and say to the victim's parents, 'I'm sorry this happened.' And I've been doing this for about thirty-five years.

"I ask the court not to maximize the sentence. I feel that if he's given a chance, at least a hope, something could be salvaged and he could be a benefit for all of us out of this society."

With no testimony or arguments left to hear, Judge O'Neill announced that the court was prepared to make a decision. He began by acknowledging the numerous letters he had received in support of Kevin from teachers, volunteers, counselors, and probation officers. My own letter was among them.

"Absolutely," he said, "unequivocally, I believe every word that is said. He is a model prisoner. But once he's on the streets with his colleagues, his fellow Bloods, he becomes an animal . . .

"It's almost like there are two individuals. It's tragic. It's really sad. We've got a very young man here who tragically lost his parents. And where did he turn for family? He turned to the Bloods. That's what he did. But that was his choice. And his choice was to go to that movie armed, and his choice was to shoot three individuals. Bad choices."

Declaring no factors in mitigation, the judge gave Kevin the maximum sentence allowed by law: twenty-six years and eight months for the second-degree murder conviction, fifteen years to life for each attempted murder conviction, plus ten years for the use of a gun, all to run consecutively. Kevin didn't visibly react to this news. When the sheriff's deputy led him out of the courtroom to be transferred immediately from county jail to state prison, he kept his head lowered and didn't turn to look back at any of us.

"This is some good-ass food, Wong."

"Yeah, but where's the dogs' toes?"

"That's Filipinos, not Chinese."

Benny Wong's mother had delivered enough Chinese food for a party. The occasion was Benny's upcoming release. He had taken a three-year deal which meant that with time served, he could be sent home any day.

Benny, Victor, Dale, Toa, Sal, and the newest members of the writing class, Carlos Bours and Antonio Siddique, stuffed themselves to capacity. Then they leaned against the walls of the small kitchen and joked around. The mood was festive; everyone seemed to share in Benny's good news.

"Man, you Asians are always passin' the buck," Mr. Granillo said. "Chinese say it's the Filipinos, Filipinos say it's the Koreans, Koreans say it's the Vietnamese. I wanna know right now: Who eats dogs' toes?"

"Dogs don't have toes," Benny pointed out. "They have paws."

Mr. Granillo sighed. "I liked it better in the old days, when everybody used to kick Wong's ass." He stacked some egg rolls on his plate like firewood. "So who's gonna bring in food next?"

"My mom could bring in Mexican food," Victor said.

"Mine too," said Antonio.

"What about you, Jones? Your mom do any cooking?"

Dale burped. "Hellyeah. KFC."

"That ain't cookin', Jones. That's buyin'."

"Sheput somekinna sauceonit."

"OK, then it's cookin'."

"Guys," I said. "If we're going to do any writing today, we'd better go over and do it now. It's already ten-thirty."

"Can't we write in here?" Antonio asked. "Then we could keep eating."

"If we stay here, no one's going to get any writing done."

"Yes we will! C'mon, Mark, we—"

Mr. Sills cut him short with a look. He pointed at the door with his plastic fork, and the boys began filing out toward the library.

"Speaking of writing class," Mr. Granillo said, "I got a bunch of kids saying they wanna join. And I know Jenkins got a few, too. You takin' anybody new right now?"

I didn't want the class to grow beyond its present size, but I felt badly that so many boys were not being given the opportunity to join. On impulse, I asked Mr. Sills what he thought about my starting a second writing class.

"When would you teach it?"

"I could start the first one at ten, then the second right at eleven, and be finished by twelve."

Sills dipped an egg roll in hot sauce and thought about it. "Lemme discuss it with the committee." He waved Dale and Toa back into the kitchen and told them what I'd just proposed. Then he asked me to leave the library. "Excuse us, Mark. We gotta talk this over."

I stepped out of the library and waited in the dayroom. Through the window set in the door I saw Mr. Sills put his arms around Dale's and Toa's shoulders, pulling them into a huddle. With their heads together they held a brief meeting, then waved me back in.

"The committee has reached a decision," Mr. Sills said.

"No second class," Toa told me. "You'll get burned out. A man only got so much to give, and you already givin' it. Too many kids, not enough you."

"But what about all those other guys?"

Dale shook his head. "Gottawait. Sadbut true."

When I got to the library the other boys were already writing. Toa, who loved being challenged, handed me his notepad and asked for his word. I no longer had to think of topics for him; all I had to do was write a single word at the top of a page and he would do the rest. This time I gave him the word "substitute." Ten minutes later he slid the notepad back for me to look over.

I remember growin' up I used to look up to my oldest brother. He was the baddest muthafucka I knew. Everything he did I wanted to do, every word he said I repeated. To me he was God. My substitute dad. My whole attitude was formin' from his influence. When I got jumped in my hood my older brother was there. I took up as his Li'l Homie under his name. To me that was for life. Incarcerated, I phoned home, hearin' that my brother just got released. I felt like my sergeant was back in command. But he came at me funny. The things I expected him to say, he didn't. I was like, "Aw, man, he getting soft." Time passed and I phoned home. He told me he was havin' a kid and he finna get married. I started baggin' on him, hopin' that he'd get angry. But you know what he told me? "It's all right Li'l Uso, I still love you."

That hit me hard. I was so angry, disappointed, 'cause I felt that what kept us close together was disintegrating. I now know that gangbanging, killing, 211s ain't life. Happiness is. And the disappointment I felt wasn't in my brother. It was in myself.

I smiled, opened his notepad to the next page, and wrote the word "regret" at the top. He nodded and started a new essay.

When everyone had put down their pencils, I asked the two new boys to read first. Carlos explained that he used to hate writing, but that changed after being locked up. "Now I got a different view. So today I decided to write on why I write."

> There are many reasons why I write. Some are unexplainable, others I can explain are my way of expressing emotion, my way of getting free, my mental vacation, my way to vent anger, my way to throw emotional blows without using my physical ability, a way that no one gets hurt. A way to get through life and keep the peace. It's my joy, my shining light. If I had no pencil and paper my mind would fail, with no real vocals to express myself it would overload my brain. My writing is how I maintain.

Antonio had written about his father's death from leukemia when Antonio was eight. His family, thinking they were protecting him from this terrible news, had lied to Antonio, telling him that his father had simply gone away somewhere for a rest when, in fact, he was dying in the hospital:

> . . . That day I found out that my father passed was the last day I cried in front of my family. I felt a burden fall on me that I was the man of the house now, that I had to look over my family. The day of the funeral everybody was crying but me. I felt if I cried it will make my family, especially my mom, cry more, so I held it in. But I was so busy holding my feelings for my family that I ceased to think about myself, and I held myself to a high standard. I thought, if I can take it, then so can my family.

The truth is I was still a kid, but I covered my feelings so that they thought I could handle it, but the truth was I couldn't. I thought I did, but that's why I now have so much trouble showing my feelings. I am able to show my anger, but not my sentimental self. I never had a real childhood. It's weird that a person who passed when I was eight can have such a big impact on my life. After his death my sorrow turned into anger. My ignorant mind painted a picture that my mom lied, so did my family, they all lied that my father just left us, so that's why I have a lot of inner anger.

"I feel what you sayin'," Toa said. "Sorrow turn to anger 'cause it stay inside you."

"Turntopoison," Dale said. "Youbecomin'thatsnake, waitin'tobite."

"Huh?"

"He sayin', you got poison inside you, you become like a fuckin' snake. You in a bad mood all the time. You just waitin'. Anybody look at you funny, anybody get in your way, you bite 'em to get that poison out."

Dale nodded.

"Yeah, same as what I was sayin'," Carlos said. "It gets that shit out without hurtin' nobody. Man, some of the stuff I wrote, if you read it you'd think I was some kinda ax murderer."

"You *are* a murderer, fool."

"Not a *ax* murderer."

"Anyways," Toa said, "Siddique an' me must be readin' each other's mind today. Mark give me the word 'regret,' an' here's what I come up with."

The day I thought would never end was the day I had to bury my cousin. I felt like shit the whole day. I woke up thinking of how I was gonna get the fools back who killed him. How I was gonna catch these punks slippin' and smoke they ass. But most of all I was thinking of how was I going to look my auntie straight in the eyes again. How was I going to tell her everything was going to be all right, knowing I was lying to myself? He was gone and there wasn't nothing any of us could say or do to bring him back. Life cut me short a heartbeat.

The funeral also made me mad. All these old people that used to talk shit about the boys in my family standing up in front of the church talking about how they felt about my cousin. What the fuck did they know about him? Shit. Nothing. Even putting him in the ground felt like forever. How I gave people dirty looks who were there, hoping they would say something stupid so I could have a reason to trip. But the main reason why the day seemed so long to me was because I tried not to cry that day and succeeded, regretting it, wishing I would've.

"That's real," Antonio said, nodding. "Whoever come up with that shit in the first place? That a man not supposed to show how he feels?"

"It always been that way."

"No wonder we so fucked up."

"Yeah, but check it out. Girls show how they feel, they cry all the time, and looka what good it does them? They just as fucked up as we are."

"They worse! Why you think we call the man we hate the most a bitch? 'Cause he sneaky on top of everything else."

"Yeah, just looka the way girls treat other girls! They *cruel*, homeboy. And none of it straight up, it all behind the back. Never one-on-one, always with they little group, like fuckin' hyenas. They cheat, they lie, they weak. If that's what cryin' does, I'ma hold off on them tears."

"Maybe girls should cry less, and we should cry more," Benny suggested.

Toa rolled his eyes. "This prob'ly be your last class, huh, Wong? Let's hear what you wrote. Wrap it up for us today."

"It's not about emotions or anything like that," Benny said. "It's about time."

Dale groaned. "Don'wannathinkabouttime. Time all-wegot."

"Looka the bright side," Toa said. "Everybody on the outs say they want more time, never enough time, can't buy time. Fuck 'em. We got more time than anybody. We rich."

THE TREE

I've been housed here at Central Juvenile Hall for nearly twenty-two months. Doing the same routine every day, time seems to have gone by fast but I have just realized how long it has been. I remember there was this one tree by the main school on the other side of this facility. The tree was right by one of the back doors of the school and was possibly a way of getting over these walls. Then one day about two months after I got here, the tree was cut down, I guess because the probation people had realized the possibility of it being used as an escape attempt.

Recently, as my unit made a routine movement to school, I saw this young, bright, green tree a little taller than me. Then suddenly, I realized that this young tree was actually the tree that had been cut down. It had already grown back. That's when I started to realize how long I have been inside these walls.

Victor looked out toward the yard. "If you cut down a tree, you can tell how old it is by how many rings it got inside, right?"

"Everybody know that, fool."

"But I'm sayin', if it got cut down once, then come up again, does it still got the original rings?"

"Who the fuck knows."

"Peoplegotringstoo."

"Huh?"

"Youcutoffaman'sleg, yougonnaseethemrings."

"Fuck no, Jones, that only trees. People got blood vessels and bones an' all that shit."

"No waya'knowin' howoldaniggagets, then."

"You could ask him, fool."

Victor frowned. "I still wanna know if a tree that gets cut down got the original rings, or does it start over?"

"Why you askin' that, Martinez?"

He shrugged. "I'm just sayin', if you get locked up for twenty, thirty years, then get out . . . I'm sayin', what if you could, like . . . ah, fuck it."

"That's whacked, Martinez."

"Hey Mark—you heard anything from Jackson?"

"Not yet."

"Who's Jackson?"

"Before your time, fool. An OG from back in da day."

"The tall guy with the scar? Who could break-dance on his head?"

"Nah, the quiet guy who was always cookin' shit."

"On L side?"

"Nah. K side."

"See that?" Victor said, looking at me. "As soon as you leave this place, you're gone. Forgotten. Who talks about Wu anymore? Or Hall? Or Javier? Nobody. Hell, just now's the first time I thought about those guys in like a year. That's what it's like on the outs for us. Like we never existed."

"Might as well be dead."

"Not me," Antonio said. "I'ma live. I'ma squeeze every

drop outta this fucker, no matter what happens." He reached into his pants pocket, took out an egg roll he'd stashed there, then stuffed it into his mouth before anybody could steal it from him. "Like I said," he mumbled, speaking with his mouth full, "that is some good-ass food, Wong."

27 / Dear Friend

Kevin's letter arrived a year later. He had been assigned to a maximum-security prison near Sacramento, about five hundred miles north of Los Angeles. Heeding my oft-repeated advice to write in specifics rather than generalities, he described the layout and furnishings of his cell, a typical day's schedule, and a few representative menus from the cafeteria. (The food in prison was better than at juvenile hall, he reported.) He also told me that his cell mate was an older fellow and that they got along well. He asked how I was doing, if I was still teaching at Central, and if I'd ever finished that book about the nun.

I wrote back and told him that I was fine, the class was going strong, and, yes, I'd finally finished the book about the nun. It happened unexpectedly, after nearly six years of groping my way from one unsuccessful draft to the next. I'd been invited to spend a couple of months at an artists' colony in New Hampshire where I was supposed to write, of course. By the time I got out there, I was so fed up with my book and with writing in general that I decided to relax instead.

Maybe it was the silence—my cabin was isolated from the others by acres of forest and had no radio, television, or telephone in it—maybe it was the fall colors, or maybe it was the Wine-in-a-Box I'd set up next to my chair on the porch; whatever the reason, within a few days my mind did begin to relax. I started to think playfully again, and one afternoon while playing with ideas I realized what had been wrong with the nun story all along. Once I'd seen the problem, its solution came effortlessly; I sat down and started writing and by the time I left New Hampshire the book was done. I told Kevin that the lesson I'd learned from this was that I had no idea how creativity worked, none at all.

I also told him that, while at the colony, I gave a brief presentation about our writing class at juvenile hall. I shared several examples of the boys' work with the audience, including two of Kevin's essays. The response was overwhelmingly positive, but one woman wanted to know why I chose to volunteer at a detention facility, rather than at, say, an after-school program in a troubled neighborhood.

"I think what you're doing is wonderful," she said, "but wouldn't you be having more of an impact if you worked with kids *before* they become serious criminals?"

I had to admit that, yes, early intervention programs for at-risk youth are highly effective, whereas rehabilitation programs for chronic offenders show poor results. But I told her that, in all honesty, my primary goal with the boys at K/L had never been to save them or improve them or even to get them to take responsibility for their crimes. I was there because they responded to encouragement and they wrote honestly; surely that sort of interaction between teacher and student has value, even if it does not lead to success beyond the classroom.

"But doesn't it depress you," another colleague asked, "knowing that they'll have this brief time with you, where they'll get in touch with themselves and bond with you and each other, only to be sent off to prison?"

It was my father's question all over again. Before I could answer, someone else added, "And do you ever worry that you might actually be making their lives *harder*? I mean—they're facing a brutal environment in prison. You're teaching them to become vulnerable, which is important for life in society, but won't they have to unlearn it to survive where they're going?"

All valid questions. Since starting the class two years earlier, I'd had plenty of opportunities to wonder: What is the value of a positive experience if it is only temporary? How do you weigh the advantages against the disadvantages of affection, or of aspiration? After all I'd been through with the boys—some of it wonderful and some of it terrible—all I could say was that a little good has got to be better than no good at all. That, I wrote Kevin, was my answer to his question of why I went there: not because I always enjoyed it, and not because the boys always enjoyed it, but because most of us seemed to agree that it was a good thing to do. Even Jose, who claimed it had all been for nothing, had never skipped a class.

I reported that all of the boys Kevin had known from class were gone: Victor, Dale, and Toa had all been convicted and sent to prison. Benny Wong was home and doing well, working for his father's company and taking classes at a community college. Duc Bui had gone to prison, but before he left he surprised us all by walking into class one day with a huge smile on his face and a Vietnamese-American magazine under his arm. "I get publish!" he said, and it was true; the boy who could barely speak English when he entered juvenile hall became the first member of the class to appear in print. Copies of his poem "This Is My Life" circulated around Central for months afterward.

Sal Frontuto fell victim to the county hit list and disappeared one day, only to come back six weeks later with a gruesome scar across his neck. A gang of adult convicts had attacked him and slit his throat from ear to ear but somehow missed the jugular vein. After he'd been sewn together the authorities sent him back to juvenile hall "due to safety concerns." He rejoined the class and became something of an elder statesman to the younger inmates, but whereas his writing had once been searching, it turned hopeless and angry after the attack.

Carlos Bours puzzled me at first. His writing went all over the place, from tender love poems one week to violent, self-hating manifestos the next. Then, one day, he wrote about a Little League game where he'd made the winning play in front of his dad:

> . . . As I stepped out of the dugout I was stopped. "Good game, son." Thanks, Dad. You're such a good dad when you're not beating me, is all that kept running through my adolescent mind.

A week later he wrote a poem about crouching in a corner while his father beat and cursed him. The poem ended:

> But yet I smiled to everyone,
> As if nothing was wrong,
> Now two and a half years later,
> My wonder years are almost gone.
> I've now learned to always
> Speak what's on my mind,
> But I think what I've learned
> Is just too late this time.

Not long after that he wrote an essay titled "The Dream," but would not read it aloud or let anyone read it aloud for him. He simply handed it in and asked me to type it for him.

The dream my dad had for my life ended on June 27, 1997. It died with him. For the fourteen years prior to that, that was all I had lived for and his dream had become my dream. It was like I was living his life over again for him. But on that day the dream left both of us. Late that night I was arrested for murder.

A religious volunteer confirmed what I was beginning to suspect. "Does Bours ever write about his father?" he asked me.

"Yes, sometimes. Why?"

The man shook his head. "I hope there's such a thing as a 'battered child' defense. That boy should be in a safe house somewhere, getting counseling, not in here facing life in prison."

I described the newest members of the class to Kevin: a Russian-speaking Armenian with terrible stage fright; a boy with a stuttering problem who told me that what he really wanted out of the writing class was the opportunity to speak with me about his writing—about anything, in fact—as he had so few chances while incarcerated to talk; a boy from a group home who had beaten one of his fellow foster kids to death after an argument, and whose deadbeat father (the man had abandoned his son to be raised by grandparents when the boy was only two years old) showed up at the trial and gave the following quote to a *Los Angeles Times* reporter, which appeared in the next day's paper: "I would say he is pretty mean. I know kids that are raised by grandparents and they came out just fine. Sometimes kids are just bad kids. The prisons are full of them. It's not necessarily anyone's fault but their own."

In closing, I told Kevin that things were more or less the same as always, but that I missed having him in the class and wondered if he still wrote sometimes.

Two months later I received his answer:

DEAR FRIEND

Hello there old friend
At the moment I'm kind of down
It seems as though this is the end
I haven't had the chance to see you around.

I've been sitting here bereft,
Alone, locked down
But now I have a window
And see you every night.
Times are hard, but I'll be all right.

Gun towers, barbed wire is all I see
No matter how far I travel
I glance up, and there you'll be.
It's good to have a friend like you
At times you help me shine through.

I still have a long journey to go
But I'll be free again
I'll use this time to grow
In not just one way, but all
There's a lot for me to learn
So I'm gonna start like a baby, with a crawl.

Though the road may seem
Long and far
Eventually I'll make it

Dear old friend, North Star.

Author's Note

This is a work of nonfiction, but not of journalism. I did not use a tape recorder or take notes during my visits to Central. The dialogue in this book has been re-created from memory. Naysayers in the sciences—and, sad to say, even in the humanities—insist that human memory is unreliable. Hard evidence supports this claim but I can cite dozens of personal anecdotes to refute it, and anyway it is a bleak view so I say *pshaw*.

The examples of student writing reproduced here are unaltered except for the spelling and punctuation corrections I suggested during class. Where alternate spellings, grammar, and so on were used deliberately, I left them alone.

Some names have been changed, but most haven't.

A Note of Thanks

I first went to juvenile hall because Duane Noriyuki invited me and I couldn't think of a way to say no. I went a second time because Sister Janet Harris invited me and—well, you try saying no to her. Duane and Sister Janet have become mentors, role models, gentle critics, tireless supporters, and great friends to me; they are all that and more to countless young people who might otherwise feel completely alone in the world. It has been my privilege and pleasure to work with them.

I'd like to thank the staff of K/L unit for their patience and support. Volunteers are needed in places like juvenile hall, but some, like me, come with broad smiles and good intentions but no prior experience. Others show promise as mentors only to disappear after a few weeks. The K/L staff had good reason to be wary of me at the beginning, but with their help the class evolved into something valuable and then they did everything they could to make me feel welcome. I forgive Mr. Sills and Mr. Granillo for making fun of Schubert's Quintet in C Major. The poem "Window Tappers" appears here courtesy of its author, Ms. Tory Brigade.

On behalf of all the teachers and students in the Inside Out Writing program, I would like to thank the Los Angeles County Probation Department for the opportunity we have been given. Special recognition must go to William Burkert, former superintendent at Central, and Dr. Arthur McCoy, principal of L.A. Central Juvenile Hall School, who supported and promoted the program from the beginning. Tragically, Mr. Burkert was killed in an automobile accident in 2002. He is fondly remembered by all of us.

Most of all, I want to thank the boys who participated in my class over the years, who dared to make themselves vulnerable and who have so generously allowed their work to appear in this book. I hope that writing serves them as a tool for exploration and discovery for the rest of their lives. Although I don't touch on this subject in the text of the book, I'll say it now: they made me decide to have children of my own. It's a debt I can never repay.

A Note About Inside Out Writers

The nonprofit Alethos Foundation and its program, Inside Out Writers, has professional writers teaching classes in detention facilities and public schools throughout Southern California, and is recognized statewide for its results in education and violence prevention. The Alethos Foundation received the Child Welfare League of America's 2002 Award for Excellence in Community Collaboration for Children, Youth, and Families. It has published a book of student writing titled, *What We See: Poems and Essays from Inside Juvenile Hall*, and publishes a literary magazine, the *InsideOUT Quarterly*.

For information concerning publications, volunteer or donation opportunities please contact:

The Alethos Foundation
23679 Calabasas Road #621
Calabasas, CA 91302-1502
Tel: 818-710-7469
e-mail: InsideOutWriters@aol.com
web site: www.insideoutwriters.org

IRON & SILK

Mark Salzman vividly captures post–cultural revolution China through his adventures as a young American English teacher and his master-student relationship with China's foremost martial arts teacher. Charming and marvelously evocative, *Iron & Silk* recounts Salzman's experiences dealing with regulations, training under a ferocious master of wushu, trying to convey the plot of *E.T.* to a roomful of students, and everywhere glimpsing the hidden face of China.

Biography/Autobiography/Travel/0-394-75511-1

THE LAUGHING SUTRA

In this original and witty novel, a naïve but courageous orphan named Hsun-ching and the formidable and mysterious Colonel Sun travel from mainland China to San Francisco, risking everything to track down an elusive Buddhist scripture called The Laughing Sutra. Part *Tom Sawyer*, part *Tom Jones*, *The Laughing Sutra* draws us into an irresistible narrative of danger and comedy that speaks volumes about the nature of freedom and the meaning of loyalty.

Fiction/Literature/0-679-73546-1

THE SOLOIST

As an adolescent, Renne Sundheimer showed promise of becoming one of the world's greatest cellists. But at the age of eighteen his gift deserted him, and he now makes a living as a cello teacher, hoping his gift will return. Suddenly his life changes dramatically when he becomes involved in a murder trial for the brutal killing of a Buddhist monk, and he takes on a new pupil—an unprepossessing nine-year-old Korean boy whose talent, potential, and brilliant musicianship remind Renne of his own past.

Fiction/Literature/0-679-75926-3

LOST IN PLACE
Growing Up Absurd in Suburbia

At the age of thirteen, Mark Salzman had already made up his mind to become a wandering Zen monk. He practiced kicks in his parents' basement while wearing a pair of dyed pajamas and a Surprise Bald Head Wig ordered from the back of a comic book. As Salzman recalls coming of age with one foot in Connecticut and the other in medieval China, he tells the story of a boy pursuing a dream in spite of his father's skepticism, his kung fu teacher's withering abuse, and the patent absurdity of a teenager trying to attain enlightenment before he's learned to drive.

Biography/Autobiography/0-679-76778-9

LYING AWAKE

Sister John's cloistered life of prayer has been electrified by ever more frequent visions of God's radiance, leading her toward a deep religious ecstasy. Her writings have become examples of devotion, but her visions are accompanied by shattering headaches that compel her to seek medical help. When her doctor tells her an illness may be responsible for her gift, Sister John faces a wrenching choice: be cured and risk losing her intimate glimpses of the divine or continue to have her visions with the knowledge that they might be false—and might even cost her her life.

Fiction/Literature/0-375-70606-2

VINTAGE BOOKS
Available at your local bookstore, or call toll-free to order:
1-800-793-2665 (credit cards only).